THE NEW NATURALIST

NATURE CONSERVATION
IN BRITAIN

SIR DUDLEY STAMP

Late Member of the Nature
Conservancy and Chairman
of the England Committee

with a list of Conservation Areas in England,
Wales and Scotland compiled by James Fisher,
Deputy Chairman, the Countryside Commission

COLLINS

ST JAMES'S PLACE, LONDON

DuHTA

<S>

c.1

First Impression 1969
Second Impression 1970
SBN 00 213152 8
© Sir Dudley Stamp, 1969
Printed in Great Britain
Collins Clear-Type Press
London and Glasgow

CONTENTS

EDITORS' PREFACE   x

AUTHOR'S PREFACE   xii

I THE BACKGROUND OF CONSERVATION   I
World population and the pressure on land. The British
position – only one acre of land per head: many demands on
land. Nature conservation more difficult than in most countries.
A very varied country with great range of natural habitats.
Rapidly changing conditions.

2 THE MOVEMENT TOWARDS CONSERVATION   7
Early love of nature. Inconsistent attitudes to wild nature.
Commons Society 1865. Society for the Protection of Birds 1889.
Rise of ecology. Vegetation survey. Society for the Promotion of
Nature Reserves 1912. *British Islands and their Vegetation* 1939.
Influence of A. G. Tansley. Norfolk Naturalists' Trust 1926.
Land Utilisation Survey of Britain 1930. Barlow Report 1940.
Scott Report 1942. Classification of land. Central Planning
Branch, Ministry of Agriculture, 1942. Dower Report 1945. Con-
cept of National Parks. Wild Life Conservation Committee 1947.
The Acts of 1947 and 1949. Atlas of Britain. British Ecological
Society. Nature Conservancy founded 1949. Council for Nature
1958. Field Studies Council. I.U.C.N. Conservation overseas.

3 INTRIGUING INITIALS ON THE MAP   22
M.T.C.P. N.C. N.N.R. S.S.S.I. M.A.F.F. S.D.A. R.L.U.O. C.W.A.E.C.
C.A.E.C. Common Land. M.L.N.R. N.P. A.O.N.B. Green Belts.
N.P.C. N.C.C. N.T. Enterprise Neptune. F.C. C.P.R.E. O.S. N.T.S.

4 HABITATS   35
The New Naturalist Series of Habitat and Regional volumes.
Science Out of Doors. Woodlands, Wetlands, Grassland. Arctic –
Alpine Vegetation Reserves. Geological Monuments.

v

5 THE NATURE CONSERVANCY 1949-1965 47
Royal Charter 1949. The First Report 1953. *The First Ten Years.*
Some early reserves. The Report of 1958. Scientific Policy Com-
mittee. Committees for England and Wales. National Collection
of Nature Photographs. Dr. E. B. Worthington. Merlewood,
Monks Wood, Bangor. Dr. J. Berry. Research. Conservation in
the Regions. Acquisitions. I.U.C.N. International Congresses.
Royal Commission on Common Land. Countryside in 1970.
N.E.R.C. I.B.P.

6 THE CHANGING CONCEPT OF CONSERVATION 61
From the hobby of a few to a national concern. Haphazard
observations to systematic study. Fundamental importance of
applied ecology. The Council for Nature and its work. County
Naturalists' Trusts. Conservation and Ethics.

7 CONSERVATION AND CONTROL 69
Ecology. Applied ecology: farming and horticulture. Balance in
grazing. Plant indicators. Significance of unique habitats. Teesdale. Life cycles. Large Blue butterfly. Control by gamekeepers.
Squirrels. Problem of the grey seal. Culling.

8 THE LAW AND THE LAND 84
Game Laws. Falconry. Game Act 1831. Protection of Birds Act
1954. Amenity Clause 1952.

9 FARMING AND WILD LIFE 90
Farming changes through the ages. Deforestation. Enclosures.
Board of Agriculture. Corn Laws and their repeal. Decline of
Farming. Farming in 1900-1914. Farming between the wars.
Post-war Farming. Mechanization. Chemicalization. Present
dangers.

10 FORESTRY AND WILD LIFE 107
The native vegetation of Britain. Deforestation and devastation.
The Forestry Commission and its work. The new landscape.

11 WETLANDS AND WILDFOWL 118
Wildfowl defined. Wildfowl counts. Wildfowl Trust. Refuges.
Wildfowling. Caerlaverock. St. James's Park.

12 BOTANICAL GARDENS AND ZOOS   123

13 CONSERVATION IN THE SOUTH-WEST   129

14 THE SOUTH-EAST AND SOUTH   135

15 CONSERVATION IN EAST ANGLIA   145

16 CONSERVATION IN THE MIDLANDS   151

17 CONSERVATION IN THE NORTH   156

18 WILD WALES   163

19 CONSERVATION IN SCOTLAND   169
   Conditions different from England. Effect on conservation.

20 THE MANAGEMENT OF RESERVES   179

21 SURVEY AND RESEARCH   184

22 THE PROBLEM OF INTRODUCTIONS   193

23 OPPOSITION TO CONSERVATION, AND THE FUTURE   198

   BIBLIOGRAPHY   205

   APPENDIX I *Council for Nature*   211
         II *The Nature Conservancy*   217
        III *Field Studies Council*   220
         IV *Conservation and allied areas*, by James Fisher   221
   INDEX   261

ILLUSTRATIONS

1 Sir Arthur Tansley FRS *Crown Copyright*   *facing page* 18

2 Editorial Board of the New Naturalist Series, 1945-66
  Eric Hosking   19

3 Juniper Hall Field Centre *Nature Conservancy*   34
  Flatford Mill Field Centre *J. Allan Cash*   34

4 Ospreys at Loch Garten, 1962 *S. C. Porter*   35

5 Field activities of the Council for Nature *J. R. Ridges*,
  Eric Hosking   50

6 The Hooked Spit of Spurn Head *Aerofilms Ltd*   51
  The Shingle Ridges of Dungeness *Cambridge University Collection*   51

7 Weathered Durness Limestone (Sutherland) *Nature Conservancy*   66
  Marram-grass covered sand-dune (Anglesey) *Crown Copyright*   66

8 Gibraltar Point, Lincolnshire *Aerofilms Ltd*   67

9 Two problems of nature conservation: Aston Rowant,
  Oxfordshire-Buckinghamshire *Nature Conservancy*   74

10 Deer in the Scottish Highlands (winter 1965) *between pages* 74 *and* 75
  Planair

11 Gulls and grey seals in nature reserves   *facing page* 75

12 Ashwood on limestone, Rassal NNR   98

13 Path in the Cairngorms NNR   99

14 Barnacle Geese near Caerlaverock NNR *N. Charles*   114

15 Two views of conservation in the back garden *Eric Hosking*   115

16 Tree hide in the Minsmere Nature Reserve *Eric Hosking*   146
  Cage for Large Copper larvae, Woodwalton Fen   146

17 Scarp of Carboniferous Limestone, Denbighshire *Cambridge
  University Collection*   147

18 Nature Conservancy staff studying the stabilising of scree, N.
  Wales *Nature Conservancy*   162

19 Air view of the Highland Boundary Fault across Loch
   Lomond *Cambridge University Collection*   163

20 Guillemots and Kittiwakes, Farne Islands *Eric Hosking*   178

21 Golden Eagle and young *Eric Hosking*   179

22 The Red Grouse investigation *Adam Watson*   194

23 Grey Squirrel *John Markham*   195

MAPS

1 National Parks, Areas of Outstanding Natural Beauty,
   Green Belts   *page* 28

2 Some centres used for field studies   38

3 Nature Conservancy areas in Scotland   56

4 Nature Conservancy areas in England and Wales   57

5 Extent of Forestry Commission areas in England, Scotland
   and Wales   113

The publishers are grateful to the Controller of Her Majesty's Stationery
Office for allowing them to reproduce Maps 3 and 4 from the Nature
Conservancy publication, *Handbook to Nature Reserves*. Map 2 is based on
the plan in *Science out of Doors* (Longmans).

EDITORS' PREFACE

Sir Dudley Stamp died in August 1966. He had been a prime mover in initiating the New Naturalist series, for which he was a devoted and energetic editor and writer for a quarter of a century.

In this period, certainly the most important ever to the evolution of our island's land use, planning and conservation systems, Dudley Stamp earned a central and scientifically benign position in an arena which can only be entered by a keen polymath. The arena is generally known as geography; but to Dudley's fellow editors and (they suspect) to Dudley himself it was simply an area of general natural history in the old broad sense, embracing human husbandry and exploitation of natural resources as facets of nature.

If the New Naturalist has come to represent, to the young geographer, a series of analyses that proves that natural history and geography share the same facet of the crystal of learning, it has Dudley Stamp to thank. His own books in our series—*Britain's Structure and Scenery, Man and the Land, The Common Lands of England and Wales*, and now this present volume—are marvels of collative scholarship and profound synthetical thought on geology, physiography, ecology, land use and management. Dudley's foreword to this book confesses his own deep conservationist inspiration. It was the last thing he wrote, for he lived to see no proof of a work which has been seen through the presses by his fellow editors. These accept far more blame than their departed friend for such errors, inconsistencies and out-of-date references that may have survived in it.

As Director, President or Chairman, Dudley Stamp served, amongst others, at one time or another, a legion of bodies dedicated to scientific progress—at home, the Royal Geographical Society, the Geographical Association, the Institute of British Geographers, the geographical section of the British Association for the Advancement of Science, the Natural Resources Advisory Committee, the National Committee for Geography, the English Committee of the Nature

Conservancy, and (most famously) the Land Utilisation Survey. Internationally, he was quondam President of the International Geographical Union, Chairman of the World Land Use Survey Commission, Chairman of the host committee when the International Geographical Congress met in London in 1964.

In all these responsible posts Dudley Stamp was the same sort of committee-man as he was on our New Naturalist editorial board—a servant of the truth and orderly scientific progress by simple (but not simplistic) dialogue and disputation. His mastery of geography and geography's organisation and strategy never gave him the master, as opposed to servant, image in his administrative work. He got things done by Socratic persuasion, leavened by a happy humour and the most patent love of his multifarious subjects.

Dudley Stamp's obsession and scholar's skill with so many sciences were deployed in a style that earned him not only undying fame and honour but eternal respect and affection. His fellow New Naturalist editors and their publishers are witnesses to this, and their meetings in the future will never be the same. They will not, however, be without him, for he has set principles and approaches to our *New Naturalist* policy that can never be lost. His mantle as geographical editor in our series is now worn by Dr. Margaret Davies. Mrs. Davies's polymathic knowledge of general natural history and geography is much in the Stampian tradition, and the rest of us venture to declare that the old master would have approved of his successor as much as we do.

JAMES FISHER
JOHN GILMOUR
JULIAN HUXLEY
ERIC HOSKING

AUTHOR'S PREFACE

The first meeting of the Editorial Board of the New Naturalist was held on January 7th 1943. Our original intention, at the request of our publishers, was to draw up a detailed scheme for thirty-six volumes which should cover the whole field of British natural history. We soon realized that it would be better to have an elastic series giving our authors scope to develop their own particular fields of study, and that we could in this way interest the cream of scientific workers who would never agree to write within a framework laid down by others. We believed that the time had come to break away from the long-held belief that books on natural history must be written in popular style – a belief common to most publishers. We believed on the contrary that there was a large public waiting to be introduced to serious work and research in progress, provided it was presented in an attractive manner.

A little later we were called upon to put our creed succinctly into words to assist in advance publicity for the series, and I well remember the draft we produced, having after much discussion coined the general title 'The New Naturalist' towards the end of a long meeting. It read:

> 'The aim of this series is to interest the general reader in the wild life of Britain by recapturing the inquiring spirit of the old naturalists. The Editors believe that the natural pride of the British public in the native fauna and flora, to which must be added concern for their conservation, is best fostered by maintaining a high standard of accuracy combined with clarity of exposition in presenting the results of modern scientific research. The plants and animals are described in relation to their homes and habitats and are portrayed in the full beauty of their natural colours, by the latest methods of colour photography and reproduction.'

This has stood with but minor modification for nearly a quarter of a century as our aim – printed opposite the title page of each successive volume.

Right from our very first meeting it was a declared aim that in due course the five editors should collaborate in a volume on Nature Conservation. Looking back, the inception of the whole series was a tremendous act of faith in the future at a time when that future looked black indeed. Few of our early meetings passed without an air-raid warning; we occupied a succession of temporary offices in different parts of London and rather took the view that if a bomb were intended for us that would be that. To some extent perhaps the excitement of thinking out this great and imaginative scheme took our minds off the everlasting contemplation of a war which was not going too well for us – though I doubt if anyone ever really envisaged eventual defeat – and in a sense our work for the New Naturalist was a form of escapism.

We knew that many of the older publishers were shaking their heads and prophesying a colossal flop. But such was the obvious interest aroused, even in advance of publication of the first titles, that the initial printing order was increased from 5,000 to 10,000 and then at the last minute to 20,000 of each. The war, both in Europe and the East, came to an end while those books were actually passing through the press. Though publishers were rationed for paper and had to use their scant supplies to best advantage, the public were never rationed for books – if they could get them. A bright new series was a godsend to harassed seekers after presents as well as to a public hungry for peace and forgetfulness of war. What better than natural history?

Most of us were old enough to remember the disaster of the early twenties, following the First World War, when there was a dismal failure to produce the promised world fit for heroes. All during the years of the Second World War was the determination to be ready for the peace.

The better life must include not only food, clothing and homes – the general satisfaction of material needs – but also the satisfaction of the less obvious demands of the spirit. To use much misused words: cultural needs. Daily hunger is countered by daily food, but the need to deal systematically with the demands of the spirit, the vital need for recreation, had long remained less obvious.

Planning for the future was in the air. As, one after another, our cities were bombed, plans were put in hand for their rebuilding. They were to have a green ring of rural land, productively used but not urbanized. There were to be large tracts set aside for quiet enjoyment. But enjoyment of what? Clearly the natural or semi-natural vegetation of mountain, moorland and coast, and with it the wild life – the animals.

Gradually the concept of nature conservation began to fit in as part of the picture of our land in the future. Naturalists met town and country planners; they did not clash.

The story of the rapid rise of interest in conservation after the war is told in outline in the pages which follow. Developments were so numerous, so kaleidoscopic, that the book the editors had planned to write became more difficult as the years went by. The volumes of the New Naturalist series continued to grow in both number and scope: the editors were presented with an *embarras de richesses*.

So our attempt to deal in general – at long last – with the Conservation scene cannot be other than a snap-shot picture of the present stage of progress. It is as much an indication of what remains to be done as it is a record of achievement to date.

My fellow editors entrusted the task of writing this general volume to me. It covers a wide field and I am indebted to many friends for help and guidance. I would mention particularly those on the Nature Conservancy in England (especially Mr. Max Nicholson), Wales, and Scotland (especially Dr. John Berry). No one has been more closely associated with the expansion of voluntary efforts in the conservation field than Mr. A. E. Smith; to him I render very sincere thanks for reading critically through my typescript. I need scarcely add that comments and constructive criticism are always welcome.

L.D.S.

CHAPTER I

THE BACKGROUND OF CONSERVATION

Nature conservation should be viewed as part of the world-wide problem of resource conservation. World population, expanding at an explosive rate never before reached in the whole history of mankind, must derive its needs from a known and static land area and the surrounding oceans which, if little exploited to date, are also of known and fixed extent.

At present, population pressure varies greatly from country to country. Britain is among the most densely peopled countries in the world, which makes the problem both urgent and acute. Nature conservation is both vital and difficult.

These are large claims and need to be substantiated. Within recent years much more has become known concerning the world population: there are few countries now where no census has yet been taken, and in the majority the rate of increase has become a matter of fact rather than speculation. The last major country to conduct a national census on modern lines was China in 1953. Now it may be said that the figures published annually by the United Nations give a total accurate to within 2 per cent.

For mid-1966 the world population is of the order of 3,400,000,000; the net annual increase is now known to be over 2.1 per cent per annum, so that the world is adding to itself over 70,000,000 persons a year. Tersely expressed, the phenomenal rise in the net increase, boldly estimated at 0.8 to 1 per cent per annum only a couple of decades ago, is the result of the knowledge and practice of death control spreading more rapidly and widely than the knowledge and practice of birth control. One after another the old killing diseases of mankind have been brought under control or even eliminated: only a few still defy the skill of the doctor, the attention of the nurse and a large range of new drugs. Population increase is greatest in those less developed parts of the world where modern medicine and health services are penetrating for the first time, for, broadly speaking, there is little change in the birth rate in most countries.

But even in those countries which, like our own, have long enjoyed the advantages of advanced medical skill and care, the changes are considerable. In 1900 nearly a quarter of all deaths recorded were under the heading 'infant mortality' – of babies in their first year. By 1961 this figure had dropped to 1.85 per cent. In 1900 TB killed 10.4 per cent – in 1961 this figure was down to 0.62, but cancer was up from 4.5 to 17.95. The net effect in Britain is an expanding but ageing population. Every baby born alive has an average expectation of life of over three score years and ten: already one person in every seven or eight can qualify to be called an old-age pensioner, being over 65 (men) or 60 (women). Whatever the sceptics may say, seen from many parts of the world Britain looks an attractive place in which to live, hence the steady flow of immigrants. A couple of decades ago a dark face was rare: now there are over a million.

Whereas demographers of the 'thirties confidently prophesied that 1936 would see the peak of Britain's population, the actual figures have been as follows:

	England and Wales	Scotland	Great Britain
1921	37,886,699	4,882,497	42,769,196
1931	39,952,377	4,842,980	44,795,357
1951	43,757,888	5,096,415	48,854,303
1961	46,104,548	5,178,490	51,283,038
1962	46,669,000	5,197,000	51,866,000
1963	47,023,000	5,205,000	52,228,000
1964	47,401,000	5,206,000	52,607,000
1965	47,763,000	5,204,000	52,967,000
1966	48,075,000	5,191,000	53,266,000
1967	48,391,000	5,187,000	53,578,000

But the area remains unchanged – England and Wales at 58,347 square miles (37,342,080 acres), Scotland 30,405 square miles (19,459,200 acres) totalling 88,752 square miles or 56,801,280 acres.

It is usual to express density in persons per square mile. England

and Wales with over 812, or the whole of Britain with nearly 600, are immediately seen to be the most densely peopled in Europe, except the Netherlands.

Personally I find it more instructive to look at population density in another way – in area per person. In Britain as a whole there is now only a little over 1 acre per head – 1.08 to be more precise. Taking England and Wales apart from Scotland this total is reduced to a little over three-quarters of an acre—0.79 to be exact, an area which is becoming rapidly less year by year as the population grows.

In simple words we in Britain must satisfy all our needs of land on the basis of an acre a head. Land is essential for industry, including mining and quarrying, for housing and urban development, for sport and recreation, for airfields, roads, railways, car parks, and other needs of transport, for training grounds for the services. All these may be classed as man's urban needs and surprisingly enough accurate statistics do not yet exist, though they are being collected by the Ministry of Land and Natural Resources. We have more exact figures for agricultural and forest land, though rough grazing, especially common land, is still largely a matter of guess-work. In 1964 crops and grass (i.e. improved farmland) occupied 24,378,343 acres in England and Wales, and 4,305,086 in Scotland. If the Ministry of Agriculture's estimate of rough grazing in England and Wales is 4,856,000 acres and of the Department of Agriculture for Scotland of 12,386,000 acres in that country, we get a rough total of *all* agricultural land in Great Britain of 45,925,000 acres, leaving roughly 10,900,000 of all other land, out of which forests occupy about 4,250,000 acres.

However one looks at the figures of land use in Britain, the assessment must be the same. Every acre is precious, for land as a whole is in short supply. Yet with an increasing standard of living our people have a right to expect more space in which to live: slum dwellings and back-to-back houses 64 to the acre belong surely to an age which is past. At our present population growth we need another 100,000 houses a year, plus those for replacement of obsolete and sub-standard houses. These demands, added to those for industry and other urban uses, are eating into the remaining open land at a rate of between 35,000 and 50,000 acres a year.

Where, and how, with such a limited land bank and such constant withdrawals, can we find the land for nature conservation? That is the crux of the problem.

How does Britain stand in comparison with other countries? Nearly all are better off than we are in terms of available land and to that extent their task is easier.

If the land surface of the globe were to be divided equally between the present 3,400,000,000 people, each person would have about 11 acres or nearly eleven times the area available in Britain. The eleven acres would be of most varied type—a fifth covered with snow or ice or permanently frozen, a fifth desert or semi-desert, a fifth rugged mountain, a tenth bare rock, leaving 30 per cent for all farmlands actual or potential. In the world as a whole land is not yet in short supply.

Many countries are still rich in land resources. A good example is the United States with about 12 acres per head (better than world average), of which roughly half has a range of rainfall and temperature enabling it to be classed as cultivable. Quite apart from the contrast in total area, density of population in Britain or, in other words, scarcity of land, makes it quite impossible for us to adopt, without great modification, nature conservation of the type and scale possible in the United States. This is important because we are so often urged to take the United States as our example in so many ways. We cannot afford the vast national parks, the huge nature reserves any more than we can afford the huge land-consuming highways of the U.S.A.

Nature conservation, considered as an aspect of planned land use, must work out its own salvation in the cramped conditions of Britain. Shortage of land is the background of our problem.

On the other side of the picture conditions in Britain are unique in another way. It has often been stressed that no other country in the world can show such a range of environmental conditions within so small an area. In large measure, as a result of a long and complex geological history, Britain can show representative rocks laid down during nearly all the periods of geological time and can fairly claim to be a microcosm of world conditions. Geological history is reflected in physical build with the marked contrast between the wet wind-swept masses of Highland Britain of the north and west, and the relatively dry sunny fertile lowlands of the south and east, almost frost-free in the extreme south-west. In soils the range is from bare rock, acid blanket bog and tundra of the highlands and west to some of the most fertile soils in the world, interspersed with wetlands of fen type, in Lowland Britain in the east. Within what may be called a very small area may thus be found an extreme range of habitat conditions.

The later phases of geological history are important also. At their greatest extent the ice sheets of the Great Ice Age, when Man was already inhabiting Britain, covered nearly all of the country north of a line from the Severn to the Thames estuary; southwards we were still united by land with continental Europe. But with the retreat of the ice Britain's land bridge was severed and we became an island ecosystem. Against the varied physical background successive human invasions have played very different roles in the evolution of the man-land relationship. Severance from the continent came before the country had been re-invaded by more than a limited range of plants and animals so that deliberate introductions have been, and continue to be, an important element in our biota. In general the older introductions are accepted as part of our native and natural inheritance, the newer are frequently damned as exotics and aliens.

Indeed there is a danger that nature conservation may become confused with what is really a wrong view of preservation. When their aims and objects are analysed dispassionately (talk of preservation usually arouses passion) it often becomes apparent that what exponents of preservation seek to preserve is the countryside of their childhood as they happen to remember it. It is not the 'natural' countryside but one particular stage in the evolution of a man-controlled land-use pattern. Very little of our moorland and heathland is 'natural' or even 'semi-natural': it results from the medieval destruction of forest and woodland. The lowland checkerboard of small fields divided by hedgerows with hedgerow trees is highly unnatural – the creation of the last two centuries when enclosure changed what must have been a prairie-type landscape.

Whilst major changes have thus taken place in the past over the face of Britain it is true that today the pace of change is speedier than ever before. We are in the midst of the new agricultural revolution. Farming is no longer a way of life which dominates the countryside: it has become a highly organized industry devoted to the production of food by a small, skilled minority on behalf of a largely urban majority. Increased output per man, per man-hour and per unit area often means depopulation of rural areas and paradoxically the decay of the village. It is achieved by mechanization, chemicalization and applied genetics. Mechanization involves larger units whether of fields or farms and farm buildings; chemicalization involves fertilizers on the one hand and pesticides on the other; applied genetics involves the substitution of specialization with selected strains of plants and animals for the old, rather haphazard, mixed farming.

The incidental impact of the new agricultural revolution on the countryside pattern is enormous. Familiar wild flowers of field and hedgerow – just weeds to the farmer – are disappearing and with them the whole associated fauna. Mechanization makes land drainage economic where it was previously impossible or prohibitively costly, so wetlands with associated flora and fauna disappear.

It is accordingly against this background that nature conservation becomes vital and urgent. But, fortunately, quite tiny areas can have a function and significance wholly incommensurate with size and, so varied is our terrain, almost every county has its own special problems and interests. Therein lies the importance of the work of County Naturalists' Trusts and of the realization that nature conservation is the concern of all: indeed there must be few who play no part. The harassed housewife hurriedly shaking the breakfast crumbs into the backyard is a conservationist encouraging the now remarkable symbiosis between wild life and man.

CHAPTER 2

THE MOVEMENT TOWARDS CONSERVATION

It would seem that a certain love and appreciation of nature has long been a basic characteristic of the British people. I use the word 'certain' deliberately because there are those who will say the love was too closely associated with the pleasures of the chase – with hunting, shooting and fishing – and that it was a love of destruction rather than of life. To a considerable extent the paradox persists to the present day. Many a true countryman is at one and the same time an enthusiastic supporter of his County Naturalists' Trust and a devotee of fox-hunting: wildfowling may even be used as a means of maintaining a balance in the conservation of species.

Actually the British public is very inconsistent in its attitude to conservation. Birdwatching, otherwise prying into the private lives of birds, has become a national sport and the ever-present danger is that birdwatchers may become more numerous than the birds ot be watched. There is now a nation-wide appreciation of birds and bird-life to such an extent that a single pair of ospreys, superciliously regarding their admirers from the sanctity of a precariously perched nest, may command an army of sixty day-and-night volunteer guardians to control their 37,000 visiting fans. It is perhaps natural that birds should hold pride of place in public interest. They are largely diurnal and sleep by night as do the best people; though many delight in display, the majority, again like the best people, hide sufficient of their charms or charming customs as to be intriguing. Many of our mammals, unfortunately, are nocturnal; those like the squirrels displaying themselves by day are popular, but it is difficult to arouse enthusiasm for the conservation of rats and mice. Going down the scale, viper-enthusiasts are rare, and I personally am sorry that so little stir has been caused by the tragic disappearance of the little lizards from our Cornish walls. Some rare butterflies have evoked much interest, but the rest of our insects secure little public attention. Fish, and we think of the pollution of our streams and rivers; few seem to rate salmon-gaffing as cruelty to animals. We are reminded, too, of the children's book presumably in the tradition of St. Francis of Assisi which puts prayers into the mouths of his adoring animals and birds. 'Give us plenty of little slugs and other luscious things to eat,' pray the ducks. But there is no prayer for the slugs.

There is evidence, of course, that our ancestors appreciated wild life to some extent for its own sake. If the Roman legionaries stationed in Britain shared the interests of the soldier-naturalist, Pliny, it is possible that bird-watching from Hadrian's Wall whiled away the time and mitigated some of the tedium of guard duties. Chaucer reminds us that pilgrims to Canterbury favoured the early spring, though the quotation from the Prologue suggests that ornithological research had far to go:

'Whan that Aprill with his shoures soote
The droghte of March hath perced to the roote,
And smale foweles maken melodye,
That slepen al the nyght with open ye.'

Although it may be claimed that one of our bird sanctuaries – the famous Abbotsbury Swannery – has been a nature reserve since the fourteenth century, swans were long a source of food regarded as a delicacy, and the reserve, like the early coney warrens, had an economic rather than a purely scientific basis. It is, of course, to be noted that our naturalists were early in the field in their careful descriptions of both plants and animals.

Broadly speaking, primitive peoples, or peoples few in number in vast spaces, fear wild nature whether it be dense forest or desert waste, and wild animals are enemies, not friends. This is especially true of people emerging from a close dependence on their environment to become tillers of the soil or herders of cattle. They seek out the best soils – as our Anglo-Saxon forebears settled on the loam terrains; they live together for protection and shun the unfriendly wilds.

This attitude persisted for long in Britain. The King's Highway is a reminder that His Majesty's loyal subjects might look for a certain protection there, not to be enjoyed on by-roads and tracks. In the latter part of the eighteenth century Samuel Johnson, eccentric though he was, did but echo the sentiment of the majority of his fellow countrymen in regarding the Scottish Highlands as a 'dismal and perilous wilderness.' Half a century later William Cobbett, riding through the length and breadth of England, had praise only for the neat well-farmed lands, and his description of Surrey's beloved Hindhead as 'the most villainous spot that God ever made' reflects the assessment of our uncultivated lands at that time.

One of our oldest amenity societies is the Commons, Open Spaces and Footpaths Preservation Society, formed in 1865. But it came into existence to protect the rights of commoners against attempts to enclose and 'develop' – to use a modern term – the remaining commons, especially in the metropolitan area. It really had nothing to do with nature conservation, though its indirect effect in that direction has been very important. The establishment of Yellowstone National Park, with its natural wonders in the geysers and wild bears, took place in 1872 and stirred the imagination, but the demarcation of 3,350 square miles – a greater area than the largest English administrative county – of practically uninhabited forest seemed to have little relevance for Britain.

It was our birds which inspired the first major move towards conservation – the founding of the Society for the Protection of Birds in 1889. Its Royal Charter came later, in 1904. The story of the founding of the National Trust in 1895 is discussed below. The protection that ownership by the Trust has afforded to some of our most important areas of wild vegetation is incidental rather than deliberate.

The early years of the present century saw the awakening of interest in the study of ecology: at first the study of living plants in their natural habitats, later extended to the associated animals. The German botanist, Haeckel, coined the word 'oekology' or 'oecology' in 1873. It reached Britain as oecology, but it was some time before the simpler spelling, ecology, became general (*Nature* in 1902). Personally I regard the publication by the Clarendon

Press of an English translation in 1903 of A. F. W. Schimper's great work, *Plant Geography*, as really marking the awakening to ecology. More than any other one book it shaped my own thinking and I determined to take an Honours degree in Botany specializing in ecology. I had spent the formative years of my boyhood among the dry chalk valleys of the North Downs, and at the age of eight started a herbarium (plants mounted two to a foolscap sheet) with a space for every plant described in Johns' *Flowers of the Field*. But alas! in 1913 there was no provision for field work in the Botany Courses of King's College, London, and we passed three years without even seeing a plant growing naturally. I completed the course, but took my finals in geology, relegating botany to my subsidiary. But things were moving both in the university study of ecology and in nature conservation.

Robert Smith initiated his scheme for a Botanical, actually a Vegetation, survey of Scotland in the 'nineties, and the first two sheets on the scale of 2 miles to one inch were published in 1900 (Edinburgh and North Perthshire). On his untimely death his brother, W. G. Smith, continued the work and two further sheets (Forfar and Fife) were published in 1904-5. Marcel Hardy published a reconnaissance survey of Scottish highland vegetation in 1906. In England a great pioneer in vegetation mapping and ecology was C. E. Moss (Yorkshire in 1901-2), but in the development of ecology the name of Arthur G. Tansley overshadows all others. *Types of British Vegetation* under his editorship was published in 1911. The Committee for the Study of British Vegetation was established in 1904 and nine years later became the British Ecological Society. The first number of the *Journal of Ecology* was published in 1912; it was not till 1932 that papers on animal ecology were separated and the *Journal of Animal Ecology* made its appearance.

The year 1912 marked the birth of the Society for the Promotion of Nature Reserves (S.P.N.R.), largely through the initiative of the Hon. Charles Rothschild. It immediately undertook the task of preparing a schedule of areas in England, Wales, Scotland and Ireland considered worthy of designation as nature reserves. But war broke out before this task was complete and it was not till 1915 that the list was submitted, with a memorandum, to the Board of Agriculture with the proposal that responsibility for nature conservation should be accepted by the Government. It was the first major attack, but there the matter rested for the twenty inter-war years. It was not, however, true that nothing happened. Ecology continued to develop: major contributions included the multi-author volume edited by T. F. Chipp and A. G. Tansley, *Aims and Methods in the Study of Vegetation* in 1926. In 1939 there appeared the first edition, in one magnificent volume, of Professor Tansley's *magnum opus*, *The British Islands and their Vegetation* (Cambridge University Press). Tansley had already in the American journal *Ecology* introduced the term 'ecosystem' and the concept (1935), but the basic ideas were made familiar to British readers in this volume. He defines ecosystem as follows:

'A unit of vegetation considered as such a system includes not only the plants of which it is composed, but the animals habitually associated with them, and also all the physical and chemical components of the immediate environment or habitat which together form a recognizable self-contained entity. Such a system may be called an *ecosystem* (Tansley, 1935), because it is determined by the particular portion, which we may call an *ecotope* (Greek τοπος, a place), of the physical world that forms a *home* (οἰκος) for the organisms which inhabit it. A prisere is the gradual development of such a system, the climax represents the position of relative equilibrium which it ultimately attains, and a subsere is the redevelopment of the same type of system after partial destruction.'

The development of the ecosystem concept has, in the last twenty-five years, played a major part in the development both of ecological studies and nature conservation – especially since the acceptance of man himself as an integral part of the whole.

In 1926 there occurred an event, perhaps little noticed at the time, which was to mark the beginning of an era. It was the establishment of the Norfolk Naturalists' Trust, the first of the County Trusts which thirty years later were destined to play a major role in nature conservation throughout the country and whose work is discussed in a later chapter.

The Society for the Promotion of Nature Reserves returned to the attack in 1941, calling together a conference which led to the setting up of a Nature Reserves Investigation Committee which published several reports. Indeed, since 1942, the S.P.N.R. has initiated many important developments in conservation. In particular it set up in 1958 its County Naturalists' Trusts Committee (on which all the County Trusts are represented) with an important advisory function and undertaking liaison with bodies such as the Nature Conservancy at Headquarters level.

It may reasonably be claimed that the development of land-use mapping and studies played its part in the general advance. The Land Utilisation Survey of Britain began work in earnest in October 1930 and in the three seasons 1931-3 recorded, with the help of thousands of volunteers, the then existing use (or non-use) of every acre of England, Wales and Scotland. The record was made on 15,000 sheets of the 6-inch maps, the results published on a series of 1-inch coloured maps. It happened that the period 1931-3 was that of world-wide depression when British farming was at its lowest ebb and much former farmland had been abandoned.

Among the many worries of the government in the 'thirties was the uneven distribution of industry and industrial workers. Greater London, with the South-East generally, was expanding and prosperous; so too were Birmingham and the West Midlands. The older industrial regions on the other hand were depressed and unemployment serious, even desperate. So the Government in June 1938 – many would say very tardily – set up the Royal Commission on the Distribution of the Industrial Population under the chairmanship of Sir Montague Barlow. Although the Barlow Report was not issued until January 1940 after the outbreak of war in 1939 and is a complex document with majority and minority reports and various notes of reservation, there emerged from it the general conclusion that there must be forward planning in the location of industry and that the days of *laissez-faire* producing a satisfactory answer were over.

If industrial development was to be directed to new areas, there would be an increase in the transfer of open land to urban uses.

But the transfer was already running at the rate of 50,000 acres a year: new land, often the best farmland, was being absorbed, whilst many of the older industrial areas were being abandoned and unsightly noxious wastes left behind. So the Government of the day wisely set up a strong inter-departmental committee on Land Utilisation in Rural Areas under the chairmanship of Lord Justice Scott. It was appointed in October 1941 jointly by Lord Reith, recently appointed Minister of Works and Buildings (later to be Works and Planning) and Mr. R. S. Hudson (later Lord Hudson), then Minister of Agriculture and Fisheries. The terms of reference of the Committee are interesting:

'To consider the conditions which should govern building and other constructional development in country areas consistently with the maintenance of agriculture, and in particular the factors affecting the location of industry, having regard to economic operation, part-time and seasonal employment, the well-being of rural communities and the preservation of rural amenities.'

I had recently published, at the request of the Barlow Commission, my attempt at land classification in Britain with a generalized map on the scale of 1:625,000 (roughly 10 miles to the inch). It divided the land into 10 types, not, it should be noted, graded from 1 to 10 in order of direct agricultural productivity, but 1 to 4 are the good agricultural lands, 5 and 6 medium, 7 to 10 poor. It served to show that really first-class loam soils, capable of intensive cultivation of vegetables and foodstuffs for direct human consumption, covered less than 2.4 m. acres or only 4.2 per cent of the surface of the country. On the other hand much of the land of primary interest in nature conservation – the yellow land or rough grazing of the land-use maps – belongs to the four lowest categories of the Land Classification map. The classification used and the small-scale maps produced were first approximations only, but after 30 years are still not superseded.

As Vice-Chairman of the Scott Committee, I undertook the drafting of much of the Report—most of it done over week-ends enjoying the hospitality of Lord Justice Scott's country home at Brightwell-cum-Sotwell in Berkshire. There we tested out our ideas concerning the future of the countryside by tramping many miles over the land itself.

We interpreted our terms of reference very widely and our Report was hailed as a 'blueprint' for the countryside. It must indeed be almost unique in that our recommendations (with the exception of our plans for the government machinery required) were embodied in legislation within a few years.

I well remember drafting the paragraphs which deal with national recreation and nature conservation. We postulated a Central Planning Authority and hence Sections 178 and 179 read:

'178. *National and Regional Parks and other open spaces* – The establishment of National Parks in Britain is long overdue. In so far as the character of the country it is desired to include within a national park is determined by the type of farming (e.g. mountain sheep farming) it is essential for that form of utilisation to be continued with the proviso that in the case of a national park it becomes secondary to the main purpose which is public recreation.

'We recommend that the delimitation of the parks be undertaken nationally and we recommend the setting up of a body to control National Parks under the Central Planning Authority or other appropriate Central Authority.

'We view with appreciation the work of the Forestry Commission in the establishment of National Forest Parks, and the magnificent work of the National Trust.

'As part of a National Parks Scheme we recommend that the coast of England and Wales should be considered as a whole with a view to the prevention of further spoliation.

'So far as smaller regional open spaces are concerned the remaining common lands of the country form a natural nucleus for a national scheme. We recommend that the Central Planning Authority should, in conjunction with the Ministry of Agriculture, take steps to record details of common lands, to safeguard any public rights of access or use, and otherwise to ascertain the position of commoners' rights. We recommend further that the question of the upkeep of commons be investigated.

'179. *Nature Reservations* – While some of the larger National Parks will naturally form or contain "nature reserves" and it may be possible to set aside portions of them specifically for the purpose, it is essential in other cases that prohibition of access shall be a first consideration, and for this reason nature reserves should also be established separately from National Parks. We recommend that the Central Planning Authority, in conjunction with the appropriate Scientific Societies, should prepare details of areas desired as nature reserves (including geological parks) and take the necessary steps for their reservation and control – which must be strict if rare species are to be safeguarded.'

The determination to be ready for the Peace was in the air. Already before the Scott Committee had begun its sittings, Lord Reith, on appointment as Minister of Works, had set up a high-powered Advisory Committee on Planning. We met only once, in May 1941, and agreed to work by sub-committees. The Maps Sub-committee supervised the setting up of the Maps Research Office and I released the Organizing Secretary of the Land Utilisation Survey (Dr. E. C. Willatts) part-time to head the new development.

The Scott Committee was fortunate in its two secretaries – Dr. Thomas Sharp, already with a considerable reputation as a town planner with special interest in village life, and Mr. Basil Engholm of the Ministry of Agriculture, who prepared the basic material from the agricultural angle. Even before the Committee reported, the Ministry of Agriculture, which only a few years before had declared it had no interest in planning, decided to set up a Central Planning Branch. I was invited to become Chief Advisor on Rural Land Use, a post I held for more than fifteen years whilst the Branch with its ten Rural Land Utilisation Officers – all like myself part-time advisors who did not become civil servants – expanded and was eventually merged with the Agricultural Land Service. All during that time we were immediately concerned with trying to dovetail the demands of agricultural improvement with the needs of nature conservation – interests which at times met head on, as with the proposed draining of some interesting piece of marshland.

When the Scott Report was issued in August 1942 some government machinery was thus already in existence to forward its proposals. In due course, with much further study, the Ministry of Agriculture drew up the famous Agriculture Act 1947 which it may be said revolutionized the whole concept of farming. It gave the farmer a guaranteed market for commodities considered desirable at guaranteed prices, and a security of tenure in exchange for certain sureties of efficient farming. At the same time the equally important Town and Country Planning Act 1947 made planning compulsory for the whole country with the county as the unit area.

But the Government decided that certain recommendations of the Scott Committee required further study – in particular the recommendations regarding National Parks, Nature Conservation, Footpaths and Access, and Land Transfer.

A comprehensive investigation into the case for National Parks was put into the hands of John Dower and the result was the well-known Dower Report. John Dower was a sufferer from advanced tuberculosis and he knew that he had only a few years to live. With the self-sacrificing approval of his wife (daughter of Sir Charles Trevelyan and so scion of a family steeped in the traditions of the English countryside) he determined to devote his last years to forwarding the cause of National Parks. As far as possible he avoided the office work in town which was particularly dangerous, and striding over moorland and mountain saw the problems at first hand. He did not long survive the publication of his Report (May 1945) and it is appropriate that his widow should become a founder member of the National Parks Commission and later its Deputy Chairman. Although concerned primarily with National Parks, the Dower Report recommended 'a permanent organ of Government . . . called the Wild Life Conservation Council'.

The concept of the National Park varies from country to country and perhaps the real function in Britain has never been resolved. Broadly speaking the main National Parks of the United States are large areas of outstanding natural beauty where facilities are provided so that visitors can reach and appreciate the scenery, the vegetation and wild life, and find accommodation of different types provided for that end. Hunting, shooting, and gathering of wild flowers are strictly forbidden, so that the National Parks serve also as nature reserves. 'Wilderness areas' difficult of access provide the necessary seclusion for wild life and the parks are, in general, without farmers or foresters, and are managed by the National Park Service. Just across the border in Canada, the National Parks perform all these functions, but parts are also developed for ordinary recreation. Banff, for example, has its palatial Banff Springs Hotel with tennis courts, swimming pools, riding schools and its extensive golf courses set in magnificent scenery. Many of the Canadian National Parks have facilities for winter sports.

Britain is in a different position. Few areas, even of the remoter mountains and moorlands, are uninhabited or the land unused; the attraction is often as much in the border villages as in the moorland heart. The function of the ten National Parks we have established in England and Wales (Scotland has not adopted the idea) never seems to me to have been decided. Should they be kept as far as possible for the few able and wanting to tramp the miles over the hills, or should their beauties be made more accessible to the fifty million town dwellers by providing better access for cars and accommodation of different types? In any case our areas are too small, too populated and developed to serve automatically as nature reserves. So in Britain nature conservation becomes a separate consideration.

The Scott Committee was particularly concerned with the question of country footpaths and recommended the setting up of a small Footpaths Commission which should be responsible for the survey of footpaths, the recording of their legal status and their representation on maps. The Government rightly considered that more study of this proposal was needed and likewise that, although the Dower Report had made a good case for national parks, a detailed plan was needed. Consequently in July 1945 (the Dower Report had appeared in May) the Government set up the National Parks Committee (England and Wales) under the Chairmanship of Sir Arthur Hobhouse. Its nine members included John Dower himself and Dr. Julian Huxley. It soon became clear that both Nature Conservation and Footpaths needed detailed and special consideration apart from the main problem of national parks, and so two special committees were created. One was the Wild Life Conservation Special Committee under Dr. Huxley as Chairman, and consisting of seven co-opted scientists with special knowledge of the field, including Professor A. G. Tansley (Vice-Chairman) and Mr. John Gilmour, one of my fellow-editors of this series. The other was the Footpaths and Access Sub-committee under Sir Arthur Hobhouse himself and to which I was co-opted.

We are concerned here with Dr. Huxley's group which reported to Mr. Lewis Silkin (later Lord Silkin), then Minister of Town and Country Planning. The report, entitled *Conservation of Nature in England and Wales* (Cmd. 7122, 1947) is the definitive document (together with the corresponding report for Scotland) upon which the work of the Nature Conservancy has been based. In it the work of the various previous committees is fully acknowledged.

The recommendations of these Committees were very quickly embodied in legislation—for the most part in the National Parks and Access to the Countryside Act 1949 which set up the National Parks Commission and laid down the sphere of work of the Nature Conservancy. Actually the Nature Conservancy had been set up in advance of this Act as a Research Council comparable with the Agricultural and Medical Research Councils under the Privy Council. It received its Royal Charter from H.M. King George VI on March 23rd 1949 and offices were opened in both London and Edinburgh. The story of the Nature Conservancy is separately considered (Chapter 5).

Despite the exigencies of war-time conditions, there had in the meantime been activities in other directions. The desirability of a stocktaking of national resources was uppermost in the minds of those who had been advocating the preparation and publication of a National Atlas. The project was taken up by an inter-disciplinary Committee of the British Association for the Advancement of Science and a careful scheme prepared which included maps showing the distribution of a large number of species of plants and animals. The report was published (*Advancement of Science* no. 2, Jan. 1940, 361-8), but war intervened; the project, revived after

1 The late Sir Arthur Tansley F.R.S., from the painting by L. J. Watson

2 The Editorial Board of the New Naturalist Series, from 1945 to 1966.
Standing: James Fisher, W. A. R. Collins, Sir Dudley Stamp
Sitting: John Gilmour, Sir Julian Huxley, Eric Hosking

the war, was turned down utterly by the Treasury and it was
eventually due to the initiative of the Oxford University Press that
the *Atlas of Britain* was at last published in 1963.

The British Ecological Society had been continuing its efforts.
In 1943 the Society published a Memorandum on Nature Conservation and Nature Reserves. Then the Biological Committee
of the Royal Society took up the cudgels and published recommendations for a 'Biological Service'.

In general it may be said that the creation of the Nature Conservancy in 1949 marked the culmination of all these hopes and
efforts. Its first Chairman was A. G. Tansley, Professor Emeritus
of Botany at Oxford (he had retired in 1937), when he was already
seventy-eight. He was knighted in 1950, served as Chairman till
1953 and died in November 1955. He had lived to see his new
approach to the study of vegetation vindicated and a life's ambition
fulfilled with the work of the Nature Conservancy. The first
Director-General of the Nature Conservancy was Captain Cyril
Diver (1949-52). He was succeeded by E. M. Nicholson (1952-66),
under whose guidance the phenomenal development recorded
in Chapter 5 took place. The first National Nature Reserve to be
declared was Beinn Eighe in the Scottish Highlands of Ross-shire
in 1951 (November 1st); the first in England was Scolt Head on
the coast of north Norfolk in March 1954.

At the same time Local Nature Reserves were also coming into
the picture: Aberlady Bay in East Lothian was the first (July 1952),
followed only a month later by Gibraltar Point in Lincolnshire.
The great burst of nation-wide activity which resulted in the setting
up of many County Naturalists' Trusts, each with an active programme, was deferred mainly till the 'sixties, by which time Wildfowl Refuges (starting with the Humber in 1955) had become
firmly established.

Whilst the Nature Conservancy as the official government agency
may be said to have led the field, the need for a widely representative
public body resulted in the establishment of the Council for Nature
in 1958. In January 1959 an interesting development was the
creation by the Council of the Conservation Corps—essentially a
volunteer band of young men and women willing to spend their

summer vacations helping to manage nature reserves by such work as scrub clearance, bracken cutting, and so on.

A period or periods of field work had long been required of undergraduates in many universities preparing for degrees in geology, botany, zoology and geography. In geography it was made a condition of entry to the examination right from the start (the first Honours examination was held in London in 1921). The Easter vacation was a popular time: it was out of season for hostels and hotels which might and did provide accommodation. But facilities for meeting to discuss work in the evening, for the display of maps and specimens, were often absent and a small group, in which the late Professor S. W. Wooldridge of King's College, London, played an important part, set up a Committee for the Promotion of Field Studies (1943) – later the Field Studies Council. With a lukewarm reception and no visible means of support the Council acquired Flatford Mill as its first and Juniper Hall, Mickleham, in the lovely Mole Valley of Surrey, as its second (1946-8) Field Centre – spartan accommodation for students, simple labs and lecture rooms, simple fare. Gradually the Council has gained strength and has established (amongst others) stations at Malham Tarn (Yorkshire), Dale Fort (Pembs.), Slapton Ley (Devon) and Preston Montford (Shropshire) (see Appendices 3 and 4). Many more are needed and, encouraging use by senior forms from schools, all centres have normally more applications for use than can be filled throughout the open season.

In this brief summary of the conservation movement it remains only to refer to the international aspects. The I.U.C.N. (International Union for Conservation of Nature and Natural Resources) has helped many nations to see the need for National Parks and Nature Reserves. Many of the less developed countries have come to realize their wild life is a valuable tourist attraction of immense cash value. Steadily the hunter's rifle has given place to the naturalist's camera. Such remote and formerly inaccessible areas as the Kruger National Park in South Africa, Murchison Falls and Queen Elizabeth Parks in Uganda, and others almost the world over, are now the most powerful magnets in attracting visitors. That delightful Scottish-Canadian naturalist the late Dan McCowan, who spent his winters touring the United States lecturing on the wild life of the Canadian Rockies and his summers guiding the resulting visitors on Nature Trails, delighted in saying that his joy in selling scenery and the wonders of wild life was that when you've sold them you've still got them.

CHAPTER 3

INTRIGUING INITIALS ON THE MAP

One of the minor irritations of the present day is the proliferation of initials. When one is told that N.E.R.C. has taken over N.C. and so is responsible for both N.N.R. and S.S.S.I. as well as P.N.N.R. but not A.O.N.B. or N.P., there is the automatic implication that if one does not follow this important information one is indeed ignorant: so much so that there is often a pretence at understanding rather than a confession. The disease affects almost every walk of life: in the field of nature conservation it is particularly rampant because of the many interests which are involved. Some of the initials have begun to appear on maps in use by the general public who can scarcely be expected to know what it is all about. Even when the initials are understood there remains a very complex situation.

In the first place several government departments are concerned in matters directly or indirectly affecting nature conservation; in some cases the departments concerned are responsible for England only, more frequently for England and Wales, sometimes for Great Britain – England, Wales and Scotland.

When, prior to World War II, some concepts of town planning were introduced into housing legislation, they were the concern of the Ministry of Health – in a section where George L. Pepler soon became the leading spirit. However, during the war it was the Minister of Works and Buildings that appointed the Scott Committee and even before that Committee had reported, the Ministry had become the Ministry of Works and Planning. Shortly afterwards the planning functions were split off to form the nucleus of the separate Ministry of Town and Country Planning, which finally took over the housing and planning functions of the Ministry of Health. M.T.C.P. administered the Town and Country Planning Act 1947 under which physical planning was made compulsory for the whole of England and Wales on a county basis. The financial provisions of that Act, based on the recommendations of the Uthwatt Committee and not in accord with the Scott proposals, allowed for the State to assume ownership of 'development' values, leaving owners with 'existing use' values. Not unnaturally owners, for example of agricultural land near towns wanted for housing, refused to part with their land at 'existing use' value (i.e. as farmland); the supply of land ceased and that part of the Act was repealed. Planning became very largely negative; 'planning' came to be regarded as implying restriction on private enterprise. The Ministry was abolished, its functions being transferred to a new Ministry of Housing and Local Government, indicating the emphasis which the Government wished to place on the importance of housing. During all this time planning in Scotland had continued to rest with the Scottish Department of Health.

Despite these ministerial changes, the practical work of town and country planning remained the same. Each county (and county borough) was required within five years of the coming into operation of the 1947 Act to prepare (a) an outline plan for the area, (b) separate detailed plans for any towns included. Both were designed to cover the 'foreseeable future' – generally equated with twenty years. Generally speaking, the work proceeded steadily according to the requirements of the Act, but the time schedule fell behind and not many counties completed their task within the allotted five years when they were required to submit their plans for approval to the Minister. A County plan when approved showed permitted areas for different types of development, likewise areas to be preserved for such specific purposes as open spaces (public and private). Clearly this is where Nature Reserves were to be shown and fitted into the general pattern. Provision was made for details of National Nature Reserves (N.N.R.) and Sites of Special Scientific Interest (S.S.S.I.) to be communicated to the planning authorities and thus shown for all to see.

Although the Ministry of Town and Country Planning had been made the ministry chiefly concerned with land-use, it was the Ministry of Agriculture and Fisheries (M.A.F.), later Agriculture, Fisheries and Food (M.A.F.F.) and its counterpart in Scotland, the

Scottish Department of Agriculture (S.D.A.) which retained the controlling interest over rural land – some three-quarters of the surface of the country. Two important principles were established: first that agricultural buildings were exempt from planning control, and secondly that change of agricultural use (including from farming to forestry) did not constitute 'development' and so did not require planning permission. For some years the land-use aspects of M.A.F.'s interests were handled by the Central Planning Branch, with myself as Chief, and my team of ten R.L.U.O.'s (Rural Land Utilisation Officers), one in each of the regions. We early reached a useful working arrangement with M.T.C.P. Around each town we agreed an imaginary line, the Urban Fence, which enclosed all developed land plus any open land so 'urbanized' as to have little interest agriculturally. Whatever was done *within* the urban fence was a matter for M.T.C.P. and we did not require to be consulted, except with regard to allotments. *Outside* the urban fence M.T.C.P. had to consult M.A.F. before proposing any developments. Soon we evolved a system of 'brown land'—areas so coloured on outline maps – where M.A.F. would look favourably on proposals for development.

The system worked smoothly but made no provision for interests of nature conservation. Because of grants available to the farmer for draining, ploughing and general improvement of farmland, there was actually increased danger of scientifically important swamps, marshes, moorland, heathland and woodland areas being drained, ploughed up and converted to improved farm land. The difficulty has not yet, in fact, been finally resolved.

It always happens in time of war that governments assume emergency powers, and the Second World War in Britain was no exception. In particular increased home food production was vital, together with a restriction of demands on shipping for imports of such items as animal feeding stuffs. Actually the year between Munich and the outbreak of war in 1939 was well used in preparation and the county organisations – the C.W.A.E.C. (County War Agricultural Executive Committees) were ready for their task which, efficiently performed, did so much to secure Britain's food supply. On the outbreak of war only some 35 per cent of food consumed was home-produced; by 1944 it was over 60 per cent. A key enterprise was the 'plough up' campaign. A field of potatoes or swedes can provide either animal or human food, a field of grass is for animals only. So vast areas of permanent pasture were ploughed, with a consequent very wide change in the environmental habitats for wild life. Interestingly enough, farmers, formerly so independent, came to appreciate the help of the C.W.A.E.C.'s – to the extent that they demanded their continuance after the war as C.A.E.C.'s. Attention was also focused on the possibility of cultivating much of the common land of the country. Normally the Lord of the Manor (who may be a public authority) is the owner of the soil (and minerals), but may do nothing which would prejudice the rights of the commoners – rights which vary but which generally include that to pasture commonable animals, and that to gather firewood and turf. So the Lord of the Manor may not enclose, plough, sow or otherwise improve common land as by planting trees. During the war the temporary legislation gave the Ministry of Agriculture (there is no common land in Scotland) the legal right to do all or any of these things, but provided that in due course the common land had to be restored as common land to the Lord of the Manor. In actual fact much land on which public money had been spent on improvements was thus 'handed back' and allowed to revert to scrub and waste. The Royal Commission on Common Land was set up in 1955 to look into the problem and reported in 1958. Legislation to cover the first requirement, that of registering common land and common rights, did not, however, reach the Statute Book until 1965. It is obviously essential to know the factual, including the legal, position before the next step which is that of integrating common lands into the national economy and land-use pattern of the present day.

Common land is of vital importance in Britain's nature conservation programme. With my colleague on the Royal Commission, Professor W. G. Hoskins, I have discussed the position and given a complete list of all known commons, with details of area and character, in England (the Welsh record was so fragmentary as to defy similar treatment). The summary is as follows (England only):

Commons		Village Greens		Other		Total	
No.	*Acreage*	*No.*	*Acreage*	*No.*	*Acreage*	*No.*	*Acreage*
2,596	1,054,551	1,354	3,905	801	7,316	4,751	1,065,772

Thus common land in 4,751 parcels covers 3.3 per cent of the surface of the country – a larger proportion if Wales is included. The Royal Commission found that nearly 80 per cent was grazed, but no less than 7.8 per cent is scrub and derelict, against 10.4 per cent with amenity and recreational use, 1.9 per cent forest and 0.6 per cent bog, fen and marsh.

Our commons have been described as the last 'uncommitted area of our countryside' but the public is generally wrongly informed as to the position. A common may not be enclosed but it is privately owned land and the public has no general right of access. Only when a common lies within a metropolitan area, wholly or partly within an urban district or when the owner has made the necessary statutory declaration granting the privilege, does this right exist. When enclosure took place from the Middle Ages onwards, the peasants would have become landless had it not been that certain land had to be left open or certain definite 'allotments' set aside to provide grazing and space for them and their few animals or geese. But few cottagers remain who have geese or commonable animals to use the grazing rights, fewer still go out to gather sticks or cut peat for winter fuel, scarcely a parish exists which maintains local roads by digging gravel or stone from the common quarry. Common land as such no longer fits into the economy of the countryside.

But if not grazed or otherwise used, common land reverts to a thicket of scrub with neither economic nor social value. Neglected, it can lose its habitat value also. In brief the Royal Commission recommended that all common land, found to be true common on registration, should be declared as such and that with certain safeguards it should be made legally free for public access. It thus becomes part of the all-important space-network of the country as open land. But also the Royal Commission recognized that all common land needed to be *managed*. It is recognized that some will be managed primarily as recreational land, some may be improved as agricultural, normally grazing, land, some as forest and wood-land. But undoubtedly an important proportion should find its first use and function in nature conservation, to be managed as nature reserves. There are many tracts of common land which are already listed as S.S.S.I. (Sites of Special Scientific Interest) and others as Local Nature Reserves (L.N.R.).

Up to October 1964 common land was primarily the concern of the Ministry of Agriculture, Fisheries and Food in that it provided important and extensive areas of rough grazing. Indeed, in the annual statistics acreage figures were given of rough grazing in individual ownership and use as returned by farmers, together with the estimated area, county by county, of 'common rough grazing' as recorded by the Ministry's officials. Metropolitan and urban commons and other legal open spaces were at the same time the concern of the Ministry of Housing and Local Government. In October 1964 when the new Labour Government set up the separate Ministry of Land and Natural Resources (M.L.N.R.), the problem of common land was placed definitely in the charge of that Ministry. The Royal Commission's Report and the draft legislation were rescued from respective pigeon-holes, carefully dusted, and in just over a year the Commons Registration Bill became law.

In addition to its responsibilities for planning, county by county, the Ministry of Housing and Local Government has been concerned with the broader pattern of open spaces and recreational areas. There have been three aspects of this activity: National Parks, A.O.N.B. or Areas of Outstanding Natural Beauty, and Green Belts.

First, the National Parks Commission set up under the 1949 Act in due course demarcated ten National Parks – the Lake District, Snowdonia, Brecon Beacons, Pembrokeshire Coast, Dartmoor, Exmoor, Peak District, North York Moors, Yorkshire Dales and Northumberland (of the Roman Wall and Cheviot). Though boundaries were varied, this is the list recommended by the 1949 Report, only the South Downs and Broadland being omitted. Though focused around sparsely inhabited country with open moor-land predominating, each of these National Parks includes con-siderable tracts of ordinary farmland. What differentiates a National Park from any other attractive part of the countryside? Mainly a

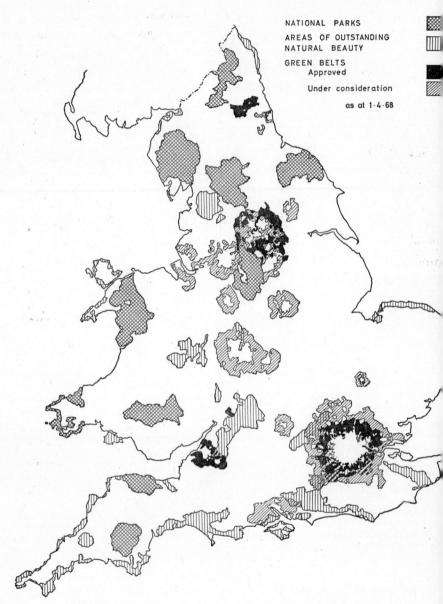

1 National Parks, Areas of Outstanding Natural Beauty, Green Belts

somewhat stricter control over 'development'. Both the Act and the Commission have been criticized, the Act because it failed to provide funds for positive action, the Commission for being content to remain negative. In 1964 the Commission was transferred to the new Ministry of Land and Natural Resources and promised extended powers. At the second Countryside in 1970 Conference held in October 1965 the Minister announced that a Countryside Commission would replace the N.P.C. and be given greater powers – including that to create, own and organize smaller 'country parks' especially for recreation of townsfolk – and funds.

Looked at from the point of view of nature conservation, National Parks enjoy a certain protection from building and development, but they are primarily for human recreation, so that increased access is not always compatible with the needs of wild life. Thus the tendency is to create, where appropriate, specific nature reserves *within* National Parks. The American pattern of combining the two aims does not fit a crowded country such as England. It should be noted that Scotland decided against national parks: there the problems are somewhat different, especially in the sparsely populated highlands.

The Areas of Outstanding Natural Beauty (A.O.N.B.) likewise enjoy a planning control stricter than elsewhere in the countryside. Not only is planning permission to build houses – including country cottages – difficult to obtain, but the construction of roads, erection of pylons and overhead power lines, permission for quarrying, and other 'urban' activities are all watched with care.

Green belts are accorded somewhat similar protection, but they are primarily related to major towns and are designed to afford open space for the enjoyment of the town dwellers concerned. In fact the concept of the Green Belt has undergone considerable evolution. The idea that a green belt should limit the growth of a town has been shown both impracticable and undesirable; a town determined to grow will leap over it and result in a still more undesirable and extensive sprawl. Many towns instead think in terms of a succession of green wedges with the advantage, well seen in Southampton, that open land can extend to the very heart of the city. The problem of trespass by both humans and their dogs makes farming in the green belt somewhat hazardous and although the ideal would seem to be that a green belt should be a tract of well-farmed land, it has tended to be made up of golf courses, sports fields, hospitals and homes with extensive grounds, schools with playing fields, public open spaces and other uses which are primarily urban. But at least the green belts maintain a variety of habitats favourable in particular to those birds which have entered into a symbiotic pact with man – the starlings coming in to roost nightly in Central London are a good example.

A special feature of the work of the M.H.L.G. is the protection of the remaining open stretches of our coastline. Although the launching of the £2,000,000 appeal by the National Trust in 1965 (Enterprise Neptune) seized the public imagination and brought home to a large public the danger of allowing continued building, in reality the Ministry has the necessary powers to prohibit such developments.

The Forestry Commission (F.C.) was established in 1919 as a direct result of Britain's experience in the First World War when much precious shipping space had to be used for essential imports of timber. The determination was to make Britain self-supporting in the event of any future three-years' 'emergency'. Actually the 'emergency' in the shape of the Second World War came before the Forestry Commission's work was sufficiently advanced. Its first mandate was to afforest or reforest 1,777,000 acres. 90 per cent of timber requirements and practically 100 per cent of priority needs are for softwoods, hence the concentration on the planting of conifers. The story of the Forestry Commission and its work has not been altogether a happy one. First, its constitution as an independent government body, not answerable to any Minister, was anomalous and raised difficulties. Its spokesman in the House of Commons was a private member. Second, financial arrangements were bad. The Commission dealt with a long-term project, but it suffered from a fluctuating annual grant always liable to cuts imposed by a government looking for some temporary economy. Yet the Commission was required to operate on commercial lines and could not legally undertake unremunerative amenity planting. In its early days public relations were bad: ignoring local feeling, large areas of moorland and mountainside were bought up and planted in rectangular blocks with usually a single species of conifer. Both the blocks ignoring contours and aspect and the use of a single species were later realized to be bad forestry, but the damage had been done. The Forestry Commission had come to be regarded as an enemy by every amenity society in the country as well as by a large proportion of land-owners, farmers and the public in general.

Although the position has completely changed, the old image dies hard. The writ of the Forestry Commission covers England, Wales and Scotland; in due course it became answerable in parliament through the Minister of Agriculture (but not to the Ministry) and the Secretary of State for Scotland. As the official body expert in forestry, the Forestry Commission is the right and proper authority to advise city and local councils in all matters relative to planting, management and utilisation of trees and woodland. The Commission began to realize its obligations, as an extensive owner and user of land, and so in due course set up National Forest Parks and indeed offers a now much appreciated service to the public. Although amenity groups like the Standing Committee on National Parks are still strongly opposed to commercial afforestation over the moorlands of National Parks, there exists a joint Committee of the Forestry Commission and the Council for the Preservation of Rural England (C.P.R.E.) to thrash out details of planting policy which will minimize the opposition of amenity interests. In 1964 the Commission went so far as to appoint a landscape architect to its staff.

It is well known that Britain can claim only one native coniferous forest tree – the Scots pine (*Pinus sylvestris*). Even that was virtually exterminated by the spread of the ice sheet of the Great Ice Age and most Scots pines are of introduced alien varieties. It was the accident of Britain's early separation from the continent which prevented the Norway spruce (*Picea abies*) from getting back into Britain on its own. It must, therefore, be accepted that the trees mainly grown have been introduced, notably the Sitka spruce (*Picea sitkensis*), now our dominant forest tree and a North American alien. There is a curious anti-conifer cult still quite widespread at least among a vocal minority which tends to refer to 'exotic conifers' as a term of damnation.

What is the position of the nature conservationist? There is no doubt that the new forests of Britain extend the variety of habitats and encourage the breeding especially of many species of birds which do not thrive in the native oakwoods. Our natural storehouse is enriched by the activities of the Forestry Commission and, where the Commission has taken over the management of such natural woodlands as the New Forest and Forest of Dean, a distinct benefit is conferred upon nature conservation.

The Ordnance Survey maps of Britain, including the very popular and widely used one-inch-to-a-mile series, now show – edged in green and marked N.T. – the properties of the National Trust. There is still much misunderstanding regarding the status and functions of the National Trust—to give it its full title, The National Trust for Places of Historic Interest or Natural Beauty – and it is difficult to better the statement given by the Trust itself in the introduction to its list of properties:

'When England was at the height of its prosperity towards the end of the Victorian era, among the few people who perceived the heavy price paid for industrialization – cities strangling the country-side; valleys choking under slag-heaps; chimney-stacks standing where oaks had grown – were Miss Octavia Hill, Sir Robert Hunter and Canon Rawnsley. These practical idealists conceived the idea which took shape as The National Trust. Their plan was to set up a body of responsible private citizens who would act for the nation in the acquisition of land and houses worthy of permanent preservation. They would hold such properties as trustees, protect them from destruction or undesirable development, and allow the public to enjoy them.

'Having started modestly in 1895, The National Trust today (1966) owns over 350,000 acres, comprising well over a thousand properties. It has also accepted many covenants which protect beautiful land or buildings. The Trust's possessions in England, Wales and Northern Ireland include stretches of common, moor, down, mountain, hill, cliff and wood; lakes and waterfalls; nature reserves in which rare birds, insects and plants find sanctuary; farms; prehistoric and Roman antiquities; mansions and manor houses; ancient castles, villages, cottages, bridges, mills, barns and dovecots; many of the best viewpoints in the country; formal and informal parks and gardens; houses in which famous people lived or worked; collections of pictures, furniture, tapestry, books, sculpture and china.

'The public are given free access to the Trust's open spaces, subject to the requirements of farming, forestry and the protection of nature.

'The Trust is controlled by a Council, partly appointed by various public bodies and societies and partly elected by the members of the Trust. Local committees help in administration. Many properties are supported, and some managed, by Local Authorities. Though "national" in name and function the Trust is independent of the State, and is *not* a Government department. Parliament and successive governments have given it valuable assistance, particularly in relief from taxation, but its main sources of revenue are endowments, legacies, donations and members' subscriptions.

'Any person or organization can become a member by paying a minimum subscription of £1.

'Scotland has a separate National Trust.'

In its early days the National Trust was concerned especially with historic buildings and, largely by gift, has become one of the largest landowners in Britain, as well as one of the largest landlords, since most of the properties are let and occupied – often by agreement with their previous owners. But more and more the Trust has become concerned with rural land, recognizing the great importance of the preservation of the countryside. To describe the countryside as the playground of our predominantly urban population is to over-emphasize one aspect of the national estate: the maintenance of the peace and serenity of the countryside as an antidote to urban hustle and stress has become an essential part of national life. It is now becoming generally recognized how easily selfish or thoughtless individual action can destroy, in a crowded country such as ours, the very features which give enjoyment. A single bungalow in an expanse of moorland or on a lovely stretch of coast may give pleasure to the owner, but mars the whole for everyone else. Therein lies the justification for planning, for the restriction of development in our national parks and above all along our still unspoiled stretches of coast. Although the coast can be, and is, protected by planning powers, positive control with maintenance where needed is more satisfactorily achieved by ownership. It was an imaginative concept of the National Trust to launch in 1964-5 Enterprise Neptune with a target of £2,000,000 to acquire or otherwise control the remaining stretches of our coastline – at the start of the campaign it already owned about 165 of the 3,000 miles of the coastline of England, Wales and Northern Ireland.

Much of the open land owned by the Trust forms a natural refuge for wild nature, but fifteen of its properties are specifically listed as Nature Reserves including the Calf of Man, Farne Islands, Brownsea Island in Poole Harbour, Scolt Head, Blakeney Point, Horsey Mere, and Salthouse Broad in Norfolk and the famous Wicken and Burwell Fens, Cambridgeshire.

The National Trust for Scotland (N.T.S., 5 Charlotte Square, Edinburgh 2) has broadly similar aims. It maintains close working arrangements with the Scottish Tourist Board (2 Rutland Place, West End, Edinburgh 1).

3 The Field Studies Council. *Above*: the Juniper Hall Field Centre, Michelham, Surrey. *Below*: Flatford Mill Field Centre

4 Ospreys at Loch Garten 1962 — female returning to nest

CHAPTER 4

HABITATS

The varied fauna and flora of Britain can only continue to exist so long as the varied habitats are themselves maintained. Whilst the wide range of conditions is due primarily to the complex geological history and the siting of the islands in a favoured part of the earth's surface where contrasted air-masses are constantly meeting, it has become necessary, in view of the increasing pressure of population and urban development, to take positive steps to maintain many of those habitats. Improvements, desirable from some points of view, may be disastrous from the naturalist's angle. This applies particularly to agricultural improvements, notably drainage of wetlands, upgrading of hill grazings, realignment of farms, removal of hedgerows, and the whole range of control by chemicals.

It has become necessary to select characteristic examples of habitats and, remembering that they are in greater or less degree the result of man's activities, to maintain them. This is the essence of nature conservation.

All the volumes in the New Naturalist Series are concerned in one way or another with nature conservation in Britain, but they fall into several groups.

There are first what may be called the background books. My own book *Britain's Structure and Scenery* and its sequel *Man and the Land* describe how the complex pattern of the British countryside has arisen from natural causes and the long-continued occupancy by man. Gordon Manley discusses the influence of weather and climate in *Climate and the British Scene*; Sir John Russell deals with *The World of the Soil*; H. L. Edlin with *Trees, Woods and Man*.

Then there are the habitat volumes – Sir Alister Hardy's *The Open Sea*; Dr. C. M. Yonge's *The Sea Shore*; Professor J. A. Steers's *The Sea Coast*; T. T. Macan and Dr. E. B. Worthington's *Life in Lakes and Rivers*; the late Professor W. H. Pearsall's *Mountains and*

Moorlands. Some volumes in this group deal with part of the eco-system only – J. E. Lousley on *Wild Flowers of Chalk and Limestone*; Ian Hepburn on *Flowers of the Coast*; John Raven and Max Walters on *Mountain Flowers*; or James Fisher and R. M. Lockley on *Sea-Birds.*

A third, large group deals with various groups of animals and plants naturally closely associated with habitat conditions.

Fourth are the regional volumes: *Highlands and Islands* of Scotland (F. F. Darling and J. Morton Boyd); *The Weald* (S. W. Wooldridge and F. Goldring); *Dartmoor* (L. A. Harvey and D. St. Leger-Gordon); *The Peak District* (K. C. Edwards); *The Broads* (E. A. Ellis) and *The Snowdonia National Park* (William Condry). With all this wealth of material already published in the New Naturalist series it is not necessary to repeat here – which indeed would be impossible – an account of the varied habitats to be found within the confines of Britain, but we should remind ourselves first of their great range, second of the inter-dependence of one on another, and third that nature conservation must be broadly based to cover all.

In the handy little volume *Science Out of Doors* (Longmans 1963), which was the report of the Study Group on Education and Field Biology set up by the Nature Conservancy in 1960 'to examine the role of field studies and their relation to school education and to science teaching in particular', there are interesting figures and statistics showing the habitats used in field studies by both school children and university students. Freshwater, woodlands and marine habitats head the list; high up are banks and hedgerows, meadows and pastures, wasteland, parkland and moorland. Other habitats included are sand dunes, arable land, marsh, bog and fen, chalk downs, heath, commons, and railway embankments. Two things strike one about this list. First, many of the habitats are part and parcel of the ordinary farmed and used countryside and could not be contained within specific nature reserves. Second, many of the habitats are peculiarly vulnerable to change, whether it be the modernization of agriculture or the disappearance of railways. Nature conservation is far more than the demarcation and management of reserves, it involves the study of the whole range of plant and animal ecology. The Nature Conservancy early realized this and has tried to maintain a balance between conservation applied to its reserves and research broadly based and fundamental.

As noted previously, the work of the late Professor Sir Arthur Tansley played a major part in the conservation movement. Although various modifications have since been introduced, it will be of value to recall his classification of British vegetation because the suggested lists of reserves on which the acquisition programme of the Nature Conservancy was based had, of necessity, to include representative samples of each of the main habitats.

At the beginning of the Christian era, at the time of the Roman invasion and long after the disappearance of the ice sheets, we may postulate the broad picture of Britain's vegetative cover. Doubtless oakwoods covered much or most of the lowlands, grading locally into beechwoods on calcareous soils and loams, into ash-woods on limestone, into pine and birch on sandy lands and high-lands and in the north, and into alder on wetlands. The forest cover was interrupted by marsh, fen and bog on low ground with a high water table. Then forest probably passed into thin scrub, possibly open grasslands, on chalk and limestone ridges, and above the tree-line of the mountain regions into mountain grasslands and tundra. For the most part the grasslands, whether the chalk downs or enclosed lowland meadows, are the result of man's activities and his grazing animals. So too are most, if not all, of our heathlands and moorlands. Hedges have all been planted – largely at the time of enclosure – and so have many woodlands.

The types of vegetation described by Tansley and of which we now seek to conserve representative portions, are thus as follows. Tansley described pedunculate oakwoods (Querceta roboris) and several types of sessile or durmast oakwood (Querceta sessiliflorae) with considerable variations between those in lowland England, the Pennines, Wales, Ireland, and Scotland. Local variation results from a range of moisture conditions, associated species and ground vegetation, so that reserves in several parts of Britain are essential. The beech is believed to have migrated or have been introduced into Britain in Atlantic or Sub-Boreal (early Bronze Age) times, so that beechwoods can fairly qualify as native. There are considerable differences between the beechwoods on steep slopes of the chalk

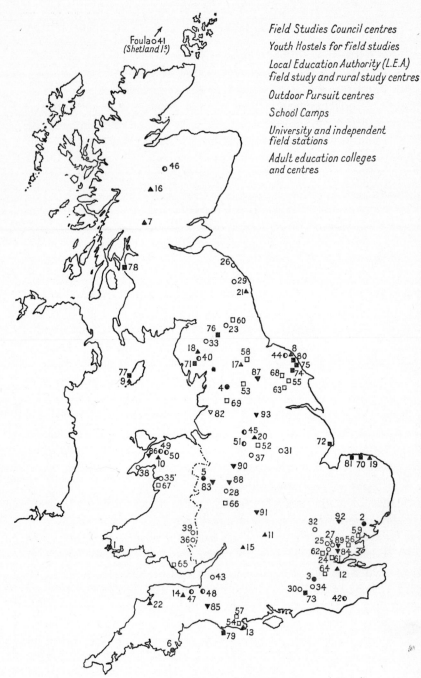

Field Studies Council centres

Youth Hostels for field studies

Local Education Authority (L.E.A.)
field study and rural study centres

Outdoor Pursuit centres

School Camps

University and independent
field stations

Adult education colleges
and centres

Foula o 41
(Shetland I.s)

2 Some centres used for field studies

KEY TO MAP *(this list is not comprehensive)*

Field Studies Council Centres

1 Dale Fort, Haverfordwest
2 Flatford Mill, East Bergholt
3 Juniper Hall, Dorking
4 Malham Tarn, Settle
5 Preston Montford, Shrewsbury
6 Slapton Ley, Kingsbridge

Youth Hostels with work room facilities

7 Balquhidder, Loch Voil
8 Boggle Hole (Robin Hood's Bay), Whitby
9 Bradda Head, Port Erin
10 Bryn Gwynant, Nant Gwynant
11 Charlbury, Oxfordshire
12 Cleves, Sevenoaks
13 Cluny, Swanage
14 Denzel, Taunton
15 Duntisbourne Abbots, Cirencester
16 Garth, Perthshire
17 Grinton Lodge (Swaledale), Richmond
18 High Close, Ambleside
19 'Hillside', Sheringham
20 Leam Hall, Grindleford
21 Rock Hall, Alnwick
22 Worlington House, Instow

Local Education Authority (L.E.A.) Field Study and Rural Study Centres

23 Catton Centre, Allendale
24 Chingford Jubilee Hut, Epping Forest
25 Epping Forest
26 Ford Castle, Berwick-on-Tweed
27 High Beech Field Centre, Epping Forest
28 Hillend, Claverley
29 Howtell Centre, Wooler
30 Marchant's Hill Rural Studies Centre, Hindhead
31 Nottinghamshire Rural Studies Centre, Southwell
32 The Priory Field Centre, Hitchin
33 Patterdale Hall, Glenridding
34 Sayers Croft Rural Studies Centre, Ewhurst
35 Shropshire Schools Field Centre, Arthog
36 Talgarth, Breconshire
37 Tissington Rly. Stn., Ashbourne
38 Towyn, Pwllheli
39 Tregoyd, Three Cocks, Brecon
40 Brathay Exploration Centre, Ambleside
41 Brathay Exploration Centre, Foula
42 Burwash Place, Burwash
43 Charterhouse Outdoor Activities Centre, Charterhouse, Blagdon
44 Danby Fryup Expedition & Field Centre, Lealholm, Whitby
45 Edale Centre, Edale
46 Glenmore Lodge, Aviemore
47 Greatwood Camp, Over Stowey
48 Kilve Court, Bridgwater
49 Plas-y-Brenin, Capel Curig
50 The Towers, Capel Curig, Bettws-y-Coed
51 White Hall, Buxton

School Camps

52 Ashover School Camp, Ashover
53 Bewerley Park Camp School, Pateley Bridge
54 Blashenwell Camp Site, Dorset
55 Castle Howard, East Yorkshire
56 Danbury Park Youth Camp, Chelmsford
57 Dorset County School Camp, Dorset

58 Ear's Orchard Youth Hostel, Sleegill
59 East Mersea Youth Camp, Colchester
60 Gateshead County Borough Camp School, Hexham
61 Hainault Forest, Barking
62 Herts. County Council Camp School, Potters Bar
63 Kirkham Abbey, East Yorkshire
64 Pilgrim Fort, Caterham
65 Silver Jubilee Camp School, Porthcawl
66 Smethwick School Camp, Ribbesford
67 Ty Gwyn Camp School, Llwyngwril
68 West Hartlepool Children's Camp, Carlton-in-Cleveland
69 Whitehough Camp School, Barley

University and Independent Field Stations

70 Blakeney Point, Norfolk
71 Brantwood, Coniston
72 Gibraltar Point Field Research Station
73 Haslemere Educational Museum
74 Hutton Buscel, Scarborough
75 Marine Laboratory, Scarborough
76 Moor House Field Station, Garrigill
77 Port Erin Marine Biological Station
78 Millport, Gt. Cumbrae
79 Portland Bird Observatory and Field Centre, Portland
80 Robin Hood's Bay Field Centre
81 Dial House, Brancaster Staithe, King's Lynn

Adult Education Colleges and Youth Centres

82 Alston Hall, Longbridge, Preston
83 Attingham Park, Shrewsbury
84 Debden House, Debden Green
85 Dillington House, Ilminster
86 Glynllifon College of Further Education, Caernarvon
87 Grantley Hall, Ripon
88 Pendrell Hall, Codsall
89 Wansfell Adult College, Theydon Bois
90 Wedgwood Memorial College, Barlaston
91 Westham Memorial College, Barford
92 Wicken House Youth Centre, Wicken
93 Woolley Hall Teachers Refresher College

valleys of the North Downs (beech hangers) and those on better soils in the Chilterns and elsewhere. Locally on the chalklands of the south-east beechwoods give place to yew woods and elsewhere to juniper scrub, very locally to box, so that a number of reserves are needed to cover the various types. The ash (*Fraxinus*) also favours limestone soils and ashwoods are a feature of Carboniferous Limestone of the Pennines. There are no certainly native pine-woods left in Britain which adds a special interest to such remnants of the Caledonian forests as may come into this category. In Scandinavia Scots pine, Norway spruce and birch are often co-dominants; on the poleward margins the birch survives and a belt of birch scrub usually lies between the coniferous forests and the tundra. The spruce did not succeed in re-entering Britain after the Ice Age, so conditions are different – indeed unique and so of special interest. Tansley did not deal with the vast forests and woodlands created by the Forestry Commission, but they have now become an essential element of the British scene.

Alder woodlands, characteristically developed as 'carrlands', form a bridge with the hydroseres – the very varied vegetation of marsh (with a water-logged mineral soil), fen (with an alkaline, neutral or slightly acid peat soil) and bog (with an acid peat base) passing into fresh water. Not only are these wetlands botanically of great interest, but they are of special significance to insect and bird life. Reserves are vital and the spacing of reserves is important relative to migration. Among areas with which the conservationist is concerned, the wetlands are particularly vulnerable. When drained many of them afford naturally fertile and easily worked agricultural soils: they are susceptible to great changes with alternation in the water level which may easily happen when surrounding lands are themselves subject to improvement by drainage and in other ways. Wetlands take run-off water from surrounding farmland, and with the increased use of chemical fertilisers and pesticides there is an ever-present danger of pollution. Very definitely wetland reserves need careful management: the control of water-level, control of intake and outlet of water, control of vegetation often involving periodic cutting. These remarks apply equally to salt-marsh.

Some parts of Britain have numerous lakes and ponds, particularly in hill areas where glacial debris blocked the outlets of pre-existing valleys or on lowlands where lakes, like the meres of Cheshire, occupy hollows in the boulder clay surface. Strange as it may seem, however, many of our most important areas of fresh water are man-made. The canal-building era was at its height a couple of centuries ago; today we value many of our remaining canals and their reservoirs mainly as reserves. Subsidence hollows due to mining and filled with water are also important; so are flooded gravel-pits.

A very large proportion of the surface of lowland Britain is occupied by grassland of various types. Very little, if any, can be described as 'natural'. In Tansley's own words, 'while the majority of our deciduous woodlands are properly regarded as more or less modified climax communities, as seral woods clearly leading to climax, or as planted but roughly equivalent representatives of one of these, the vast bulk of our "permanent" or semi-natural grass-lands are subclimax or (better) biotic plagioclimax vegetation, i.e. vegetation stabilized by pasturing. If pasturing were withdrawn their areas would be invaded and occupied, as they were originally occupied, by shrubs and trees' (p. 487). This applies not only to the 'neutral' grassland of lowland meadows, but to the famous downlands – the basic grasslands of chalk, other limestone and some basic igneous rocks – and the rough hill grazings dominated by *Agrostis-Festuca*, *Nardus* and *Molinia*. The associated flora and fauna (notably of the richer chalk grasslands) are varied and highly specialized so as to include the majority of Britain's orchids and a wonderful range of insects. Yet the whole habitat can disappear either by removal of grazing and reversion to scrub (easier than formerly because of the diminution in the rabbit population) or by ploughing which has become profitable with a subsidy for barley. A particular effort is needed to save representative tracts of chalk grasslands and may involve conservationists in maintaining flocks of sheep for controlled grazing, just as cattle are already being used by the Nature Conservancy to maintain the present character of other grasslands.

Above the tree-line Britain has some very interesting types of

Arctic-Alpine vegetation. Several factors have combined to bring many of the areas concerned into increasing danger of elimination. The very increase of interest in natural history has led to plant hunting for rare mountain flowers on an extensive scale; the only solution is to keep secret important localities since control is very difficult. Another danger is the increase in ski-ing and winter sports with construction of chair-lifts as popular in summer as in winter. It has been realized that some mountain plants, such as *Rhacomitrium*, are slow-growing and hence slow to recover from trampling.

Danger from trampling (and motor-car erosion) affects also a very different type of vegetation – coastal sand dunes and lowland heaths on very light soil. Blow-outs, otherwise wind-erosion hollows, are liable to occur where the binding vegetation has been removed along footpaths.

This brief review of types of habitat is intended to remind us of the complexity of the problems of conservation. It will help to explain the numerous, often small, reserves set up by the Nature Conservancy and County Naturalists' Trusts. It should also serve to remind us of the delicacy of balance which so often exists between the physical factors of the environment, its plant cover and faunal assemblage. In later chapters some examples, such as that of the large blue butterfly on the coasts of Cornwall, will be given to illustrate the intricate symbiotic relationship between the fauna and its food, i.e. the vegetation. In very many cases our knowledge of the exact conditions needed is still inadequate and there are everywhere problems of research.

The majority of plants are fixed, the majority of animals are mobile. The establishment of a nature reserve protects the vegetation, the plants, but only indirectly protects the fauna. In later chapters the protective measures afforded by legal enactions for mammals and birds will be discussed.

Not unnaturally nature conservation tends to be regarded as restricted to animals and plants. It is, of course, realized that the physical conditions of a habitat must be maintained, hence physiography, hydrology and pedology enter fully into conservation research. But separate issues are involved in regard to geology and the conservation of sites of geological importance. The first time this was noted in a public document was, I think, when I inserted the words '(including geological parks)' in para. 179 of the Scott Report. Discussion in scientific circles was sparked off by a typical clash of interests. A famous geological section, mecca of successive generations of students, was the deep gorge of a burn – Bilston Burn – near Edinburgh. The local authority discovered it to be an ideal site for tipping rubbish or for the waste from a new colliery. The late Professor W. J. Gordon, a patriotic Scot and graduate of Edinburgh, took up the cudgels and ventilated the matter through the local press and meetings of the British Association.

When the Wild Life Conservation Committee started work in September 1945 it did so with the help of Dr. A. E. Trueman, then Professor of Geology at Glasgow, as a full member. As a result a list of forty-two proposed 'geological monuments' was included as appendix 7. There are some considerable tracts, such as Pentire Head, Cornwall, and some caves, such as Kent's Hole, Torquay, and Victoria Cave, Settle, but many of the monuments are quite small, such as single glacial erratics. We may note the inclusion of the Piltdown Skull site, Sussex, 'site of the discovery of the famous skull in 1912', later to be proved a hoax. In due course the Nature Conservancy took over responsibility for including certain geological sites as National Nature Reserves. They create some problems: a quarry face is liable to become overgrown, a sand or gravel pit to cave in and become completely obliterated.

In fact the problem of geological 'monuments' is still very much with us. The Nature Conservancy has a geologist on its staff and a watch is kept on the position. There is little difficulty over such features as the main cliff sections round the coasts, or even such areas as the Warren at Folkestone or the Axmouth-Lyme Regis Landslip area, already a NNR. But whereas the biologist is happy to see vegetation clothing a rock exposure, the geologist wants a clean face. There is a need to protect some natural sections which are classic ground – the Avon Gorge at Bristol, for example, with its type section of the Carboniferous Limestone – and there may be danger of building or even obscuring sections by concrete walls constructed for safety. In the past, railway cuttings have provided some key exposures and need to be watched. More difficult are quarries which soon become overgrown even when not used for tipping rubbish. The Wild Life Conservation Committee was compelled to exclude the famous Charlton Sand Pit with its complete sequence from the Chalk up through the Lower London Tertiaries as a NNR: it required regular working of the Thanet Sand to keep the face clean. An interesting example of the problem is afforded by the famous Rhynie Chert of Aberdeenshire. By a million-to-one chance a set of circumstances allowed, in far-off Devonian times some 300-400 million years ago, the delicate tissues of a primitive plant *Rhynia* to be impregnated with colloidal silica, so that the cell-structure is perfectly preserved. Quite small pieces of the chert can be sliced and thin sections prepared for microscopic examination. The exposure of rock in a field is small: pieces of the chert could be sold for as much as £5 and it was impossible to say, although the chert could possibly be traced elsewhere, whether it would still include these wonderfully preserved fossils. Clearly a case for protection! Even a few years ago, when geological students went on a field class armed with geological hammers, they were encouraged to knock off pieces of fresh rock and to make their own collections of rock specimens, minerals and fossils. But now, with our ever increasing population, is this permissible? Certain type-sections are liable thus to damage; stalactites and stalagmites in caves must certainly be protected and so must some limestone pavements. There is another, perhaps more serious danger, in the vogue for rock gardens. Large areas of limestone fells have been ruined by the removal of 'weathered Westmorland limestone' – quite irreplaceable and such areas are badly in need of protection, just as are Sarsen stones and interesting erratics – many of which are listed in the Conservation Report.

Early in 1966 the Nature Conservancy carried out a review of its work and reconsidered the selection of Nature Reserves, having in mind particularly the necessity of covering each of the main types and sub-types of habitat present in this country. For this purpose the Nature Conservancy drew up the following list of habitats which has now been further revised in the 1969 Nature Reserves Review (see Appendix II):

Maritime and
Sub-maritime
1. Maritime grassland
   (a) On shell sand
   (b) Other
2. Salt-marsh
3. Mudflat or sandy shore
4. Sand-dune
5. Shingle
6. Sea cliff
7. Estuary
8. Off-shore island

Inland Grassland and Heath
1. Upland Grassland
   (a) Base-poor
   (b) Base-rich (inc. limestone)
2. Lowland Grassland
   (a) Chalk
   (b) Southern limestone
   (c) Other
3. Lowland Heath
4. Northern 'Wet' Heath
5. Arctic-Alpine

Fen and Bog
1. Fen and fen-woodland
2. Raised Bog
3. Blanket Bog
4. Southern Valley Bog

Freshwater
1. Still
   (a) Base-rich, over 100′ deep
   (b) Base-rich, under 100′ deep
   (c) Base-poor, over 100′ deep
   (d) Base-poor, under 100′ deep
2. Running
   (a) Fast-flowing, base-rich
   (b) Fast-flowing, base-poor

      (c) Slow-flowing, base-rich

      (d) Slow-flowing, base-poor

  3. Freshwater island

Woodland

  1. Oak

      (a) Base-poor Soil

      (b) Medium Soil

      (c) Base-rich Soil

  2. Beech

      (a) Base-poor Soil

      (b) Base-rich Soil

  3. Ash

  4. Birch

  5. Alder

  6. Mixed Deciduous

  7. Pine

  8. Juniper

  9. Yew

  10. Mixed Coniferous and Deciduous

  11. Other

Other Habitats

  1. Inland Cliff

  2. Gorge

  3. River Shingle

Geological or Physiographic

Species Reserves

CHAPTER 5

THE NATURE CONSERVANCY 1949-1965

The gradual development of interest in nature conservation covering the first half of the present century has been traced in Chapter 3. The definitive documents which were to set in motion government action were the two reports of the Wild Life Special Committees (Cmd. 7122 for England and Wales, Cmd. 7235 part II for Scotland), both published in July 1947. In the words of the First Report of the Nature Conservancy (December 1953): 'Emphasis was laid on the need of increased facilities for ecological studies because of the value of the ecological approach to many activities of Government as well as for the conservation of the native flora and fauna. The recommendations made included: the selection, management and study of a well-balanced representative series of Nature Reserves, together with some areas chosen specially for experimental work; the establishment of research stations; the conduct of a biological survey of Great Britain; the maintenance of facilities for the training of ecologists at university level; the making of grants for approved researches; and the setting up of suitable machinery to achieve these purposes.'

On 29th April, 1948, the Lord President announced in the House of Commons that the Government had accepted, in principle, the recommendations made in the two reports. It was at first intended that the Agricultural Research Council should take general charge of these new activities, but it soon became apparent that a new body with separate legal entity was preferable to rank as a research body parallel with the ARC (Agricultural Research Council) under the Privy Council.

On 29th March, 1949, a Royal Charter constituted the Nature Conservancy as a separate body:

'to provide scientific advice on the conservation and control of the natural flora and fauna of Great Britain; to establish, main-

47

tain and manage nature reserves in Great Britain, including the maintenance of physical features of scientific interest; and to organize and develop the scientific services related thereto.'

The Charter laid down that the Conservancy should consist of not less than twelve members and not more than eighteen, being at all times persons chosen for their scientific qualifications or interest in matters of nature conservation. The Charter named fifteen initial members, gave the Conservancy powers to appoint necessary staff, subject to Treasury approval with regard to numbers and remuneration, and required the Conservancy to appoint, with the approval of the Secretary of State for Scotland, a Scottish Committee.

It should be noted that, right from the start, the Conservancy was concerned with the whole of Great Britain and that its duties were fairly defined as threefold: the general ones of providing scientific advice on conservation and the encouragement and conduct of research, and the specific one of establishing, maintaining and managing nature reserves.

The further powers and duties of the Nature Conservancy were laid down in the National Parks and Access to the Countryside Act which received the Royal Assent in December 1949.

The quite remarkable success story of the Nature Conservancy is told interestingly, if prosaically, in the successive annual *Reports*. The first issued covers the whole period up to 30th September 1952, but was not published till 8th December 1953, the same day as the *Report* for the fourth year which ended 30th September 1953. These first slender pamphlets of thirty-three and thirty-one pages respectively had swollen to 173 by the time the *Report* for the year ended 30th September 1964 came to be issued. On the last day of March 1950, a year after the grant of the Royal Charter, there was a total staff of eighteen in London, including four scientists, and eight in Edinburgh, including four scientists. For the first full year, October 1st 1949 to September 30th 1950, a grant of £100,000 was sanctioned, but owing to the difficulty of recruiting staff and obtaining premises only £36,185 was spent. For the year ended 31st March 1964, General Expenses account balanced at £691,928, plus a capital account of £58,034. By September 1969 the Conservancy had established 127 National Nature Reserves, covering 262,551 acres, of which 67,077 acres were owned, 35,844 acres leased, and 159,630 acres covered by agreements.

In March 1959, the Conservancy published for public consumption a well-illustrated booklet of thirty-six pages entitled *The First Ten Years*, which summarized something of the varied activities with which it is concerned. Without in any way decrying the enthusiasm and energy of the many who have taken part in the work of the Nature Conservancy, it is not too much to say that its phenomenal success is due to the genius, coupled with relentless toil, of Mr. E. M. Nicholson – and the wonderful team he inspired. Max Nicholson, civil servant and amateur ornithologist, was one of the original members of the Conservancy; in 1952 he resigned in order to accept the post of Director-General on the retirement of Captain C. Diver, who had held that position for the first three formative years.

The Conservancy in fact got off to a good start. The first Chairman was Professor Tansley himself, who guided the early moves as head of a powerful team. A Royal Charter, an initial grant of reasonable proportions, right of direct access to the Treasury, a carefully worked out list of reserves to be acquired and scientific sites to be studied and notified, were good foundation stones. The Scottish Committee was set up immediately in accordance with the Charter and was fortunate in securing early both its energetic Director, Dr. John Berry, and its permanent home, a large Victorian house with a garden large enough to take care of expansion (which in fact took place in 1965-6), conveniently situated at Hope Terrace, Edinburgh, reasonably far from St. Andrew's House and reasonably near the University. London was not immediately so fortunate regarding premises, and occupied temporary accommodation in Victoria Street before joining the embassies in Belgrave Square.

It was not long before the Conservancy was reminded of its wider function – to give advice on many problems. Local authorities wanted to know what were their duties regarding local reserves, the War Department were worried as to the effect of continued training amongst coastal sand-dunes in Devon; should there be a rabbit-control exercise (this was before myxomatosis arrived in 1953), was it advisable to introduce reindeer into Scotland, should there be control of chemical sprays on roadside vegetation and would there be secondary effects? These early inquiries of course revealed the lack of factual knowledge and the need for research, research not only to be initiated but to be envisaged on a continuing basis.

An immediate priority was the notification to the local planning authorities of sites of special scientific interest (SSSI) to be included in the development plans then in hand. Under the 1947 Town and Country Planning Act these plans were due for submission to the Minister within five years – by 1952 – so time was short. The Wild Life Conservation Committee had recommended thirty-five large 'conservation areas' covering such very large tracts as the Lake District, the Lizard Peninsula and the South Downs, with a further twenty-three in Scotland. The 'conservation area' concept had to be abandoned in favour of specific areas of smaller extent to be shown precisely on the development plans. The Conservancy wisely decided that only the areas of the highest scientific interest should be included in the top category of 'National Nature Reserves' to be directly managed by the Conservancy itself. Notwithstanding the difficulties, by the 30th September 1952, covered by the first report, seven had been declared in England and two in Scotland.

In the north-west Highlands some 700 acres of old pine forest near Kinlochewe in Wester Ross had been on the list of reserves recommended by the Scottish Wild Life Conservation Committee, but it proved possible to buy on advantageous terms a much larger area, including a large red deer herd, so the first reserve to be acquired, Beinn Eighe, totalled 10,450 acres. The other reserve initially acquired in Scotland was of a very different character – in Fife, near Tayport, 47 acres with Morton Lochs and their immediate surroundings: artificial lochs important for the study of wildfowl population.

In England the early acquisitions included Yarner Wood, oakwood already the subject of detailed ecological study on the eastern margins of Dartmoor. The Moor House property of 10,000 acres of moorland ranging from 1,600 to 2,780 feet above sea level, on the north-east borders of Westmorland, was purchased at auction: the farmhouse provided accommodation for a warden and serves as a field station conveniently near the northern Research Station,

5 *Above*: Council for Nature — a conservation corps at work clearing *Rhododendron* scrub at Rostherne Mere National Nature Reserve, Cheshire. *Below*: bird-watching from a shore hide at Minsmere

6 *Above*: the Hooked Spit of Spurn Head, Yorkshire. *Below*: the Shingle Ridges of Dungeness — unique in Europe, now the site of an atomic power station; but bird-watching is continued here

Merlewood. In southern England 352 acres on the South Downs of West Sussex (Kingley Vale) has some of the finest yew woods in existence. Ham Street Woods near Ashford, Kent, are coppice with oak standards, and so are the Blean Woods near Canterbury, but very different. In East Anglia 132 acres of Cavenham Heath (a typical section of Breckland), and 640 acres of Holme Fen were acquired from the Crown Land Commissioners, and 114 acres with Calthorpe Broad were presented by Mrs. Gurney.

This list of early acquisitions is given because it illustrates how soon the Conservancy started on its task of setting up really important National Nature Reserves. It was not long before a major problem asserted itself. The proper management of even these early reserves required a considerable and well-qualified staff. Should the Conservancy consolidate its gains by undertaking this work, or should it go ahead and acquire more reserves, hoping for staff and facilities for management later? The obvious soon happened: criticism that the Conservancy was not undertaking proper supervision of the properties it already had, and should not, therefore, be allowed to acquire more.

But the policy of acquiring reserves was actively followed and by September 1958 the total had reached seventy, covering 133,081 acres. It was in that year, early in 1958, that I joined the Conservancy and its Scientific Policy Committee. I soon formed the view that it was 'now or never'. Everywhere farmers were being encouraged to undertake land improvement, commercial afforestation was taking its place alongside the Forestry Commission in extensive planting, a multiplicity of new chemicals was being used to destroy not only pests and diseases but to eliminate large numbers of wild plants deemed undesirable in pastures and hedgerows. I was mindful of an experience some years previously in the United States when lecturing in the University of Nebraska at Lincoln. I had asked to be shown a specimen of the old typical prairie. We had a long hot tiring day, covering some 300 miles by car, but I returned with my ambition still unfulfilled. I felt that it might soon be just as impossible to find in Britain a typical section of the chalk downland of my youth, or a lowland moss, or a stretch of fen and carrland. Reserves must be secured while the types of habitat were still there; consolidation in the form of management plans must come later.

We were much encouraged during that same year, as recorded in the *Report* for the year ended 30th September 1958. The respected, but sometimes dreaded, Select Committee on Estimates of the House of Commons carried out a thorough investigation, visited several Nature Reserves and Research Centres and put 576 questions to the Chairman (then A. B. Duncan, Scottish landowner, knighted on his retirement in 1961), the Director-General and officers. As a result the Committee

'were impressed with the potential value of the work carried out by the Conservancy. This included the study of soils and their improvement, water conservation, the effects of burning and of grazing on vegetation, the regeneration of woodlands, planting against erosion and flooding, and the study of animal and insect populations. The accommodation and equipment seen by members of the Committee seemed in no way extravagant. . . . Your Committee believe that the scope for scientific research in the field is almost unlimited and that therefore it is important that wisdom and common sense are brought to bear in selecting projects for research which will redound to the prestige and prosperity of the nation.'

The Conservancy were grateful for this authoritative appraisal of their work. They had undoubtedly been labouring under the difficulty that their task was novel and little understood. There had been press criticism and those who thought only in terms of setting up selected Nature Reserves tended to regard research activities in broader fields of ecology as 'empire building'.

It is perhaps here appropriate to note how the organization has evolved. The main Conservancy meets four times a year, normally in London, but with one meeting in Edinburgh and an occasional one in Bangor. The Scottish Committee likewise meets four times a year, normally in Edinburgh; the Scottish Committee has an overlapping membership, but a majority are Scottish members; its first Chairman was Professor J. R. Matthews, followed by Sir Basil Neven-Spence (1955) and Sir Charles Connell (1962).

A very important Committee is the Scientific Policy Committee 'to consider matters affecting general scientific policy, in regard to conservation and research; and to make recommendations accordingly'. This was set up almost immediately, being composed of all the scientific members of the Conservancy and of the Scottish Committee. It remained under the energetic chairmanship of Professor W. H. Pearsall, F.R.S., for ten years until 1963, when he handed over to Professor A. R. Clapham. Professor Pearsall died shortly afterwards.

The Committee for England and Wales was early, on 1st October 1953, divided into two separate committees for England and for Wales. They are concerned especially with all matters relating to nature reserves and conservation generally in their respective areas. Successive Chairmen for England have been Lord Hurcomb(1953-61), Professor A. R. Clapham (1961-3) and myself (1963-6), and for Wales, Professor R. Alun Roberts, C.B.E. (1953-6) and Professor P. W. Richards (1956-67).

The Finance Committee and Staff Selection Committee are self-explanatory, but the Conservancy has also an Advisory Committee on Photography under the chairmanship of Eric Hosking, and a National Collection of Nature Photographs was inaugurated in February 1955.

In 1956 a major advance was marked by the appointment of Dr. E. B. Worthington as Deputy Director-General (Scientific), who also functioned as Chief Conservation Officer. Although there is an intimate connection between research and conservation, to some extent the two functions are kept separate. Research covers (a) the work of the Conservancy's own research stations and (b) the large volume of research in universities and elsewhere which is grant-aided by the Conservancy, the applications for assistance being considered by a sub-committee of the Scientific Policy Committee.

It was clear from the beginning that the Conservancy had a major task in putting across to the public the concept of conservation. This meant education at all levels – work in which Mr. R. E. Boote, apart from his administrative duties, has taken a leading part.

The Conservancy's own research stations deserve separate consideration. The first to be opened was Merlewood at Grange-over-

Sands in July 1953 (Director, J. B. Cragg 1961-6), conveniently situated in the north and having its field station at Moor House. In the following year Furzebrook near Wareham was established: a large house and grounds to which laboratories were added. This became the centre for the Conservancy's physiographic work. A major adventure was the decision to build a completely new and modern research station at Monks Wood near Huntingdon: sufficiently near the Great North Road as to be readily accessible, sufficiently near Cambridge to enjoy the scientific contacts, and actually on the margin of an important and extensive reserve with facilities for field experiments on the spot. This was opened in October 1961, with Dr. Kenneth Mellanby, c.b.e., (first Principal of University College, Ibadan) as Director.

Wales has a combined Headquarters and Research Station, specially built on the outskirts of Bangor and opened on 20th July 1960, under the direction of Dr. R. Elfyn Hughes.

In Scotland the Edinburgh headquarters, under the Director, Dr. J. Berry, were extended in 1965 to afford a fine commodious research station. Scotland also had the small Speyside Research Station, a large house, Achantoul, on the outskirts of Aviemore, facing the Cairngorm reserve, which has been the centre of climatological research under F. H. W. Green. There is a field station on the Beinn Eighe Reserve, and a Research Station for Mountains and Moorlands at Banchory.

Every year a formidable list of publications bears witness to the research activities of members of staff of the Conservancy. Fine volumes issued by the Conservancy itself include a comprehensive study of wildfowl and of vegetation in Scotland.

The conservation work is carried out on a regional basis; each region has a Regional Officer with staff. Some of the larger reserves have resident wardens or honorary wardens; others are administered from regional headquarters.

The four regions into which Scotland is divided are administered by regional officers based on Edinburgh. Clearly this involves a great amount of travelling and it means that reserves can only be visited at long intervals. The famous Isle of Rhum is administered

direct by the Conservation Officer, Scotland (Dr. W. J. Eggeling*).
Nowhere could there be clearer evidence of how much the Conservancy are trying to do with a staff very thin on the ground.

Wales is divided into North and South, with the South administered from an office at Aberystwyth.

In England there are six regions and six regional offices. The
North Region is administered from Merlewood, the Midlands from
offices at Attingham Park near Shrewsbury (a mansion which is
now an educational centre), East Anglia from Bracondale, Norwich,
the South-West from Taunton, the South Region from Brimpton,
Berkshire, the South-East from Wye, Kent, conveniently near Wye
Agricultural College of the University of London.

Steadily through the years the list of National Nature Reserves
has grown. Some details will be noted in regional chapters which
follow, and it is only possible to notice here, chronologically, some
of the milestones of progress. In July 1954 the Cairngorms NNR
was declared partly owned, partly under agreement, but covering
(with later extensions) 64,118 acres in the heart of the Scottish
Highlands. Its size makes it by far the largest reserve, and one of
the largest in Europe. A large part was difficult of access and so
this reserve, by its size and its combination of wilderness area with
only parts used by the public, approached the American concept of
a national park. But great changes have taken place with the
growing popularity of ski-ing and the provision of ski lifts. The
latter are as popular and as much used in summer as in winter, and
what was inaccessible mountain top is now subject to much
trampling by walkers.

In 1957 (extended 1962) Caerlaverock NNR in Dumfriesshire
was declared – another large reserve of 13,514 acres, and in the same
year the whole island of Rhum, 26,400 acres, was purchased. Rhum
was overstocked with red deer – the 1957 count was 1,544 – and
was grazed by a few cattle and sheep by a tenant farmer who,
shortly after, left. The island, isolated yet within easy reach of the
mainland, is an ideal reserve for large-scale experimentation, but the
Conservancy has had to move warily in restricting public access.
The islands of the St. Kilda group (2,107 acres), which were

* Now Director, Scotland

National Nature Reserves

Forest Nature Reserves

Local Nature Reserves

Headquarters

Field Station

Research Station

Regional Boundaries

Hermaness

Haaf Gruney

SHETLAND ISLANDS

Noss

ORKNEY ISLANDS

North Rona & Sula Sgeir

Invernaver

Strathy Bog

Inchnadamph

Inverpolly

Mound Alderwoods

Corrieshalloch

St. Kilda

Anancaun

Beinn Eighe

Rassal Ashwood

Allt nan Carnan

Monach Islands

Loch Druidibeg

Craigellachie

Sands of Forvie

Cairngorms

Dinnet Oakwood

Rhum

Caenlochan

St. Cyrus

Arriundle

Rannoch Moor

Glasdrum Wood

Meall Nan Tarmachan

Glen Nant

Ben Lui

Morton Lochs

Tentsmuir Point

Loch Leven

Isle of May

Loch Lomond

EDINBURGH

Aberlady Bay

Glen Diomhan

Tynron Juniper Wood

Silver Flowe

Castle & Hightae Lochs

Kirkconnell Flow

Caerlaverock

0   40   80

miles

3 Nature Conservancy areas in Scotland

National Nature Reserves
▲ Forest Nature Reserves
○ Local Nature Reserves
〰 National Wildfowl Refuges

⌂ Headquarters
⌂ Regional Offices
▼ Research Stations
🚌 Field Stations
■ Experimental Stations
–– Regional Boundaries
☐ Sub. Regional Offices

Lindisfarne

Coom Rigg Moss
Newcastle ☐
Castle Eden Denes
Glasson Moss
Moor House
Upper Teesdale
Drigg Dunes & Gullery
Blelham Bog
North Fen
Rusland Moss
Merlewood
Roudsea Wood
Ling Gill
Leighton Moss
Colt Park Wood
Wyre-Lune
Farndale

Fairburn Ings
Humber

Southport Sanctuary
Ainsdale Sand Dunes
Sandall
Beat
Rostherne
Mere
Gibraltar Point
Scolt Head
BANGOR
Coed Gorswen
Newborough Warren
Coed Dolgarrog
-Ynys Llanddwyn
Cwm Glas Crafnant
Holkham
Cwm Idwal
Coed Cymerau
Wybunbury Moss
Winterton Dunes
Y Wyddfa-Snowdon
Coed Camlyn
Hickling Broad
Coedydd Maentwrog
Coed y Rhygen
Chartley Moss
Bure Marshes
Coed Tremadoc
Rhinog
Castor Hanglands
Norwich ⌂
Morfa Harlech
Coed Ganllwyd
Morfa Dyffryn
Cader Idris
Attingham Park
Wren's Nest
Holme Fen
Aberystwyth ⌂
Woodwalton Fen
Weeting Heath
Coed Rheidol
Monks Wood
Thetford Heath
Cors Tregaron
Chippenham Fen
Westleton Heath
Nant Irfon
Cavenham Heath
Orfordness
Allt Rhyd y Groes
Knocking Hoe
- Havergate
Craig Cerrig
Wychwood
Hales Wood
Gleisiad
Craig y Cilau
Colchester
Skomer
Penmoelallt
Cwm Clydach
Tring Reservoirs
Island
Waterperry
Beacon Hill
Cothill
Ruislip
Whiteford
Blackcliff &
Slimbridge
High Halstow
Gower
Oxwich
Wyndcliffe
Fyfield Down
Aston Rowant
Coast
High
LONDON
Swanscombe
Blean
Pewsey Downs
Standing
Skull Site
Woods
Bridgwater
Hill
Brimpton
Wye ⌂
Temple
Braunton
Bay
Rodney Stoke
Hothfield Common
Ewell
Burrows
Ebbor Gorge
Old Winchester
Ham Street Woods
Downs
Shapwick Heath
Lyndhurst Hill
Kingley
North Common
Wye &
Bramshaw
Vale
Chailey
Crundale
Black Tor Copse
Exe Estuary
Mark Ash
Matley
Lullington
Downs
Bovey Valley Woodlands
Hartland Moor
Morden Bog
Denny
Heath
Yarner
Arne
Pagham Harbour
Wistman's Wood
Dendles Wood
Wood
Newtown
Furzebrook
Marshes
Axmouth-Lyme Regis
Studland Heath
Stanpit Marshes
Undercliffs

0   40   80
miles

4 *Nature Conservancy areas in England and Wales*

acquired the same year, are, by way of contrast, so isolated and difficult of access as to seem safe, but almost immediately occupancy by the Air Ministry under national defence schemes brought new difficulties.

Later acquisitions in Scotland included 26,827 acres of Inverpolly in Ross and Cromarty (1961-2) and Loch Leven, 3,946 acres, in 1964.

In Wales some of the exciting acquisitions included over a period the coastal sand-dunes of Newborough Warren, Anglesey (1,566 acres) and glorious views of the whole Snowdon range. Morfa Harlech was obtained in 1958, the exciting Skomer Island in 1959-63. Various inland mountain and moorland reserves preceded the final agreement for 4,145 acres on Snowdon in 1964 and 1966.

Many Reserves were only acquired after much consideration and sometimes protracted negotiations.

Acquisitions in England illustrate the Conservancy's wide range of interests: the marvellous landslipped masses which make up the Undercliffs of Axmouth-Lyme Regis (793 acres) were obtained between 1955 and 1964; the lovely beechwood of Aston Rowant on the Chilterns in 1958-68; Wychwood in Oxfordshire in 1955; the extensive stretches of marshland (6,076 acres) along Bridgwater Bay in 1954-8. An early acquisition of downland was Fyfield Down (612 acres) in 1956. Wye Downs followed in 1961. East Anglia received considerable attention: the Bure Marshes (1,019 acres) by agreement in 1958, Hickling Broad (1,204 acres) by agreement with the Norfolk Naturalists' Trust in the same year. The fascinating meres and mosses of the Lancastrian-Cheshire plain are represented by Chartley Moss (104 acres) 1963, Rostherne Mere (327 acres) 1961, and Rusland Moss (58 acres) 1958-64. Braunton Burrows, Devon (560 acres) in 1964, Shapwick Heath, Somerset (546 acres), in 1961-4, Studland Heath, Dorset (429 acres), in 1962, and Lindisfarne (7,368 acres) in 1964-66 may be noted.

The position of National Nature Reserves, whether owned, leased or established by agreement, is clear. But the Nature Conservancy is interested in many other areas and is in something of a quandary. As already noted, there is a very large number of SSSI (Sites of Special Scientific Interest) of which the Conservancy maintains careful county schedules and which are notified to the planning authorities and the significance of scheduling explained to owners. It may happen, however, that the landowner (especially after a sale) may be unaware that some of his land has been thus scheduled: only in a few cases have the lists been published. In our book on the *Common Lands* Dr. Hoskins and I recorded all SSSI which were on commons. The Planning Department Cambridgeshire and Isle of Ely County Council issued a Survey Report in 1965 entitled 'Nature Reserves and Sites of Scientific Interest'. In this details are given of two Reserves (Chippenham Fen and Wicken Fen) and forty-four SSSI. Of the latter fifteen are woods, ten are fenlands, six are grasslands and thirteen are pits or quarries. Looking at this list from one small agricultural county, it will be realized that the total of SSSI for the country is very large – too many to be included, as was intended, as an appendix to this volume. Publication of such a list as the Cambridgeshire one may be undesirable as it discloses the exact location of rare species. The Nature Conservancy is in a still more difficult position over its PNNR (Proposed National Nature Reserves). Premature disclosures of such aims and ambitions may easily alienate owners and prejudice delicate negotiations.

For its own internal use the Conservancy distinguishes as an SSSI (A) an area which is of NNR status in the possession of a public body or other responsible organisation so that, by a formal exchange of letters, it can be managed so as to preserve its scientific interest. Somewhat similarly a Forest Nature Reserve (FNR) is a woodland area owned by another Crown body (usually the Forestry Commission) which, by an exchange of letters, has agreed to manage the area in accordance with a scheme of management agreed with the Conservancy.

In all these years of its many activities the Nature Conservancy, both as a body and through its individual members and staff, has been closely in touch with many national and international events in the conservation field.

In 1956 the 5th General Assembly of the International Union for Conservation of Nature and Natural Resources met in Edinburgh, and one of its commissions at Anancaun Field Station,

In 1958 the 15th International Congress of Zoology met in London; in 1964 the 20th International Geographical Congress met in London and the International Botanical Congress in Edinburgh. The Conservancy gave evidence to the Royal Commission on Common Land 1955-8 and to many public inquiries – including the famous clash over Dungeness with the Atomic Energy Authority.

Major events included the first Countryside in 1970 Congress, arranged in conjunction with the Royal Society of Arts (1963). H.R.H. Prince Philip, Duke of Edinburgh, personally presided over this Conference, with the result that leaders of commerce and industry shared platforms with conservationists, and real progress was made in mutual understanding. This was followed up by a second Countryside in 1970 Conference in October 1965.

It has been explained that when the Nature Conservancy received its Royal Charter in 1949 it was placed in a position analagous to the Agricultural Research Council and the Medical Research Council. Many workers in other fields had felt the need for other Research Councils. There were contra arguments that DSIR (Department of Scientific and Industrial Research) filled the gap, that the Nature Conservancy could be expanded as required. The Labour Government, elected in October 1964, decided to create two new research councils—the Natural Environment Research Council (NERC) and the Social Science Research Council. NERC was duly set up and the Nature Conservancy became one of its constituent committees, the Chairman of the Conservancy and the Chairman of its Scientific Policy Committee becoming members of NERC. So the Royal Charter of the Conservancy was cancelled and thus ended sixteen years of successful independent existence. The guiding spirit of those years, Max Nicholson, resigned on 31st March 1966; shortly before his scientific deputy (Dr. E. B. Worthington) had left to take over wider duties as Secretary of IBP – the International Biological Programme.

If one chapter is concluded, there is every sign of a new one opening auspiciously.

CHAPTER 6

THE CHANGING CONCEPT OF CONSERVATION

In a paper contributed to the *Handbook* for 1965 of the Society for the Promotion of Nature Reserves (published November 1964), E. M. Nicholson, Director-General of the Nature Conservancy, honoured by the University of Aberdeen with an LL.D. for his work for conservation, dealt with advances in British Nature Conservation. He lists sixteen points, and contends that the changes amount to a revolution in man's attitude towards nature. The revolution has taken place entirely within the past decade or so – since the initiation of the New Naturalist. It would be wrong to suggest that the Nature Conservancy is responsible for the revolution, but it has certainly played a major role and it may be hoped that the New Naturalist has had a share also.

In the first place, whereas the attempt to protect animals and plants by legislation was formerly regarded largely as the attempt by a few rather eccentric sentimentalists to safeguard a hobby, man's care for his natural environment is now recognized as an essential concern of civilized society in general and of governments in particular. Similarly, nature reserves are no longer the concern of a minority organized in a few voluntary groups, but are areas held in trust for the nation by national and local bodies, official and unofficial, professional and amateur, all working in close liaison.

The idea that nature reserves, selected and demarcated on a casual unplanned basis, can be left to look after themselves, has given place to a systematic selection of related, but varied, sites representing different habitats which then have to be carefully managed. Reserves are outdoor laboratories of living things to be fully and systematically studied in the field, backed up by further study indoors in properly equipped field stations or research centres.

Formerly the search was for areas of 'natural' or at least 'semi-natural' vegetation. Now it is appreciated that man has long been an essential part of each ecosystem and the many stages of an eco-logical succession are all worthy of study.

Haphazard recording of phenomena by irregular visits has given place to the systematic study and regular plotting of changes and the quantification of population studies and life histories.

The former neglect of field studies in school and university has given place to a recognition of the vital importance of outdoor science at all levels, with a corresponding increase in research at graduate level. A post-graduate diploma course in conservation was initiated by University College, London, and various courses in ecology or some branch of conservation have been developed at Aberdeen, Glasgow, Strathclyde, Newcastle and elsewhere. A major development was the transformation of the Forestry School at Edinburgh into a School of Forestry and Natural Resources, under Professor J. N. Black, who is primarily an agriculturalist. It has full undergraduate courses in Ecology and Conservation. The new University of Lancaster established a Chair of Natural Environment.

It is now realized that effective land management and the balanced development of land and natural resources are really applied ecology, whether it be forestry, agriculture, fisheries or general estate management, landscape architecture and physical planning.

The apparent antagonisms and clashes of the past are gradually being reconciled. Whereas the conservationist and the follower of field sports were previously regarded as natural enemies, experience is showing that this need not be so. Twelve years of management at the Scottish wildfowl refuge of Caerlaverock, discussed in a later chapter, have shown that carefully controlled wildfowling need not be incompatible with wildfowl conservation. Positive conservation, discussed in the next chapter, necessitates continued human control. Rarity of a species, whether of plant or animal, is frequently an indication that it is unable to compete successfully with the more vigorous or aggressive of its associates. To enable the rare plant to survive it may be essential to cut away competing vegetation threatening to choke it. So far so good, and no protests. It is much more difficult to get public approval for killing off a proportion of an aggressive species that a weaker one may survive. The villainies of that handsome rogue, the grey squirrel, are without doubt and, without human help, the little red squirrel is losing ground everywhere. Similarly, if we want to preserve a colony of breeding terns, it may be essential to kill off the rapacious herring gulls that swoop down on the young. In nature conservation an attempt is made to gloss over the unwelcome truth that slaughter of the aggressor may be essential by referring to the action as 'culling'. In many cases what constitutes a right balance is far from clear, and a special case is the grey seal (see Chapter 7); another is the red deer. Undoubtedly before the arrival of myxomatosis the rabbit population had become too large. Frequently the introduction of alien species, whether of animals, birds, or plants, is fraught with danger, as many countries have learned to their cost. The escape into the quiet well-ordered British countryside of the savage unlovable mink is a real danger; the coypu in East Anglia is already a nuisance, and the spread of the muskrat caused such damage that a full-scale operation had to be mounted against it. So it may well be that the sportsman has an important role to play in conservation; at the same time those who regard the maintenance of hunting, shooting and fishing as important must look to conservation to maintain the very possibility.

In his fine book in this series, *The World of the Soil*, the late Sir John Russell demonstrates, as his title suggests, that within the few inches of the soil there is a complete animal-plant world, inhabited mainly by microscopic and ultra-microscopic organisms and with a few occasional giants, such as earthworms and beetles. What is the effect on this world of the dressings of chemical fertilizers, now so universal? What, indeed, is the effect of the general chemicalization of agriculture? The tragic picture painted by the late Rachel Carson in *Silent Spring*, silent because of the extinction of birds and insects alike by indirect and direct effects of pesticides, may have been exaggerated, but the problem is a very vital one.

In sum, to quote Max Nicholson's words, 'scientific ecology has just reached the point of transforming concepts of management of natural areas and is beginning to make a serious impact on land use and land management, on education, and on interests concerned with the use of renewable natural resources.'

It is perhaps traditional that the people of Britain, sometimes slow to accept an idea, once they are convinced, take up a cause with widespread and tenacious enthusiasm. If the cause is sufficiently worth-while, there is always a vast reserve of voluntary effort. No one expects to be paid for doing a job which obviously must be done.

That is the present position with regard to nature conservation. In the last chapter a consideration was given to the results of official enterprise in the Nature Conservancy – even there the work is largely voluntary, since none of the members of the Conservancy or its committees has received any payment, and many of the wardens are unpaid volunteers. Parallel with the work of the Nature Conservancy has been the mobilization of voluntary effort, especially through the County Naturalists' Trusts mentioned below.

But first there is the Council for Nature. Many naturalists and lovers of the countryside had come to feel that interests had become too sectarian and specialized. Birds were well looked after by the Royal Society for the Protection of Birds; the British Ecological Society and the Botanical Society of the British Isles held a watching brief for plant life; the Councils for the Preservation of Rural England and Wales were concerned particularly with amenity aspects affecting the human population. There was no corporate body to look at and speak for Nature as a whole.

So a small group, including Lord Hurcomb (the first president), Sir Julian Huxley, Peter Scott, Aubrey Buxton, J. E. Lousley, E. W. Taylor, and the late Professor W. H. Pearsall, set up the Council for Nature in 1958 to be the voice of Britain's wild life. Its member-bodies include over 400 local natural history societies, field clubs, County Naturalists' Trusts, and many specialist national societies, its ordinary members comprising any interested individual willing to subscribe a minimum of a pound a year. The Council is under the Patronage of the Duke of Edinburgh, its president Sir Landsborough Thomson. After eight years of working from 41 Queen's Gate, London, s.w.7, the Council, through the generosity of the Wolfson Foundation, is now accommodated at the London Zoo. The Council has been working through a succession of active committees. First the Conservation Committee (in close touch with its own all-party Parliamentary Committee) deals with threats to wild life at a national level – such matters have been discussed, with the government departments concerned, as the gassing of badgers, culling of seals, control of pesticides and chemicals generally, and armed trespass. It played a leading part in calling the Countryside in 1970 Conferences of 1963 and 1965. Publicity is regarded as important: in 1963 the first National Nature Week was organized and marked by the issue of special stamps, and in 1966 a second National Nature Week. A wild life exhibition was organized, with the help of *The Observer* newspaper, in connection with these weeks. The Youth Committee has concerned itself with education and indeed regards it as a major role to make people of all ages conscious of their responsibility for the natural environment. In this connection the Council for Nature continues to publish an attractive broadsheet for the information of member bodies entitled *Habitat* every other month. A particularly imaginative action of the Council was the creation of the Conservation Corps of active young people willing to undertake manual work needed in the management of reserves – such as clearing scrub, felling unwanted trees, laying hedges in such a way as to encourage nesting birds, clearing drainage ditches and cleaning out ponds. Some of the first tasks undertaken by the Corps illustrate the range of work. At Box Hill, Surrey, property of the National Trust, dense scrub was cleared to open up chalk grasslands; at Gibraltar Point (Lincolnshire Naturalists' Trust) the spread of *Spartina* grass was dealt with; scrub clearance was undertaken at Meathop Moss, Woodwalton Fen (Huntingdonshire) and Askham Bog (Yorkshire Naturalists' Trust); field paths were constructed to facilitate access on Skomer Island for the West Wales Naturalists' Trust and the Nature Conservancy.

Largely coincident with the development of the Council for Nature as a central organization has been the quite remarkable growth in numbers and influence of county and local organizations, especially the County Naturalists' Trusts or Trusts for Nature Conservation. There have, of course, been local natural history societies all over the country for many years, and by October 30th 1959, one year after its foundation, the Council for Nature claimed 152 as 'member societies' of the Council apart from thirty-eight national societies. But the County Trusts, with a primary object of acquiring and managing local nature reserves, are a new development. They are mostly limited liability companies empowered to buy and hold land. Norfolk established the first in 1926; by October 1959 the Council for Nature listed as member societies six others – Cambridgeshire and Isle of Ely, Kent, Leicestershire, Lincolnshire, West Midlands and Yorkshire. Less than five years later Max Nicholson could refer to Somerset as virtually the last English county to create its own Trust, though of course some counties had joined to form joint trusts (see Appendix 1). In Wales the former West Wales Field Society became the West Wales Naturalists' Trust and played a leading part in safeguarding the offshore islands of Skokholm and Skomer, and later in the fight to save Borth Bog. With the sparse population of Scotland's Highland counties, it is not surprising that the County movement has not been as strong there, initiative being with the Nature Conservancy. However, a Scottish Wildlife Trust was founded in 1964 and quickly established four branches. The activities of the County Trusts are discussed later in the regional sections and the Trusts are listed in full in Appendix 1.

By way of comparison it may be interesting to mention the activities of a single County Naturalists' Trust. The Cornwall Naturalists' Trust Limited was established in 1962, to some extent continuing or taking over the Cornwall Bird Watching and Preservation Society. It keeps its members abreast of developments by a periodic cyclostyled Newsletter which records national news, such as the work of the Nature Conservancy, progress of the Trusts, new Acts of Parliament, and local planning proposals (the Trust presents the conservationist view). It runs a nest-box scheme, holds field meetings (including work on its reserves), keeps records of rare plants, animals and birds, takes part in national surveys (as of badgers) and national work such as de-oiling sea-birds. Through a series of Bulletins it gives details of some of the species of plants and animals about whose distribution in the county more information is needed, and the first lists include such diverse investigations as bird pellets (i.e. food of predators giving clue to the distribution of voles), shore collecting, bumble bees and millipedes. The county has been divided into regions, each with a responsible naturalist in charge who makes periodic reports.

7 *Above*: a glacial erratic resting on weathered Durness Limestone (Cambrian) in Inchnadamph National Nature Reserve, Sutherland. *Below*: a relict marram-grass covered sand-dune, eroded by wind. Newborough Warren National Nature Reserve, Anglesey

8 Gibraltar Point, Lincolnshire. The first local nature reserve to be established in England by a local authority

Although the economic importance of conservation, as now understood, would seem to be abundantly clear, it has other aspects. As an American writer said recently, all planning is a matter of ethics rather than economics. Many years ago my eldest brother, the late Lord Stamp, who was a leading Methodist, expanded one of his public lectures into a small book with the title *The Christian Ethic as an economic factor*. He found it a highly significant factor, the study of its influence much neglected by economists. It is interesting to find a leading ornithologist in Dr. Bruce Campbell preaching the sermon which was broadcast from Gilbert White's Selborne Parish Church at the beginning of National Nature Week 1963, on 'Conservation and Christianity'. On reflection it is curious how close in the past has been the link between nature-study and religion. So many of the great naturalists of the past were country parsons. One need go no further than Selborne itself, where the great Gilbert White was born in the parsonage, the grandson of the parson, another Gilbert White, and we know how after the naturalist had taken holy orders he turned down one attractive offer after another till he had the chance of going back, this time as the curate of a neighbouring parish, to the parish of his birth and childhood love. Gilbert White stood head and shoulders above his fellow amateur naturalists of the day in his accuracy of observation and his ability to write, but he belonged to the old school of collectors: he did not hesitate to take the life of the rarest, if he needed a specimen to confirm some point.

Therein perhaps lies the greatest difference between the old naturalist, who was basically a collector of dead specimens, and the new naturalist who is an observer of life. Indeed, the small minority of present-day collectors of the rare are, rightly, regarded as vandals. Sometimes there is the element of wanton damage, as in the senseless robbing and smashing of the ospreys' eggs which caused a nation-wide furore, which unfortunately affects so many aspects of our national life.

Humanist and Christian alike will agree with Bruce Campbell when he points out that 'today man has the power – and is exercising it – to change things almost overnight'. Only some plants and animals are able to adapt themselves to the new conditions imposed by man. Starlings, house sparrows, woodpigeons (better to eliminate the wood) and some gulls have done it: others have failed to accommodate themselves. The same is true of the plant world. There is thus a moral obligation placed on man, the superior being, to become conservationist. Bruce Campbell would urge that there is a special obligation to those calling themselves Christians. To those who 'accept the existence of God as the best explanation yet offered for the existence of the Universe, there is no difficulty in accepting the view that He should have chosen the means which we call evolution to work towards His ends on earth . . . surely, the exercise of the mind to the glory of God includes the study and appreciation of the whole of His world and the taking of thought to conserve it?'

Many may follow the dictum of Teilhard de Chardin: 'Nature is the art of God'.

CHAPTER 7

CONSERVATION AND CONTROL

The term ecology has been in use long enough to have received a variety of dictionary definitions. According to *Chambers' Encyclopædia*, 'Ecology can be briefly defined as the study of the relations between living organisms and their environment. . . . The environment . . . is . . . the whole association of factors, inert and living, of which the organism is a part'. Tansley, in his *Introduction to Plant Ecology* (1946), gives a characteristically vivid turn to the definition when he says: 'In its widest meaning ecology is the study of plants and animals as they exist in their natural homes; or, better perhaps, the study of their household affairs'.

Whilst many writers have drawn a distinction between autecology – the relation of individual plants to their habitats or the ecology of the individual organism – and synecology – the ecology of a group – the emphasis now is on the ecosystem concept already discussed in Chapter 1, where the stress is on living together or peaceful co-existence. The study of the environment itself demands the separation of a whole range of factors – elevation, relief, soil, drainage, aspect, microclimate and soil climate – and may be studied *per se*. The vegetation cover is influenced by all these factors and it is often extremely difficult to determine which are of major importance. Individual species adapt themselves in different ways to environmental factors, even individual plants may react differently. Animals are often influenced by several or all of the physical factors and frequently depend on a complex food chain, though most animals have the advantage of being mobile and thus able to move away should conditions become unfavourable or less favourable.

In any ecosystem an approximate equilibrium has been established, though it may be far from stable, and the vital lesson to be learned is that any balance established in Nature is a very delicate one. It can be upset by a change in any one of the physical factors – as when water conditions are altered by irrigation or drainage, or when soil is given added nutrients. In turn plants more suited to the new conditions will displace those which previously flourished, and so the story goes on.

The study of ecology involves basic research: when the influences of environmental or habitat factors have been isolated and defined, man is in the position of being able, within limits, to manipulate those factors to suit his own requirements. This is applied ecology.

The whole of agriculture and farming is, in reality, applied ecology. By clearing the land the basic character of the habitat is changed. By ploughing the nature of the soil and its hydrology and climate are changed – in this case to suit the crops the farmer wishes to grow. The natural struggle between competing plants becomes a one-sided struggle, with man carefully placing the seeds of his crop plants, providing them with the plant foods they desire, while at the same time eliminating competition by hoeing or other-wise removing 'weeds', latterly by chemical means with selective weed-killers, and using insecticides against enemies from the animal kingdom. The rearing of animals is, in the same way, applied animal ecology: providing the animals with the right habitat, environmental conditions and food.

Of course the whole of horticulture and gardening is similarly applied ecology, in this case often much more autecology, with the needs of a single species in mind. With forestry there is a certain difference in that the time factor is greatly extended: it takes much longer to get the right answers. Mistakes in forestry practice may only be revealed after a period of many years when trees begin to approach maturity. The study of the basic ecology of existing natural woodlands is thus often a valuable short-cut.

With the increasing pressure of population on natural resources, the proper use of different types of land in a national economy becomes of urgent practical importance. In our own country there are cases where a rare combination of environmental factors has produced a rare, perhaps unique, habitat marked by index species not found elsewhere or in a like combination. To understand why may be the key to major progress in the control of the environment.

To the uninitiated, the fight of the conservationist to conserve a particular area may be dismissed as a minority interest in some rare flower and such bigotry must not be allowed to stand in the way of 'progress', such as the construction of a reservoir. It is only the expert biologist who is able to realize that a unique habitat may hold the key to the understanding of major advances in knowledge. This problem has come to the fore many times in recent years, not least in the plan to construct a reservoir in Upper Teesdale near the old Cow Green mine. The reservoir as planned would submerge some unique habitats: if it were moved but a short distance away, those habitats would be preserved for study.

In the early stages of the development of plant ecology emphasis was placed on the climatic climax. The basic idea is quite simple: it was seen in action during the war over blitzed sites, or clear felled areas of forest; it may be seen in action where land is reclaimed from the sea, as in the drainage of the Zuider Zee in the Netherlands, or in tip heaps from mines and quarries. There are pioneer plants which move in as the first colonists – often annuals or biennials, which in due course are replaced by others more persistent and resistant, which in turn may act as 'nurse crops' to others which will finally take possession. There is thus a succession culminating eventually in a vegetation which, because it is primarily determined by the regional climate, is the climatic climax vegetation. In some instances it is the nature of the soil which decides the climax, in which case one has an edaphic climax. There are many important reasons for studying the succession of vegetation. What one may be looking at may be just a seral community: something which has been arrested in a certain stage of development and which is destined to change. Thus the rough grazing of much of our remaining common land has reached a certain stage in development towards a forest or woodland climax, and is maintained in that stage by grazing animals. If an urban authority takes it over as a recreational area and the grazing animals are removed, development will take place: it is likely to pass into a useless thicket or scrub. Many authorities are only now learning, to their cost, that the cheapest, perhaps the only, way of maintaining land as they want it is to farm it. It was not till 1965 that even the Nature

Conservancy bowed to the inevitable and became the owner of cattle and sheep required to undertake controlled grazing.

The truth is that there is very little climax vegetation in Britain. Even some of the oldest woodlands, such as the New Forest and Forest of Dean, have not only been grazed by deer, but also managed in one way or another by man. Until the invasion of Britain in 1953 by the rabbit plague, myxomatosis, grazing by rabbits was a very important factor in maintaining certain types of seral vegetation. The lovely short springy turf of the chalk downland is due to close sheep and rabbit grazing: most heather moorland is the result of periodic cutting or burning and grazing. But the best examples of all of seral communities in Britain are our pastures and meadows. Ours is a woodland climate so, when neglected, our meadows soon become overgrown with briars and brambles, more slowly pass into thickets of whitethorn and blackthorn before forest trees appear.

It may be said that a major advance in forestry was when this succession became understood. A hillside planted with young trees may fail to produce a forest, unless attention is paid to the normal succession. What the forester does is often to help Nature to speed up the process. Seeds are germinated in a nursery and two or three years saved by planting them out, but often in shade afforded by transient pioneer herbs. They are helped in their struggle to survive by cutting away coarse-growing brambles which threaten to choke them, but many of our forest trees need to be planted with others which act as nurse crops. Often a forest has to be built gradually up a hillside, the vigorous growth at a lower level affording protection to trees higher up. Whereas, too, an oak forest can scarcely spread naturally *up* hill, since the acorns always roll *down* hill – unless taken up higher by squirrels or jays – man can plant higher and higher and bring the forest quickly to a height dictated as the limit by climate.

The management of pasture is based essentially on an understanding of succession, but there is much still to be learned. It was Sir George Stapledon who, with Dr. William Davies, at the Welsh Plant-Breeding Station at Aberystwyth, did fine pioneer work in this field, though it was not fully appreciated at the time by ecologists. His earliest paper (1925) looked at pastures essentially from the farmer's point of view, and he distinguished 'fatting pastures', 'dairy pastures', 'general purposes and sheep pastures' and 'outrun pastures'. The great floristic feature of all the best pastures is the prominence of perennial ryegrass (*Lolium perenne*) and wild white clover (*Trifolium repens*) and the paucity of 'weeds'. Decreasing value of pasture is marked by the increase in proportion of *Agrostis*, especially *A. tenuis*. Stapledon notes that only about twenty of the many grasses and herbs occurring in pastures have nutritive value for animals: all the rest act as fillers. During the war Stapledon campaigned actively for the improvement of pastures: he was a great advocate of periodic ploughing and reseeding with selected seed mixtures. His work in fact has revolutionized British farming practice in that the old 'permanent pastures', once regarded as sacrosanct and never to be ploughed, have been subjected more and more to periodic breaking of the turf. But Nature is never simple. Cattle and sheep are to some extent complementary feeders: cattle wrap their tongues round tufts of grass and partly pull; sheep nibble with their front teeth and produce a turf resembling a mown lawn. It has been found that both may suffer from a pasture which is over rich: they require roughage. Some of the most nutritious plants – *Lolium* and *Trifolium* – are liable to accumulate excessive proportions of certain trace elements which, though essential in small quantities, are toxic in excess.

There is in fact quite a delicate balance between the type and quality of grazing and the stock of grazing animals. In fields which are undergrazed the animals will eat only the parts they like best, leaving the unpalatable thistles and roughage to grow up and choke the whole. If a pasture is overstocked, the animals will almost pull up the plants by the roots, so that chance of recovery is slight. If pasture is improved, stocking must be increased. Stapledon found that when he had vastly improved some of his hillsides he did not have the stock to take advantage of the improved herbage, with the result that it quickly deteriorated. Undoubtedly rabbits maintained a close turf in many areas; when they disappeared there was not only an increased growth which could support more domestic animals, but more animals were actually needed to maintain the quality of the pasture.

Since the bulk of the vegetation cover of Britain is not the climax vegetation, but some stage in the succession, there is need for constant and continuous study which is basic to conservation. In so many cases conservation is, in other words, the maintenance of a very delicate balance between plants, animals and man.

The great American botanist, F. E. Clements, was the author of a classic work which he entitled *Plant Indicators*. The basic idea on which he worked is simple enough: the plant, or rather the group of plants, in any given locality is an index of the sum total of environmental conditions – of elevation, climate, soil, soil-climate, hydrology, and biotic relationships. This concept obviously gives a great importance to the mapping of vegetation. The vegetation map of the Highlands of Scotland, for example, becomes an index-map of environmental conditions. As such it is an immediate pointer to economic potential. Certain types of vegetation thus indicate land suitable for afforestation (and may indicate the trees which will flourish), another type, such as cotton-grass moor (Eriophoretum), may signify that drainage is a first essential, and so on.

This leads us to the question: what is the significance of a patch of vegetation of unique character, perhaps with plants not found elsewhere? It is clear that a certain set of conditions, perhaps a certain combination of climate and soil, perhaps the presence of some rare trace element in the soil, perhaps living denizens of the soil, or physical character of the sub-soil, has made possible the development or the survival of the unique plant assemblage. If only we can determine *why*, we may have the key to such major problems as the economic development of a vast highland area. The non-scientist, whether a member of the public or one in authority, is apt to regard with scorn the scientist's desire to conserve such unique habitat or floral assemblage, and to contend that some silly flower must not be allowed to stand in the way of progress. We are back to Upper Teesdale and the Cow Green reservoir: a unique environment with a unique floral assemblage which may have the key to some of the great puzzles concerning what to do with our uplands.

Enough has surely been said to stress the importance of the

9 Aston Rowant, Oxfordshire-Buckinghamshire. These two views, both taken in 1964, illustrate two of the problems of nature conservation. *Left*: the Post Office tower illustrates the invasion often necessitated by modern technology in or near reserves. *Below*: the abandoned farm implement and consequent invasion of land by scrub suggest a changing environment, not necessarily for the better

10 *Overleaf*:
Deer on the Scottish Highlands in winter (November 1965) near the main Pitlochry to Blair-Atholl road

11 *Above*: at a nature reserve in Holland, maintained by the Forestry Service. *Below*: grey seal with pup on north Rona N.N.R.

study of the habitat and of its influence on the vegetation. But we are concerned with both plant and animal life. We may study the flora and the fauna: it is perhaps better to think of the biota as implying the intimate connection between plant and animal life, and we may look now at the other half of the story – the animal life.

The successful practice of nature conservation often, indeed usually, requires an accurate and detailed knowledge of the life cycle of the organisms concerned. Both the life cycle and the relationship with the environment are frequently very complex and may be but imperfectly known. It is often difficult to persuade the layman of these facts, and therein lies the criticism sometimes levelled at the Nature Conservancy and similar bodies. Whilst the need to preserve the native fauna and flora is accepted, even enthusiastically, and it is recognized as the duty of the Nature Conservancy to demarcate and manage nature reserves with this end in view, for the Conservancy to devote a considerable part of its staff and funds to 'fundamental research' is, say these critics, not its purpose or function. But research and management are inseparable. Without a knowledge, to take a single example, of the fantastic life cycle of the large blue butterfly, how could efforts at conservation hope to succeed except by accident? The story was well told in an anonymous contribution to the *New Scientist* (6 May 1965):

'PRESERVING THE LARGE BLUE'

'The Large Blue has the most extraordinary and elegant life history of any British butterfly. Although it is thought to have reached England from the continent of Europe just before the last Ice Age, it has always been only locally abundant. In fact, the first book on British insects, published in 1634 by Charles I's doctor, ignored it entirely. In the last few decades it has been reduced by changes in habitat, collectors and one of those exasperating and apparently inexplicable declines that animal populations occasionally go in for.

'Now virtually confined to a chain of coombes on the north coast of Devon and Cornwall, the Large Blue (*Maculinea arion*) depends for its survival on ants and wild thyme. A recent progress report from the Cornwall and the Devon Naturalists' Trusts suggests that the insects may have had a rather better season than usual last year. The conservation techniques being used are closely related to the Large Blue's strangely beautiful life cycle, which was first described by F. W. Frohawk in the 1920s.

'The adult, distinguished from other butterflies by its large size, deep blue colour and black-spotted wings, flies for only three or four days in June and July. During her short life the female mates and lays her eggs among the buds of the wild thyme (*Thymus drucei*). Within ten days the caterpillar is hatched, and feeds voraciously on thyme flowers and – cannibalistically – on its younger brethren. Twenty days later, after a third moult, the larva leaves its food plant, for from now on it will be exclusively carnivorous. Wandering aimlessly around on the ground, it eventually meets up with a foraging red ant, either *Myrmica scabrinoides* or *M. laevonoides*.

'The ant walks round and round the caterpillar, caressing and stroking its honey gland, a curious organ on the seventh abdominal segment. It milks the gland, gorging on the secreted droplets. After an hour or so of this, the larva's thorax suddenly puffs up and the ant seizes the caterpillar, much as a cat might grab a kitten, and carries it off into its nest. The Large Blue lives in darkness in a special chamber from August until the following summer, feeding all the time on young ants, like some tiny Minotaur. By May it has grown, without moulting and merely by stretching its skin, from 3 to 15 mm. in length, and is a bloated, shiny, pinkish-white parasite. It spins a silken pad on the roof of its chamber, hangs itself up and pupates. Three weeks later the adult insect emerges from the chrysalis, crawls up through the ants, and dries its wings in daylight.

'Naturalists have not always taken much notice of biology of the species they are seeking to protect: a recent discovery of the two trusts was that the famous Butterfly Valley at Crackington Haven, Cornwall, which had been carefully left untouched for thirty years to preserve the Large Blue, was so overgrown that it contained neither thyme, nor ants, nor butterflies.

'Since then management at other sites has been more sophisticated, in recognition of a delicate balance of factors that includes burning, toxic spraying, and grazing by rabbits, cattle and sheep.

'Last year 170 Large Blues were seen on the wing, compared with eighty-five in 1963. However, sites occupied were down from thirteen to ten, and the weather probably favoured the species. Research is still going on into the precise habitat requirements of this butterfly. The two trusts hope to colonize suitable new sites artificially, since it is known that the species does not wander far afield by itself. But with entomologists perhaps the least conscious among all naturalists of the dangers of collecting, the Large Blue's worst threat still comes from an energetic butterfly collector.'

Nature is full of such intimate and intriguing relationships. It has been pointed out that in many parts of Britain the once familiar glowworms of the hedgerows are now decidedly rare. The food of the glowworms consists of small snails, into which the insect injects a fluid which kills the snail and in fact partly pre-digests the soft parts so that later it can be eaten by the glowworm. If the supply of snails is interrupted, the glowworms cannot survive: the glowworms may escape hedgerow spraying, but the snails may succumb.

The large blue butterfly is a very interesting example of the intimate knowledge required where an insect is concerned. We come now to the consideration of birds and mammals. A very crude form of wild life control was that formerly practised by gamekeepers. How crude it was may be judged by the wide differences of opinion among gamekeepers themselves. At one extreme the old type was both indiscriminate and cruel: any bird with a hooked beak was a predator with designs on game chicks, in fact almost any non-game bird and a range of animals would be found strung up on his nauseating gibbet. The sight of a decomposing corpse presumably was to deter others by reminding them of impending fate. Often animals were caught in gin traps infrequently visited, and so left to die lingering deaths. Even if the old type disappeared, many gamekeepers retained a special hatred for hawks and had most exaggerated ideas of the amount of damage a pair of peregrines might do. Another maxim was that the first essential condition, to quote from *The Keeper's Book*, 'in order to increase a stock of game on an estate, is the destruction of vermin', and one must remember the wide range covered by 'vermin' – rats and mice yes, also rabbits, foxes, stoats, weasels, polecats, otters, as well as wood-pigeon and crows. Indeed the noblest of birds are 'vermin' to many gamekeepers – the golden eagle, the osprey, the kite, all owls. All, according to the old type of gamekeeper, to be shot in the interests of the grouse and his fellow noblemen.

Writing as late as 1946, Brian Vesey-Fitzgerald in the New Naturalist volume on *British Game*, notes how sportsmen were 'leaning towards the nature-lover's point of view – a great increase in the number of shooting men who did not want to kill every hawk just because it is a hawk', but still records those who shot the protected buzzard without a second thought. He noted the educative work of the British Field Sports Society and how it was introducing a more civilized and balanced understanding. Nevertheless, his own confessions show a very hit-and-miss approach. He contends that three cardinal rules apply: first, there should be a *reduction* of vermin; second, the reduced population of vermin should be maintained; third, no ground should carry a greater head of game than it can support in good health. He quotes from personal experience: 'I did not destroy hawks, owls, or jays. I was overrun with magpies and I did destroy them till I was left with four pairs. I did not destroy hawks because I like hawks and I did not find that they did any great damage. . . . The jay in reasonable numbers is a friend. . . . I employed my keeper's time in trapping rats and re-ducing the enormous rabbit population, and I left him stoats and weasels to help him – excellent rat catchers, deadly and skilful . . . owls, with the possible exception of the little owl – I regard as sacrosanct . . . if one now and again makes a mistake and takes a chick of mine, why, it is welcome to it. Buzzards are also sacrosanct . . . they do enormous good in keeping down the numbers of young rabbits and voles. . . . The kestrel is in exactly the same position, and the hobby should never be shot. The rook is sometimes doubt-ful . . . carrion crow and hoodie are no good and need their num-bers drastically reduced. The raven, too, is a menace, but on a lesser scale. And I regard all gulls, when away from the coast, with the gravest suspicion . . . they are ruthless robbers . . . the grey squirrel is another menace. . . . I can find no good word to say of the rabbit. . . . Disease, not the predator, is the gamekeeper's chief enemy. Nine times out of ten disease is the direct result of over-crowding. In the wild if any animal attains too great a population remedial factors (predators as well as parasites) instantly get to work. . . . A great increase in voles produces short-eared owls, almost magically, a great increase in wood-pigeons produces disease. . . .'

This extensive excerpt is reproduced because it illustrates the extent to which the need for control has long been recognized, but has in the past been based very much on personal likes and dislikes. Much more exact knowledge is needed.

In the chapter on wildfowl which follows, emphasis is laid on the growing understanding between wildfowlers who seek to kill and conservationists who seek, broadly, to maintain life. Whilst most will accept that certain types of vegetation must be cut and destroyed if habitats are to be maintained, it is much more difficult to accept that, both in the country as a whole and in nature reserves in par-ticular, it may be necessary to kill birds and other animals which are in too great numbers, if we are to preserve the rare and the weak. A special section has been devoted to the grey seal, where the problem is particularly acute.

But there are many other examples. The grey squirrel is a handsome ruffian who is undoubtedly driving the red squirrel to extinction. If, therefore, it becomes necessary to destroy excessive numbers of the more aggressive species, how far should one go in encouraging the rarities? A few years ago a pied flycatcher found a hollow tree in Yarner Wood, Devon, and nested there, farther south than previously recorded. By the simple experiment of pro-viding a couple of dozen nesting boxes tied to the trees at an appropriate height, many heard the glad news and nested there the following year. But some may ask how justified is man in becoming a dominant biotic factor in the life of a pied flycatcher?

A paper which appeared on the agenda of a Nature Conservancy meeting in 1966 was entitled 'Pesticides as a Management Tool'. At first this strikes a strange note, but the study group concerned, recognizing that the 'chemical treatment of the environment is becoming as universal as mechanical' on farm lands, very wisely looked at ways in which chemical treatment could be used in the management of reserves. Bramble and nettle patches, expensive and tedious to clear mechanically, succumb to phenoxyacetic acid herbicides, Paraquat and Diquat can be safely used for spot treatment of undesirable plants in any habitat, Dalapon can be used to control monocotyledonous species in aquatic and other habitats. Under strict control many specialized pesticides can be brought into service.

THE PROBLEM OF THE GREY SEAL

The grey seal (*Halichoerus grypus*) is Britain's largest mammal and no animal illustrates more forcibly the problem of conservation and control. Early this century the grey seal was believed to be in imminent danger of extinction, and when the first Grey Seals Protection Act of 1914 (which provided for a close season from 10th October to 15th December) was passed, the surviving population was stated to be as low as 500 individuals. In 1947 Professor James Ritchie and Mr. W. L. Calderwood estimated the population around Scotland (excluding Orkney and Shetland) at between 4,000 and 5,000, with about 1,000 pups being born annually. Although the second Grey Seals Protection Act 1932 extended the close season from 1st September to 31st December, provision was made for its suspension by the Minister of Agriculture and Fisheries in England and the Secretary of State for Scotland. The seal was becoming a potential pest, and damage to fisheries, especially the salmon fisheries along the east coast of Scotland, was causing alarm. Soon after its foundation the Nature Conservancy began to take an interest in the problem, but was soon up against an interesting case of red tape. So long as the grey seal is on land it is properly the subject of research by the Conservancy, but when it enters the water it becomes a matter of fisheries research. So the Conservancy made grants to the West Wales Field Society to study the seals of the Pembrokeshire coast, to the Natural History Society of Northumberland, Durham and Newcastle-upon-Tyne to study the

Farne Islands, and to a group from the University of London and elsewhere for the Scottish coasts. In 1959 the Treasury approved a grant for three years to a widely representative Consultative Committee under the Chairmanship of Dr. E. B. Worthington (then Deputy Director-General (Scientific) of the Nature Conservancy). Its Report, *Grey Seals and Fisheries*, was published by HMSO in 1963.

The world population of grey seals was estimated at 46,000, 78 per cent round the British Isles. Orkney alone has nearly a quarter of the world's total. The cows reach puberty in their fourth or fifth year, and they bear a single pup annually until death at up to thirty-five years. The bulls have a harem of about ten cows and each has a definite territorial status and a life span of about twenty-five years. Seals are predators on a wide range of vertebrate and invertebrate animals, but especially fish. The consumption of food fish, especially salmon, is undoubtedly high. In addition, large numbers of fish are wounded and lowered in commercial value by seal bites, and fishermen in the areas concerned claim that ten per cent of all nets are damaged by seals (adults weigh between 500 and 800 lb.) and that large numbers of fish escape through the torn nets. There is evidence that seals are intermediate hosts for the cod-worm, a nematode which causes serious damage to cod-fish and which, though not dangerous to human beings when the fish is properly cooked, are aesthetically unpleasant.

Mature seals can be, and are, shot by fishermen, but a bobbing head in the water is a difficult target and the main effect of shooting is the noise which scares them away. On the other hand, the pups which are born on land are very inactive. They can be approached and photographed and supply abundant evidence of wide-eyed innocence and the appeal inalienable from the young and helpless. It is equally easy to kill them painlessly, as far as any death is painless, by the Webley-Scott pistol commonly used by veterinary surgeons for disposing of sick animals. In the words of the Report, 'The operator should stand behind and over the pup, aiming at a point at least two-thirds of the distance from a line between the eyes to the back of the head at about 6 in. range'. Such is the practice of seal-culling.

It is unlikely that the problem of whether or not to use systematic culling to reduce the grey seal population will be solved to the satisfaction of all. The Report records that the Committee considers no operations should be undertaken on such areas as the Isles of Scilly (where the seals undoubtedly earn their keep as a tourist attraction) and other areas where there are small numbers. Where the seals are very numerous, as around Orkney, it may be justified to kill half the pups born every year. But the problem and the controversy reach their height in the two largest breeding colonies in the world – the island of North Rona and the Farne Islands. Both of these are National Nature Reserves, and there are many who find it hard to reconcile conservation with the annual carnage of 360 seal pups, which is recommended for the Farne Islands. There are still other difficulties. Human beings are not alone in their gregariousness and willingness to face overcrowded slum conditions. This seems to be happening with the seal population of the Farne Islands; though food is short there seems no inclination to emigrate or colonize other islands, even nearby. One wonders whether the answer is not to be sought rather in shooting off some of the territorial bulls who have had a good life anyway, or alternately whether scientists should not turn their attention more seriously to birth control. The problem of protected animals multiplying and outrunning food supply is becoming world-wide – it applies in parts of Africa, for example, to hippopotami and elephants.

THE PROBLEM OF THE RED DEER

The problem of controlling the deer population in Britain has some points of comparison with the grey seal problem, with the added complications that deer-stalking and hunting have long been a part of the social life of Britain, albeit a sport for the privileged few, and that venison is a highly appreciated and valuable food. The red deer (*Cervus elaphus* L.) standing about four feet high at the withers, and the much smaller roe deer (*Capreolus capreolus* L.) of about half that height, are the only true wild deer of Britain. The red deer, formerly occurring over the whole country, but now restricted to the Highlands and Islands of Scotland, the Lake

District, Exmoor, the Quantocks and the New Forest (though there possibly re-introduced) is a gregarious animal of the moorlands; the roe deer is a nocturnal woodland animal living in small family groups and has been extending in the new forests of the Forestry Commission. The reign of Edward VII (1901-1910) saw the recognized and demarcated deer forests of Scotland increase in numbers to over 200 and the acreage to over 3,850,000 acres. At the peak period of 1912-13, just before the outbreak of the First World War, the deer population may have reached 175,000; the annual kill reached 12,500 (all stags should be seven years or more), the 'industry' employed 2,000 persons and the rental of deer forests was over £100,000 per annum. Although probably 50-60,000 were killed for food during the war, the present situation began to emerge: too many deer, little disturbed by the extinct race of wealthy deer-stalkers, chasing too little food on too little land, and competing for that land with the growing economic needs in lamb, mutton, beef and timber. The townsman, thinking of the deer in Richmond Park, is very easily led to be sentimental about Britain's wild deer. He should see the emaciated carcases, two-thirds of them last year's calves, on the ground in the Highlands after severe frosts as in the winter of 1962-3. Again comes the obvious need for positive control and how our red deer should be managed under today's conditions.

Even in southern Britain the increase in numbers both of our native deer and of the several introduced feral species is creating major problems. One thing becomes clear: the worst cruelty is that inflicted by failure to take positive steps to control the deer population.

CHAPTER 8

THE LAW AND THE LAND

A multiplicity of Acts at present on the Statute Book affects the conservation of wild life in one way or another. Reference has already been made in Chapter 2 to some of the major enactments concerned with land use, including the provision of national parks and nature reserves. But there are also the laws designed to protect certain animals or groups of animals and birds. Many, perhaps the majority, of these were enacted in the interests of sport and sportsmen. They include some of the oldest still unrepealed. The notoriously harsh forest laws, guaranteeing the animals of the chase for the King and his nobles in the Royal Forests and Chases, may have been swept away long since, but others still remain. Though not comparable with their importance in the great Edwardian days, various forms of hunting, shooting and fishing are still very much with us.

Deer forests still occupy some 3,000,000 acres in Scotland, grouse moors are not only extensive but grouse shooting provides an important economic incentive to life in many upland areas. Since grouse shooting is not permitted by law before August 12th, the 'glorious twelfth' is still an important date in Britain's social calendar. It is the night of August 11th-12th when special trains of first-class sleepers take the jaded London executives to the refreshing air of the Scottish Highlands.

The laws which lay down the 'close seasons' for game animals and game birds are obviously as much an important element in wild life conservation as in the maintenance of shooting as a sport. One of the earliest New Naturalist volumes, *British Game*, by Brian Vesey-Fitzgerald, points out the significance from very early times of the sport of hawking – in England from Saxon times and probably earlier. In later times a man's rank could be known from the species of hawk assigned to him: the peregrine, gyrfalcon, and goshawk were reserved for the gentry, the sparrow hawk (associated particularly with clergy below the rank of the bishops, who were nobles) and kestrel for persons of lesser rank. The goshawk was very popular, since it was said to be affectionate and to have regarded its master's hand as its home, but was relentless in pursuit of a quarry. Goshawks apparently bred regularly in Britain: it is typical of the attitude of the nineteenth century that the last two females who tried to nest in the nineteenth century – in Lincolnshire in 1864 and Yorkshire 1893 – were both shot. When hawking was popular and fashionable in Tudor times there were most stringent laws to protect eyries and nests: Henry VII and Henry VIII both passed such laws. A good hawk was worth a King's ransom: indeed one of the Crusader princes is said to have been ransomed from the Saracens for twelve Greenland falcons. Falconry began to go out with the Restoration, when improved firearms made shooting popular. But even today there is still a Falconers' Club and hawks are flown.

Pheasants are believed to have figured on the dinner menus of the Romans in Britain but certainly disappeared when the Romans left, to be reintroduced shortly before the Norman Conquest. Pheasants and partridges continued to be reared for many centuries, the eggs being put under hens, and certainly during the eighteenth century pheasants and partridges were turned into coverts to be beaten out later, and shoots were arranged much in the modern manner. There were gamekeepers and game preservation was clearly well-established. Another example of medieval conservation was the warrener, whose work was to guard and supervise the rabbit warrens, with the rabbit an important source of food.

But modern conservation really begins with the famous Game Act of 1831. This Act legalized the status of the gamekeeper, gave him certain powers of arrest. Previously only property owners could shoot game (this is still true of Scotland and Ireland). The Game Act requires a licence with a fee payable to the Inland Revenue – an ordinary gun licence does not permit shooting of game. The Game Act lists as game hares, pheasants, partridges, 'heath or moor game', black game and bustards. Bustards are extinct, the identity of 'heath and moor game' is unknown. Uncertainties in the provisions of the 1831 Act and much subsequent legislation have made our game laws exceedingly complex, sometimes contradictory and even farcical. Woodcock, snipe, quail, corncrake and rabbits are not game, but require a licence to shoot. To quote Vesey-Fitzgerald again:

'Deer, though they are not game, do require a licence before they can be taken or killed (except by hunting with hounds) under the Game Licences Act, 1860. But they can be killed on enclosed land without a licence by the owner or the occupier or his licensee. On the other hand, they are included as Game in the Agricultural Holdings Act when questions regarding compensation for damage arise. Again, hares (which are game) and rabbits (which are not) are included in the Excise Licence to kill game but are excluded from the close seasons for killing game. In England and Wales you cannot shoot (in peace-time) a grouse, a pheasant or a partridge on a Sunday nor a pheasant or a partridge on Christmas Day. Black game are not protected on Sundays. And it is quite possible to find plenty more contradictions. Furthermore, poaching, strictly speaking, seems to be applicable only to game and rabbits. The Game Act, it will be seen, is not very easy to understand, and the position is not made any easier by such things as the Law of Trespass (particularly with regard to boundary questions), which is very technical indeed.'

Apart from game, wild birds, which attracted attention because of their rarity or interest, were in need of legal protection. Wild Bird Protection Acts came into force which have saved from extinction many of our rarer species. One difficulty was that often a protected species could not be identified until after it was shot.

A major change is marked by the very important Protection of Birds Act 1954 which came into force on 1st December 1954. Its advantage is that it is a straightforward measure which gives protection to *all* birds, making exceptions to a list of common birds which can be regarded as pests or harmful in one way or another, or are so numerous as to present a menace to other rarer species. The list of shootable exceptions can be varied.

Under Section 10 of the Act the Nature Conservancy assumed responsibility for issuing licences for necessary interference with bird life for scientific or educational purposes, and the Conservancy was also one of the bodies empowered to nominate authorized persons to deal with pest control. The Act also included a clause continuing the statutory protection which has been enjoyed by many famous reserves and empowered the Secretary of State to create others. The new Act has enabled fruitful co-operation to be developed, such as that with the wildfowlers (see Chapter 11).

The situation with regard to mammals is much less satisfactory. It is highly desirable that there should be a general protection act for mammals comparable with the Protection of Birds Act 1954. Exceptions in the case of animals regarded as pests could then be made. As things are, piecemeal legislation is unsatisfactory. The case of the grey seal has been discussed in detail; the common seal enjoys no protection from being hunted and shot when it ventures on land, but is safe so long as it stays in the sea. Red deer have been made the object of special legislation, but many of our interesting mammals enjoy no protection.

There is a recent development whereby interested conservationists have an opportunity of taking action. This is the insertion in a number of recent Acts of Parliament of what is sometimes called the amenity clause, and reads something as follows:

'. . . The Board or the Minister, as the case may be, having regard to the desirability of preserving natural beauty, of conserving flora, fauna and geological or physiographical features of special interest, and of protecting buildings and other objects of architectural or historic interest, shall take into account any effect which the proposals would have on the natural beauty of the countryside or on any such flora, fauna, features, buildings or objects.'

This clause appears in the North Wales Hydro-Electricity Acts 1952 and 1955, Electricity Act 1957, Opencast Coal Act 1958, Pipelines Act 1962, Water Resources Act 1963.

It is only right to state that with increased concern for amenity and wild life conservation, the clause is far from being a dead letter and is being widely observed.

Two major problems of the present day are litter and pollution. Both do far more than threaten wild life: they threaten the very existence of the countryside. There was a time, not far distant, when the people of Britain took pride in cleanliness – to such an extent that a continental holiday was regarded as an excursion into lands where both public and personal standards of cleanliness were suspect, where water was certainly undrinkable and most food potentially dangerous. Even if our water and foodstuffs are safe-guarded by strict laws, it must be admitted that in many other respects national standards have fallen far behind those of many, if not most, of our continental neighbours. Public transport, rail-ways in particular, are just dirty, but one conspicuous sign of a deficient national standard is litter. We have anti-litter laws, but public apathy makes enforcement difficult. Modern wrappings are excellent for the protection of food, but thrown under a bush after a picnic they do not quickly waste away as did the old newspaper or tissue. Discarded tins are slow to rust and dangerous to animals, bottles still more so.

There are several different aspects of pollution. That arising from chemicals, now so widely used in agriculture, is discussed in Chapter 10; there is also atmospheric pollution, especially from factories, which is being gradually controlled, and from the exhausts of road vehicles which is not. A build-up of toxic substances, notably per-haps lead, by certain roadside plants even casts doubts on the wisdom of eating salad vegetables grown within range of a highway, and may indeed reach human beings through milk. Then there is pollution of rivers – by waste effluents, but also in these days by detergents arising from domestic sinks. Although there are estimated to be 3,000,000 active anglers in Britain who are vitally interested in the pollution of rivers and lakes, it was not till 1965 that a body came into existence to speak for them at the national level. The large-scale pollution of the sea by oil accidentally or purposely discharged from tankers is a nuisance too well-known to need emphasis, but the annual toll on sea-birds is appalling. This is despite international agreements to prohibit dumping of oil waste at sea. The RSPCA in particular spends much time, energy and resources in attempting the de-oiling of birds, but many still perish. The larger companies and many of the nations are alive to their responsibilities, but unfortunately not all – as yet.

THE COUNTRYSIDE ACTS

An extremely important new development is marked by the Countryside (Scotland) Act 1967 and the Countryside Act of 3rd August 1968. Under the latter the National Parks Commission becomes the Countryside Commission and is strengthened with new powers and duties. Sections 6 and 7 of the Act empower local authorities to create Country Parks where the public will be able to enjoy open-air recreation and find secluded places in which to relax and picnic. They are primarily intended to meet the growing demand resulting from the increased leisure and mobility of large numbers of the population living in cities and urban areas who are looking for a change of environment within easy reach. This will relieve pressure on existing areas, especially National Parks and some Nature Reserves. The Act also requires every Minister, Government department, and public body to have due regard for 'the desirability of conserving the natural beauty and amenity of the countryside', including its flora, fauna, and geological and physiographical features. Of particular significance is the clause (in both Acts) to enable the Natural Environment Research Council, through the Nature Conservancy, to make agreements with owners and occupiers to manage certain sites for nature conservation without their becoming statutory reserves.

CHAPTER 9

FARMING AND WILD LIFE

One of the greatest difficulties facing the conservationist at the present time is to convince the preservationist that Nature is constantly on the move. The natural tendency of the young is to welcome change, sometimes indeed to welcome change for its own sake and the constant need is to be 'with it'. The natural tendency of the old is often to resist change and to regard change as inherently a Bad Thing. There is a small, but often very vocal and sometimes powerful, minority which equates conservation with preservation and preservation with the maintenance of conditions which, all too often, are already out of date. In their attitude to nature conservation and the countryside generally this group often takes as their standards conditions as they recall them in their childhood or youth. It is very difficult to convince them that there is a continuous process of evolution going on all around us and that what they seek to 'preserve' is a particular stage in this process of evolution.

Nowhere is this more true than in the progress of farming which has evolved and changed constantly since man first took to the domestication of animals and the tilling of the soil. Admittedly, just at present farming is in the midst of the new agricultural revolution and changes are taking place with bewildering rapidity and are of a far-reaching character.

A brief review of some changes in the landscape, due to evolving farm techniques through the ages, may not be amiss.

When the pre-Roman British tribes sought to tame the wild forest of their natural environment, there is evidence that they laid out and tilled by hand small square fields in the uplands where the forest was sparse and thus more easily cleared. It was the Angles and the Saxons who penetrated up the rivers, clearing and cultivating in two or three open common fields the better soils of the river valley loam-gravel terraces. Their cattle grazed in the waterside meadows, often flooded in winter but with an early bite of grass in spring; their sheep found food on the valley slopes with rough herbage; forest was left on the higher ground between fertile valleys. No doubt cultivation and controlled grazing spread till the farmers from one settlement met those from another and boundaries between their respective parishes had to be laid down. In those far away days of trial and error no doubt villages were established which failed to survive because of adverse factors in the environment – poor soils, or lack of a permanent water supply, or difficulties of access.

The bulk of the evidence is that on the best soils cultivation has continued from those early Anglo-Saxon days to the present; heavy and overdrained soils, ever hungry for plant food, were a lasting problem and probably today remain untilled. The maximum of change has always been on lands of intermediate quality.

Through the long centuries of the Middle Ages we can envisage the bulk of lowland Britain as consisting of villages of farmhouses, farm buildings and workers' cottages, clustered round a village church, the parsonage and manor house nearby, perhaps an open village green, then stretching all around, the great open common fields, with beyond rough grazing and woods. It must have been a very open, prairie type of landscape, and we know that hedgerows were rare. Rough muddy unmetalled tracks led from village or farmhouse to the bounds of the open fields, and perhaps, more by accident than design, linked up with the trackways of the adjoining settlement. In time these unfenced roads, wandering rather aimlessly, were given a coating of stone from a village common quarry. Some better trackways led to the market towns and it was the towns well sited at meeting places of the country roads which developed at the expense of others.

No doubt the Black Death of the fourteenth century led to the abandonment of many villages and the consolidation of effort on the better lands, but the major changes did not take place till the era of enclosure and improvement. I have dealt with some of the consequent landscape changes in my book *Man and the Land* in the New Naturalist series. The point which I now want to make is that it was not till the eighteenth century – some two hundred years ago only – that lowland Britain began to assume the general pattern which today is regarded as essentially the British countryside. So long as cultivation was in strips in the common open fields, improved farming by any one individual was impossible, while the others adhered to old methods. The introduction of root crops to be stored as winter feed, the introduction of the Norfolk four-course rotation, marked the early stages of the great change. With the 'improvers' of the eighteenth century, the face of Britain began to assume what is now regarded as its traditional pattern. To quote my own words (p. 80): 'The country houses with their gardens and parks became more numerous. The parks were frequently made to serve as agricultural experimental stations for no longer was it derogatory to indulge in husbandry. England in particular had become a land of hedgerows and hedgerow trees giving place to stone walls in natural stone country. In many counties the predominant land use was a patchwork of small fields in the midst of which the unenclosed arable of the common fields and the common grazing remained as a survival from the past. The hedges were planted "quick", usually of may or hawthorn (also known as whitethorn), sloe or black-thorn, crab apple, holly and elder. Ash and elm were often left to grow into hedgerow trees but other trees or shrubs, after growing for eight to ten years, were slashed and "laid" to make a barrier remarkably impenetrable. It was often considered unlucky so to treat a holly tree: hence the many holly bushes which stand up above the hedge level. Naturally hedges were set along old lines – the margins of lanes, the borders of assarts or clearings, the limits of old cultivation strips – so that the field pattern of today enshrines centuries of rural history. As the fields were thus enclosed attention had to be paid to drainage and the ditch by the hedge became standard in many areas. So important is drainage that boundaries of properties are commonly defined not by the obvious hedge but by the less obvious ditch.

'Apart from the enclosure of the common arable and common grazing which was still in many areas to take place, the eighteenth century saw what may be called the completion of the rural pattern by the people of the countryside themselves. What was to follow was in large measure the impact of town on country.'

It was not until after the middle of the last century that enclosure was nearly complete. According to the Returns made to the House of Commons in 1873, there were still 250,868 acres of unenclosed common arable fields in England and a further 13,439 acres in Wales (see W. G. Hoskins and L. Dudley Stamp, *The Common Lands of England and Wales*, New Naturalist series). In those same returns the common grazing was given as 1,484,476 acres in England and Wales – not very different from the total of 1,505,002 acres recorded by the Royal Commission in 1956, by which time the only common arable remaining was in one or two villages deliberately preserved as specimens of the medieval system, notably Laxton.

In general terms the pattern of lowland Britain as one of small fields divided by hedges has been in existence less than a couple of hundred years. The same is true of other features of the countryside now regarded as 'traditional'.

There is no doubt that enclosure made possible major advances in farming, but it also created a large class of landless rural peasantry with a very low standard of living. Fortunately this was at a time when the industrial revolution was gaining pace and it was the peasantry rendered superfluous by the agricultural revolution which provided the labour force for the industrial revolution. In due course the day was to come when the descendants of the displaced countrymen were to become the ruling democratic majority of our towns and cities.

Fortunately there are certain periods of British farming history of which contemporary records afford an adequate picture. The Board of Agriculture and Internal Improvement, as an independent body supported by public funds, was established in 1793 under an experienced Chairman, Sir John Sinclair, and with an energetic secretary, Arthur Young, already known as an agricultural writer. The Board immediately set to work to produce a long series of volumes dealing with the agriculture of each county, entitled in each case *A General View of the Agriculture of . . . shire*. The first edition was usually printed on quarto paper with broad margins and circulated for comments which were later incorporated in the final octavo volume. About the same time the (first) *Statistical Account of Scotland* (1791-9), with descriptions of each parish prepared by the local minister, was being issued, eventually to form twenty-one volumes. The establishment of the Board, like that of the Ordnance Survey in 1791, was due in part at least to the current fear of invasion of Britain by the French under Napoleon, and the need for a stocktaking of our position. The Napoleonic wars, in fact, kept corn prices high and British farming prosperous, and there was a serious collapse after the victory of Waterloo in 1815.

The extensive tours on horseback made by William Cobbett and described by him in his immortal *Rural Rides* relate to this period of depression. The Tithe Redemption Act 1836 set up the Tithe Redemption Commission which embarked on the colossal task of mapping and recording details of every piece of land, parish by parish, still subject to tithe. Coincident with this work was the *New Statistical Account of Scotland*, begun in 1834, and published mainly in 1846-9.

For centuries the complex Corn Laws had virtually made impossible any considerable international trade in grain. Protection was afforded to the home grower and prices were often kept artificially high until the famous Repeal Act of 1846 allowed the import of foreign grain practically free of duty. At first this made comparatively little difference, for the great wheat lands of Canada, the United States, Argentina and Australia had not yet been developed. So it was the period of the 1870s, the period of 'high farming' in Britain, which interests us and may be taken as the starting point for a consideration of the modern interaction between farming and wild life.

Agricultural statistics, collected in Ireland from 1847 as a result of the great potato famine, were first undertaken in England, Wales and Scotland in 1866, and from 1867 onwards the forms filled in annually by farmers on or about 4th June are the source of our agricultural statistics. In England and Wales the acreage under the plough reached its all-time maximum of 15,275,513 acres in 1869, out of a total of improved land, crops and grass, of 26,901,141. The latter figure rose somewhat to its all-time high in 1891 (28,091,134), since when it has continued to drop steadily as more and more land has passed into urban uses, and some marginal lands have been abandoned. By 1935 it had dipped below 25 million, in

1946 to 24.3 million, but in 1965 was 24,357,000. From its peak in 1869 the arable acreage declined steadily till 1915 to 10,965,707 acres, then a small temporary rise for the efforts of the First World War against the submarine menace, then a renewed decline to a low of 8,877,712 acres in 1938. This was, of course, followed by the spectacular rise through the war effort and 'plough up' campaign to 14,588,000 acres in 1944, not far short of the maximum of 1869. In 1965 it was 14,132,000 acres.

The decline of arable acreage, 1869 to 1938, was accompanied in general by the increase in permanent grass from 11.1 m. acres in 1870 to 16.1 in 1914, and an average of about 15.7 in the 'thirties. Although we know there has been some abandonment of hill lands, the figures for rough grazing are not sufficiently reliable to be used without careful analysis. But with livestock the position is clear: a steady rise in the cattle population (especially dairy cows) from a little over 4 m. in the late 'sixties of the last century to pass the 7 m. mark in 1943 and to reach 8.8 m. in 1965. The peak of the sheep population was in 1874 with 22.9 m., dropping to under 12.6 m. in 1945 but back to 20.3 m. in 1965. The career of the horse as a farm animal has been a remarkably brief one. When the Board of Agriculture started its work in 1793 the horse was replacing the ox as the plough animal, but as late as 1834 the anonymous author of *British Husbandry*, a manual for farmers, comes down in favour of the ox. The position of the horse on the farm was challenged in the early years of the present century, when progressive large-scale farmers employed two steam traction engines, one on each side of the field drawing a multi-furrowed plough between them by means of a steel rope. The days of 'one-horse' (light), 'two-horse' (medium) or 'four-horse' (very heavy) land began to disappear. With the advent of the internal combustion engine the working horse quickly became a rarity on urban streets, the pit pony disappeared from the mines and, on the farms of Great Britain, the 1,002,000 horses in 1938 had fallen to 494,000 in 1953 and to under 100,000 by 1963. By 1965 only one farm in ten still had a working horse. Since oats were mainly grown for the purpose of feeding horses, the drop in oat-cultivation has been similarly spectacular.

The history of farming development in Scotland, where two-thirds of the surface is 'rough grazing' (various types of moorland), is somewhat different. The general picture is familiar: the Highland glens, with their self-contained crofting settlements, giving place to extensive hill-sheep farming, deer forests and grouse moors, with an accompanying depopulation. In the lowlands the changes are not so different from those of England, though the Scottish farmer long remained faithful to his six-year rotation – three years in crops, three in grass – and his belief in 'taking the plough round the farm', long before it was accepted as general practice in England during the Second World War. In consequence the officially recorded arable acreage in Scotland, with a maximum of 3,686,866 acres in 1888 (an average of rather over 3.5 m. in the 'seventies), did not dip to just below 3,000,000 until 1934, and its lowest was 2,975,995 in 1936. From 1868 to 1938, just before the outbreak of war, Scottish cattle varied in numbers only from 1,017,724 in 1869 to a high of 1,318,494 in 1935, and sheep from a low of 6,360,928 in 1920 to a high of 7,916,424 in 1932.

Perhaps we are now in a position to form a mental picture of the successive stages in the recent development of the farming landscape. My own formative years of boyhood were spent in the village of Meopham at 500 feet on the chalk (with local cappings of clay with flints) of the North Downs of Kent – near enough, by going to Rochester to school, to know the tidal marshes of the Medway and the rich fruit belt of North Kent. The village was then a tightly-knit community: church and chapel, parson and minister, squire and professional men, a number of prosperous farmers, a large number of farm labourers, essential services such as the blacksmith, village store, postmistress, church school with a headmaster and two or three teachers. There was no street lighting: winter amusements depended upon the period of full moon. Large families were the rule; there were numerous governess carts and other types of pony trap; but only one progressive resident acquired a motor car. The roads were roughly metalled with broken flints rolled in with the aid of a steam-roller; and the first attempts at tarring resulted only in a thickly rutted sea of black mud. In summer every passing motorist raised a cloud of white dust which settled thickly on the verges and hedgerows, and even quite heavy showers failed to remove the coating. Farm hedges were usually well and skilfully laid and afforded excellent protection for nests; road banks and hedgerows had a remarkable wealth of flowers and, knowing not the chemical sprays to come, had an abundant insect fauna in summer and a wide range of snails and slugs in wet weather. The village greens and wayside manorial waste were well grazed by cattle (often tethered) and sheep: we protected the cricket pitch with hurdles and had a morning removing dung before the Saturday afternoon football match. The steeper slopes of the dry chalk valleys carried a very rich and specialized flora which encouraged a remarkably varied insect fauna. Also one looked upon a veritable plague of flies within the house as normal: they clustered especially on the Venetian blinds and circled endlessly round the bedroom ceiling. Outside one looked upon the swarms of wasps as inevitable: we took it in turn to spend hours with rattles keeping birds from cherries and apples. We looked upon mice in the house and rats in the stable and rabbits in the orchard as natural and likewise inevitable. Even more inevitable were the common weeds of arable fields. I am not old enough to remember the corn cockle (*Agrotemma githagos*) in abundance, but the blue cornflower (*Centaurea cyanus*) was often conspicuous and wheat fields on the lighter land were nearly always a blaze of red poppies (*Papaver rhoeas*). Farmers regarded it as normal that ten per cent of seed sown (especially of their own or of 'sown grasses') would be of weeds. Most farmers had a patch of woodland and, all over the south-east of England, it was normally managed as coppice-with-standards. The standards were commonly oak, the coppiced trees were hazel, birch and, more locally, chestnut. A delightful succession of ground vegetation followed the sequence of coppice management: an incredible spread of primroses on the open freshly cut-over land, at other times bluebells, anemones (*Anemone nemorosa*), *Oxalis acetosella*, and dog's mercury (*Mercurialis perennis*) were dominant.

Undoubtedly the major differences between the England farm-lands of my youth and today, in so far as they provide habitats for wild life, are in the hedges and hedgerows, and the arable fields.

But there are also major changes in the grass fields. The old popular belief, that cows fed largely on buttercups will yield rich milk (and bright yellow butter) dies hard, and farmers and countryfolk in general looked with pleasure and favour on the brilliant yellow of a field of buttercups in spring. There was a thrill in finding that some of the more delicate yellow might be due to cowslips (*Primula veris*) and in damp corners the meadow-sweet (*Filipendula ulmaria*) was relied upon to give a fragrance to hay. These are just a few of the differences which I remember from my boyhood; John Gilmour and Max Walters tell the story delightfully in their *Wild Flowers* in this series. It took the stern realism of Sir George Stapledon and his colleague, Dr. William Davies, to point out the low standard of most of our pastures and meadows considered as pastures for cattle rather than an attractive stage in the evolution of an ecosystem.

The next vignette of conditions may well be that of the period 1931-3, when the bulk of the field work of the first Land Utilisation Survey of Britain was carried out. It was my task, as Director, to visit practically every county in England, Wales and Scotland to organize or supervise or check the work. It was a period of depression in British farming, perhaps even to be described as a nadir when services to the national survival during World War I had been so largely forgotten. The work of the survey has been fully analysed in the ninety-two county parts of *The Land of Britain* which I edited from 1936 to 1946, and later summarized in *The Land of Britain: Its Use and Misuse* (Longmans 1948, 1950; third edition 1962). The 'thirties were a period of neglect. Much marginal land on hillsides had been abandoned and so had former arable on such light thin-soiled lands as the chalk of Hampshire and Wiltshire. It had been allowed to 'tumble to grass' which often meant invasion by useless weeds such as ragwort (*Senecio jacobaea*) and later gorse (*Ulex*) and bramble (*Rubus*). Hedges were neglected and allowed to grow up into irregular bushes affording far less protection to birds than a well-laid hedge. Drainage ditches had been neglected and so had field drains and field drainage, large areas had become waterlogged and invaded by rushes (*Juncus*). A great decrease in arable cultivation, including grain, had meant a

12 Ashwood on limestone, Rassal National Nature Reserve, Wester Ross

13 A path in the Cairngorms Nature Reserve

diminished food supply to wild life. In sum, agricultural neglect of the land and deterioration of farming had led to a return to 'semi-natural' vegetation, but, contrary to widely held beliefs, this was *not* to the advantage of wild life. Many birds had been robbed of their hedgerow fastnesses, their sure supply of surplus grain; many interesting plants were crowded out by the more aggressive dominants of waste land.

Passing over the special war-time efforts, we come now to the period after the Second World War, the period of the New Agricultural Revolution. The war years themselves saw vast changes, especially in the extension of plough lands and rapid mechanization. From the point of view of nature conservation it is essential to remember that change in farming is inevitable and that it is impossible to put back the clock. At the same time, as the preceding pages have endeavoured to show, change is nothing new. The task of the conservationist is to recognize and fit in with current changes.

In the first place, in all walks of life, this is the age of the machine and mechanization is here to stay. The horse has practically disappeared as a farm animal, oats are no longer required for feed, horse manure belongs to the past and is no longer available. An arable farm can now be run on a five- or six-day basis and Sunday and the week-ends can be complete rest-periods. It is even possible to go to the extreme, by no means unknown now in the prairie provinces of Canada or the mid-western United States, and shut the farm for the winter and enjoy the sunshine of Bermuda, Florida or Hawaii. However, the farm designed to produce only summer crops, such as grain, is scarcely known in Britain, and the American pattern is unlikely to become widespread. But mechanization is very definitely part of British farming life – indeed Britain can claim to be the most highly mechanized farming country in the world, if numbers of tractors and farm implements per unit area be taken as a criterion. Yet mechanization to this extent is not necessarily efficiency, unless the machines are more fully employed than many of them are at present.

Two desiderata arise: large field units to accommodate the larger machines; larger farm units for economic organization.

All over the country fields are being realigned and enlarged by grubbing up superfluous hedges and removing hedgerows and isolated trees. The hedgerow as a habitat is becoming less widespread, but a few well-laid hedges are better, for the associated bird life, than a multitude of sprawling unkept hedges. Those who are concerned with the effect on the scenery of our countryside must be reminded that this is only a partial *return* to the pre-enclosure scenery, and brings a feeling of greater spaciousness, a roomy landscape which offers a pleasant contrast to the close country of tiny hedged fields around the villages. Those who dislike the disappearance of the hedgerow trees, often elms, seek to secure retention of their landscape value by planting in clumps at field junctions. However, the hedges may change in character as hedgecutters cut but do not 'lay' the branches – modern trimmed hedges are less attractive to birds. Mechanization makes possible cheaper and more effective drainage and there is need for vigilance to maintain specimen areas of various wetland habitats. It is now easily possible to drain and plough extensive areas, destroying in particular such remains of past cultures as burial mounds and other archaeological features.

But the larger scale of operations brings into play other considerations. The larger farm unit, with a smaller but highly skilled labour force, means redundant farmhouses, unwanted (but often very substantial) farm buildings and unneeded farm workers' cottages. With a rising standard of living, we are rapidly becoming a two-homed people, and the desire for a week-end (or summer) cottage can absorb all the old cottages sufficiently well built or attractively sited to warrant expenditure on modernization or conversion. There are parts of the country, very fertile and desirable agriculturally, such as much of Fenland, where the physical landscape does not seem to attract the townsman, but elsewhere a tied cottage, no longer required for a farm worker, becomes a valuable asset to the farmer. Similarly many redundant farmhouses are readily marketable as country retreats and homes for the retired city dweller; all the more attractive if set within well-farmed country. Frequently one of the major attractions of the country is the wild life – especially birds – and an increasing knowledge of scientific ornithology renders safe the lives of many species which might otherwise fear extinction. Bird tables, nesting boxes, an appropriate water supply, even little wilderness areas, add to the facilities. In the three acres attached to my own thirteenth century manor house (for long a farmhouse) in Cornwall there is automatically a little nature reserve much appreciated by the local fauna and flora, despite the activities of my semi-feral cat, now however on the verge of retirement. The twenty or so collared doves know exactly feeding time for the ducks and chickens, the innumerable starlings work regularly in a neat row across the front lawn and dig up the moss between the paving stones, the rooks from the next-door rookery, the blackbirds, thrushes and magpies, with an occasional woodpecker, owl and jay, descend when the time is judged appropriate. Just so, the converted farmhouses through the countryside become little nature reserves.

More serious in farming changes is what I have elsewhere called chemicalization.

The first stage in chemicalization is the maintenance of the nutrient status of the soil. It is surely obvious that when crops are taken off any land there must be a loss of the nutrients which have gone into their growth and production. An obvious way of returning the plant foods to the soil is by natural manure – the excreta of animals together with the straw or hay used for their bedding: in many countries human excreta properly prepared plays a major role. Micro-organisms in a natural soil are also constantly at work in breaking down dead vegetation, such as leaves and other organic matter, into a form in which it is again available as plant food. A rapid return to the soil of nutrients derived from organic matter is by burning. Practically all over the grasslands and savannas of the tropics withered grass is burnt off annually, and it may generally be agreed that only when fires are so intense as to damage the soil (analogous to burning clay into a brick) is the process harmful. As every gardener knows, the treatment of a compost heap is to encourage nature, in the form of bacteria and other micro-organisms, to do the work, and so it is the living organisms of the soil which need to be encouraged – together with such other denizens as earthworms. The maintenance of a 'healthy soil' or a 'good tilth' implies this management of the soil as a home for living organisms. For long in Britain the controversy raged for and against paring and burning in our hill lands with a coating of acid peat. The process consisted of skinning off a layer of the peat and burning it. On the whole the process seems to have been beneficial. However, the main nutrient requirements of plants can be expressed by the symbols of the three essential elements – P.K.N. or phosphorus, potassium and nitrogen. A major advance was made with the realization that certain plants actually *add* to the nutrients of the soil. Various members of the pea and bean family (including the clovers) have small nodules on their roots which are the home of the so-called nitrifying bacteria – bacteria able to use the inert nitrogen of the atmosphere and to produce nitrites and nitrates which are the main source of the nitrogen required by plants. The introduction of clover, one of the plants concerned, into a crop rotation was obviously a great advantage.

It was a natural step to add dressings of chemicals containing the required elements in a form usable by plants, and so began the use of 'artificials'. It came gradually to be realized – indeed the story is not yet complete – that plants require very minute quantities of many metallic elements for their proper growth, but that the same elements, even in slight excess, can be definitely poisonous. Copper, lead, zinc, cobalt, magnesium, molybdenum, are all examples of such needed trace elements. An 'artificial' much used was (and is) sodium nitrate from the deserts of northern Chile, and a very valuable source of the required phosphorus, in a form available to plants, was, and again still is, guano – the droppings of birds and bats on dry lands, such as certain tropical islands or in caves. In a way the addition to the soil of such substances was accepted as at least 'semi-natural'. There followed the manufacture of ammonium sulphate as a by-product in the extraction of oil from oil shale, and the door was opened to the production on an ever increasing scale of 'artificials' of varied types.

Three questions now arise. First: in adding these substances to the soil to provide crop plants with required nutrients, what is the effect on the organisms of the soil itself? It may be argued that if they are killed it does not matter; their work has been superseded. Second, is there any effect on the crop-plants themselves in such a way that value as human food is affected? At any rate a minority contend strongly that flavour is changed and that the actual value as food is lowered. It is difficult to either prove or disprove the argument. Third, is the actual physical character of the soil altered? It is certainly true that we now know of certain 'soil-conditioners' which can do this, and in the future we may be able to break down a heavy clay into a friable soil, but at present costs are too high to do this on a large scale. But certainly much cultivation can now be carried out by the system known as hydroponics: the 'soil' can be of entirely inert mineral particles, since its function is simply to hold the roots of the plant and to allow water to circulate. Whatever nutrients the plant concerned may require are simply added in soluble form to the circulating waters. The system is extensively used for the production of tomatoes under glass, since the soils in which tomatoes are grown for a succession of seasons are liable to get 'tomato sick' and build up either organisms or chemical substances inimical to the growth of the plant. Now, therefore, the soil is sterilized and just essential nutrients added. But do the tomatoes taste the same and do they have the same food value?

Whilst we may not yet be thinking that nature conservation involves the conservation of the microbiota of the soil, it would seem clear that in reality this is involved.

Another development of chemicalization in farming is in the treatment of seeds. It is common practice now to treat seeds with chemicals which make them unpalatable or poisonous to animals such as mice, or to birds, whilst germination is not affected. The home gardener knows only too well how a few field mice can go through a row of peas just planted and eat every one. It is but a step from this to the general use of an ever widening range of chemicals as pesticides. The main trouble is that the researches of the chemist have been so fruitful that a succession of fungicides, insecticides and herbicides has been put on the market before the after-effects or the side-effects have been fully investigated. The rapidity of development in this field of organo-chemistry has been paralleled by that in curative drugs for human use. The success of penicillin, insulin and the sulphonamides led to a confidence which was rudely shattered by the tragic, but salutary, story of thal-idomide. Not till some hundreds of deformed babies had been born were the 'side-effects' realized. It would be quite wrong to suggest that the firms producing pesticides for the farmer are either oblivious or insensitive to the problem and the dangers. On the one hand countless millions of mankind – perhaps half of all the 3,400,000,000 human beings in the world today – are victims of malnutrition and insufficient food, and to save the 10 to 20 per cent of food crops at present lost through pests and diseases would mean life itself to the unfortunate half: similarly, with nations whose people may have enough to eat, this saving means all the difference between economic and uneconomic production of food. The industrial chemists have the weapons: we must number the giants such as I.C.I., Shell Petrochemicals, Monsanto, Fisons, as saviours of mankind. On the other hand they may all unwittingly be admin-istering slow poisons to all nature, mankind included.

Some poisons pass through the body and in due course are eliminated. Much more dangerous are those which are retained and build up in certain parts of the body till their cumulative effect may be fatal or, perhaps worse, paralytic. There is definite evidence that some of the sprays widely used in farming today get into the water of the soil and so into streams, there to build up in the head and tail of fish, such as salmon, till death results or, perhaps earlier, enters the system of human victims. In other cases, the poison gets into the milk of cows or the eggs of chickens, and again man is in danger. Certainly there is evidence of sterility induced in rats and mice eating grain or treated seeds, evidence of sterility in predators that eat the rats and the mice. The complex food-chains in Nature are not as well known as they should be: the whole situation is fraught with danger. The Royal Society for the Protection of Birds early drew attention to the problem. Public awareness owes much to the vigorous writing of the late Rachel Carson in her book already mentioned, *Silent Spring*: it had perhaps to be sensationally pre-sented and the picture overdrawn to have the required impact. The present state of knowledge – inevitably rendered in part out of date between writing and publication – is reviewed in Dr. Kenneth

Mellanby's recent book in the New Naturalist series, *Pesticides and Pollution*.

Already a number of pesticides have been withdrawn from the market, and farmers are alerted to the dangers of the substances in their hands, but two major troubles remain.

One is the ever-present danger of human carelessness – the temptation to spray when wind is present to carry the poison where it is not needed and may do much harm, or the illogical but highly prevalent reasoning of the amateur, especially the amateur gardener, who doubles or quadruples the dose on the ground that it will thereby do twice or four times as much good. Many simply do not realize the consequences of thoughtless action, as with the killing of 3,000-4,000 game fish in the Hampshire Avon when some R.A.F. personnel poured unwanted paint stripper into the river in 1965.

The second is the quite senseless wholesale spraying of hedgerows and wayside verges, especially by local authorities, and notably by their highway engineers, with herbicides. Even some of the major County Councils are, or have been, chief offenders – and here is a case for local vigilance and for county councillors to realize their responsibilities.

In these misuses of pesticides and weedkillers it is not as a rule the farmer who is mainly responsible. His sprays cost money and he must count his costs. It is the amateur, to whom the few odd shillings in the garden make little difference, and the local authorities spending the taxpayers' money rather than their own.

This is not the end of chemicalization on the farm, but it is the aspect of most importance in the side-effects on wild life. The old farm labourer no longer exists: of necessity he must be a skilled mechanic and know how to keep his tractors in trim. The old-type cowman or shepherd no longer exists: in a white coat with a hypodermic syringe in the pocket, each is a step towards being a vet. A piped water supply, clean food and other hygienic regulations have brought tiled surroundings to the dairy and a new air of cleanliness.

A third line of development in modern farming may be called applied genetics. Intensive plant-breeding has exploited the advantages of hybrid vigour; intensive animal-breeding has brought with it factory farming with barley-fed de-horned cattle and calves in stalls, and battery houses for hens. A modern well-run farm is no longer one where the farmer's animals share their daily rations with either a surreptitious rat or a bold crow. If there is a barn for the barn owl, some of his food has gone. No longer is the farmstead a natural nature reserve. Perhaps, above all, though not the fault of the farmer, the rabbit has gone – or nearly so.

CHAPTER 10

FORESTRY AND WILD LIFE

Two thousand years ago when the Roman invasion of Britain was beginning, but the large-scale settlement of Anglo-Saxon farmers was yet far in the future, we may regard the country as covered still largely by the natural vegetation which had established itself after the retreat of the ice sheets of the Great Ice Age. The climate then was not very different from what it is now.

Undoubtedly the climatic climax vegetation at that time was deciduous woodland with oaks predominating. The oak woodland probably merged into localized beechwood and ashwood on calcareous soils, into alder woodland in wet situations and into coniferous forest of Scots pine on light sandy soils of the lowlands or under the more rigorous conditions in the highlands and the north.

In the lowlands, ill-drained hollows, many with remnant glacial lakes on boulder clay, were occupied by fen, marsh and bog – the latter dominated by *sphagnum*. It is possible that woodland growth was sparser and more easily cleared on the ridges and downlands of the chalk and Jurassic limestones, accounting thus for the traces of settlement and cultivation in small square fields and for the existence there of ancient trackways.

The military urban-minded Romans drove their long straight roads to connect their well-sited strongholds with a relentless disregard of natural features and natural vegetation. The result was an open network of straight main roads: a national plan never since equalled.

The Angles and the Saxons, to a lesser extent the Danes, came as settlers looking for good land. They travelled up the rivers and chose good sites for towns and villages, either beside a stream or where a constant spring guaranteed a water supply. With uncanny precision they found the good loamy soils, cleared the woodland and used the timber for their buildings.

As the centuries passed the woodland cover steadily disappeared. The timber was needed for building, for construction of ships, and for conversion to charcoal to be used as fuel and in the smelting of iron. Four hundred years ago the depletion of our last reserves of timber caused alarm and some of the remaining woodlands were prized because of the angle oak timber needed for the ships of the Royal Navy.

The pine forests where such existed were likewise depleted; the famed Caledonian Forest came to exist only in memory and in the remnants of Rothiemurchus.

Voices like those of John Evelyn (*Sylva: or a Discourse of Forest Trees*, 1664) calling for reforestation and conservation were voices crying in the wilderness. Though a century and a half earlier, in Elizabethan times, official pronouncements had referred to the forests of Britain as 'utterly destroyed', there was little renewal of interest till late in the eighteenth century. The foundation of the Highland Society in 1783 encouraged the planting of trees by Scottish landlords; about the same time amenity planting, especially of imported species in parklands or in clumps, became fashionable. Many of the beech clumps, so much appreciated on the downlands of today, date from this period. The Napoleonic Wars produced some panic planting of oak woodland, many of oaks in open formation to produce thick-boled, low-branched trees which would provide the timber so much needed for the repair of His Majesty's ships of war. But the Royal Navy had turned to iron ships long before the oaks were mature.

Therein lies one of the great problems of forestry. It is essentially long-term. While some 'thinnings' may be useful within fifteen or twenty years of planting, mature trees to provide lumber timber are likely to be sixty or eighty years old in the case of certain conifers, 120 years for oaks. Very quick-growing trees usually produce timber which is almost worthless except for firewood, now almost unmarketable, and although all trees pass through normal growth stages of youth, maturity and old age, many timber trees are in their prime after 150 years or more and may remain sound and healthy for a very much longer time – oaks to 500 years certainly, whilst many of the redwoods of California, as almost the oldest living things on earth, are flourishing after 4,000 years.

The time factor has many consequences. Selection can be made from an annual crop – for example a cereal variety – after a year's trial, and in recent years world-wide increases in crop yields have resulted from trial and error methods extending over a few years. Not so with trees; the trial and error method involves centuries, or at least a half century, before the results of a 'trial' can be demonstrated. Although there has been management of farm woodland in Britain – especially the coppicing of oak-ash-birch-hazel woodland to provide fencing posts in south-eastern England for centuries – the practice of scientific forestry is quite modern. Many countries of continental Europe were, however, concerned with the proper use of what was rightly recognized as a major resource; and British administrators, especially in India and Burma, realized their responsibilities there and in the Colonies. It was a German forester, William Schlich, who did more than any one man to put forestry on a firm scientific basis in India, where he became Chief Conservator. Schlich's great work, the five-volume *Manual of Forestry*, was published between 1889 and 1910 and is still a valued work of reference. Sir William Schlich can be looked upon as the father of British scientific forestry, more especially as Australian-born Roy Robinson, later Lord Robinson, first Chairman of the British Forestry Commission, was one of his pupils.

The Forestry Commission was established in 1919 as a direct consequence of experience during the First World War. Imports of essnetial timber had proved a very heavy strain on available shipping, and the intensified submarine warfare of 1918 had accentuated the problem. The plan was therefore to render Britain self-supporting in timber for any future 'emergency' of three years' duration. In fact the emergency, the Second World War, came before the plantings of the Forestry Commission were sufficiently advanced to be of much value, but the central plan was to plant 1,777,000 acres in England, Wales and Scotland. It is unfortunately typical of the wavering British attitude towards forestry and failure to appreciate its long-term character that Parliament subjected the

Commission to all the injustices of getting cuts in its budget and years of stop-go directives. The Second World War produced a more balanced view and an expansion of its programme to the planting of 3,000,000 acres and re-planting of a further 2,000,000, together with plans for co-operation with owners of woodland and commercial interests.

The uncertain attitude of Parliament to the Forestry Commission is in line with the utterly inconsistent attitude of the British public in general and, unfortunately, of many of the amenity societies. It is, indeed, one of the weaknesses of the CPRE (Council for the Preservation of Rural England) that the Council has never faced squarely the necessity of formulating a policy towards tree-planting and forestry. The Council might retaliate that it was in favour of the maintenance of native British deciduous woodland of oak, ash and hazel, but in general against large-scale planting of introduced softwoods. There is, however, failure to realize that trees have a life cycle and that trees in forests and woodlands are as much a commercial crop as the annual crops of arable land. Under existing Town Planning legislation there is a provision for 'Tree Preservation Orders'. The object was clearly to prevent the wanton or unnecessary felling of groups of trees or individual trees which had an amenity value, and the orders are so used by planning authorities. On the one hand, however, there has been a tendency to extend the preservation orders to woodlands and thus to prevent economic management. On the other hand, penalties for ignoring an order are too small to deter any large-scale developer from cutting down choice specimens. Whereas in many countries developers, whether urban authorities or individual owners or builders, will plan an estate or site a house so as to keep good specimen trees, the British tendency is to clear the whole site, leaving new householders with a bare patch to develop as a garden. Too often, alas, a Tree Preservation Order will be put on a few large specimens already over-mature and likely to become rotten and unsafe in the near future, especially when the land all around is drained or the water balance changed. At other times an urban authority goes to the length of employing a 'tree-surgeon' on contract. The surgery may be successful, but too often the patient dies.

Undoubtedly the first task of the Forestry Commission was the apparently straightforward one of economic afforestation. It was not answerable to Parliament through any specific minister. If Parliament found it easy to curb its financial resources, it found it difficult to exercise any control over its policy. By comparison with the continuing need of softwoods, the demand for home-grown hardwoods is limited in both scope and quantity. Consequently the bulk of the planting has been of alien conifers – Sitka spruce from western North America, Norway spruce, Japanese larch, Douglas fir and continental strains of Scots pine. The Commission was permitted to buy land, provided it was under a certain figure; consequently it acquired much hill land previously used for hill sheep, often finding a large proportion was unplantable and had just to be abandoned. It is now admitted that not a little of the early work of the Forestry Commission was in fact what would now be called bad forestry. The blanketing of hillsides with vast single-species plantations in square blocks, irrespective of contours, produced an appearance alien to the countryside and which aroused strong opposition. It was not good forestry: forests need to be built up in such a way that they are allowed to creep up the sheltered valleys and avoid exposed spurs – in other words to be adjusted to the contours. The great continental forests, for example of Scandinavia, have frequently two or three co-dominants, such as Norway spruce (*Picea abies*) which flourishes in the damper situations and Scots pine (*Pinus sylvestris*) which reaches its best proportions on drier land. A few deciduous trees, such as birch and poplar, but especially the aspen (*Populus tremula*) add variety and life and colour at different seasons. These natural and successful forests of Europe should have served as a model to our planters in Britain, which indeed they are now doing.

But the antagonism which the Forestry Commission built up in its early days dies hard, and many find it difficult to credit that the Commission is now a powerful force in many directions working for the good of the community. It is worth-while to record some of the results of the Commission's activities.

First, it has converted a very large acreage of land which, whilst once wooded, had become moorland and grassland of low economic value, into productive forest. Some salient figures are that a total of 2,736,188 acres under forest and woodland in Great Britain in 1913-14 had increased to 4,205,000 by 1962. This is still only 7.5 per cent of the surface of the country or 0.08 acres per head – still the lowest in Europe. To the end of 1962 the Forestry Commission had planted 3,000,000,000 trees over 1,400,000 acres, comprising (in area) Sitka spruce 30 per cent, Scots pine 18, Norway spruce 12, Japanese larch 9, Lodgepole pine 6, Corsican pine 5, Douglas fir 4, European larch 3, other conifers 3, oak 4, beech 4, other hardwoods 2.

Second, it has recognized that many people are attracted by the beauties of forest land and, as soon as seedlings are safe from accidental damage by trampling, picnic fires and so on, the Commission has opened its forests to public access and created National Forest Parks. Attractive guides have been published to Argyll, Snowdonia, Forest of Dean, Glen More (Cairngorms), Glen Trool (Galloway), Hardknott (Lake District), Queen Elizabeth (Ben Lomond and trossachs) and (largest of all) the Border National Forest Park (Dumfries, Roxburgh, Cumberland and Northumberland). There are also booklets on most of the main forest areas and an indication of the Commission's attitude to public enjoyment of its forests is that the little guide, *Camping in the National Forest Parks*, is free.

In the third place, the Forestry Commission has come more and more to act in the role of technical adviser in matters relating to forestry – to local authorities, statutory bodies, landowners, individuals. The economic value of a forest may be as much indirect, as when it attracts tourists and their money to an area, as direct, so that the Forestry Commission has come more and more to regard what used to be called amenity considerations, including amenity planting of non-economic species, as coming legitimately into its sphere of normal activities. The desire of the Commission to enter into the life of the nation is indicated by the existence of such a body as the Joint Committee of the Forestry Commission and the CPRE and by the appointment of a Landscape Planning Consultant, as well as by the close co-operation with the Nature Conservancy. The Nature Conservancy has special arrangements, for example, in the

5 *Extent of Forestry Commission areas in England, Scotland and Wales*

New Forest where Bramshaw, Mark Ash and Matley-Denny are held as Forest Nature Reserves by agreement with the Forestry Commission. The Nature Conservancy also has ten other Forest Nature Reserves, and many of the National Nature Reserves are primarily forest. The growing importance of recreation, and the provision of recreational areas in forest land, has been recognized by the official forestry organizations in many countries. In our small crowded neighbour the Netherlands, for example, the forestry authority is as much concerned with the provision and maintenance of forest parks and nature reserves as it is with commercial forestry as such. In many countries, too, the provision of shelter belts for crops and stock, the stabilization of dunes liable to wind erosion, and elsewhere the improvement of drainage in poor land, are regarded as essential functions of the forester.

But what of the direct effect of forests and afforestation on wild life? In his book in this series, *Trees, Woods and Man*, H. L. Edlin reminds us that the forester creates over large areas habitat conditions which are rare in nature. In countries clothed with natural forest the competition between plant species is largely one for light. Shade-loving herbs alone can survive on the woodland floor; only when some giant tree dies does light penetrate which enables a sudden upsurge of some light-loving species. In contrast, many forests are worked by clear-felling, so that, quite suddenly, conditions are created whereby such light-loving species as rose bay (*Chamaenerion angustifolium*), ragwort (*Senecio jacobaea*) and fox-glove (*Digitalis purpurea*) and other biennials, can come in. The invasion is intense but short-lived, and the wise forester gets his planting done while this phase persists for the plants do not smother seed-lings. Later invaders such as brambles (*Rubus*), briars (*Rosa*) and bracken (*Pteridium*) are tougher and more persistent. When they are cleared, as they must be, the shade-loving bluebells, dog's mercury, wood anemone, become dominant on the forest floor. The man-agement of so much woodland in south-eastern England as coppice or coppice with standards – the species to be coppiced cut a foot or so from the ground after twelve to fifteen years and then the stumps allowed to send up half a dozen shoots each, to be cut again after a similar period – allowed a regular rotation of habitat

14 Barnacle Geese near Caerlaverock National Nature Reserve

15 Conservation in the back garden. *Above*: a feeding table with Blue, Great, and Long-tailed tits. *Below*: Mistle thrush, Pinner, Middlesex

conditions particularly favourable to a wealth of wild flowers and insects.

Mr. Edlin, in the book quoted, considers the effect of the physical and biotic environment on forest growth, picking out four factors of the latter as specially important – fungi, insects, birds and mammals. In damp autumn days 'fungus forays' in woodland areas reveal these to be the home of a large proportion of our larger species (see J. Ramsbottom, *Mushrooms and Toadstools*, in this series), but the forester is concerned with pathogenic fungal diseases. Treatment with sprays in the forest nursery is the usual control: it is scientifically possible, even simple, to spray a fully grown tree, but economically out of the question. Many fungus pests – for example the dreaded elm disease – are unwelcome invaders, and the more dangerous if the forester has planted a single species so that the disease may wipe out acres of a pure stand. Mixed planting is recognized as some protection.

Edlin divides the insects into those which may assume epidemic proportions and do considerable damage from time to time, and those which, though numerous, cause little harm. On the whole the danger of serious damage is slight.

Birds prey on good and bad insects alike and predators prey on some of the smaller birds. Something of a balance is maintained except when the gamekeeper steps in to war against the hawks and owls which may do a valuable work in controlling rodents.

Mammals may present a serious problem to the forester. Again Edlin finds the gamekeeper, at least in the past, may have upset the balance of nature by blacklisting the fox, badger, stoat, weasel, polecat and others which preyed on the destructive voles and rabbits. Man has to take on the task of ratcatcher himself, which is expensive. When deer become a nuisance they can be controlled by shooting, as can the grey squirrel, but with more difficulty. The worst enemy of the forester was undoubtedly the rabbit.

Edlin does not deal with the other side of the picture, the effect of modern forestry on wild life, except by inference. One may hazard the suggestion that systematic forestry favours wild life conservation. The habitat is varied with the successive operations, so that while some groups may suffer temporary eclipse, others have

a chance. A mature oakwood offers a single monotonous environment to both plant and animal life: it is relatively dull. The introduction of other forest trees, including a range of conifers, undoubtedly creates a range of environments and in consequence
more varied wild life. It would be hard for a naturalist to range
himself wholeheartedly against afforestation, or against the variety
of species now used by the Forestry Commission. There is in fact
a body of evidence that a given species of bird will become associated with a particular species of tree. Rennie Bere, who organized
the Murchison Falls and Queen Elizabeth National Parks in
Uganda, informed me that this is definitely the case in Africa.
Certain birds will nest only in *Borassus* palms: cut down the palms
and the birds depart though many other trees are available. It
follows that where a deciduous oak woodland in Britain is replaced
by a partial mixture of conifers, there is likely to be an increase in
bird species. This is said to have been substantiated in the Forest
of Dean.

In June 1965 Mr. G. B. Ryle, Deputy Director General of the
Forestry Commission, prepared a State Forest Memorandum (circulated to all responsible officers) defining the Forestry Commission's general policy regarding wild life (mammals and birds). The
Commission, it says, has a primary duty to prevent damage to
forest crops and to prevent damage to neighbours' property through
animals, including birds, whose habitat may be the forests. Indiscriminate destruction of most species which cause damage is both
wasteful and ineffective. Moreover the Forestry Commission recognizes its responsibility for conservation and enlightened wild life
management, since State Forests are more and more becoming
natural wild life reservoirs and there should be active encouragement of beneficial and harmless species, and its duty to protect such
rare species as pine marten and polecat, whether or not they have
legal protection. The term 'vermin' is both imprecise and inappropriate, but it is reasonable to use 'pests' for those species directly
harmful to tree or farm crops, and 'predators' for those which feed on
others. Rats, crows, foxes (in non-hunting country) and mink are
listed as 'at all times harmful to agricultural neighbours' and there
exists a bonus for the killing of foxes. Pests to be rigorously con-

trolled as harmful in the forests themselves include the rabbit, grey squirrel, rats, coypu and locally, hare, voles, mice, edible dormouse, pigeon, starling, carrion and hooded crow, and, on nursery seed beds, some finches. The Forestry Commission, when letting shooting rights, is concerned with the general maintenance of its wild life policy. It is categorically against the capture of any animals or birds or the collection of eggs for the purpose of introducing the species elsewhere. Beneficial animals in the forest, which are listed, include badger, otter, stoat, weasel, wild cat, and 'feral domestic cat'. Though the forest is an ideal habitat for deer of all species, when uncontrolled they multiply rapidly and can do great damage to trees and farm crops. The sporting value of deer-stalking in woodlands can be important and is increasing. The great majority of birds are either beneficial in forests or do no harm, and there is every reason to encourage wildfowl by improving or creating habitats, insectivorous birds by provision of nesting boxes and belts of natural vegetation especially along watercourses. The new coniferous forests 'represent a vacant niche as far as birds are concerned and there is every advantage in encouraging birds to breed in them.'

CHAPTER 11

WETLANDS AND WILDFOWL

To a considerable extent nature conservation is a national matter, but some aspects of nature conservation are *ipso facto* international. In no sphere is this more obvious than with migratory birds, moving regularly with the seasons, between the cold lands of the north for breeding and summer pasturage and the warm lands of the south for winter use.

In particular many of the migratory birds are what may be called wetland species: those whose habitat is fresh or salt water and associated marshland, those whose adaptations, such as webbed feet, are for life associated with water. They need wetland conditions at either end of their migratory journeys and a chain of wetland refuges between. In the most part they have regular migration routes and resting stations as clearly mapped out as the ocean lanes used by human beings with their shipping. When the draining of the Zuider Zee was undertaken by the Dutch it was soon realized that migratory birds were becoming confused by the disappearance of familiar landmarks and ports of call, and provision was made for new refuges not too distant from old ones.

Britain is not only on regular migration routes but also has a summer climate attractive to a wide range of visitors for breeding and spending the summer. Two words have come into general use which very conveniently cover the general situation: one is 'wetlands' to cover the varied habitats demanded for residence or temporary stay; the other is 'wildfowl' which is applied specifically to the great world-wide family of Anatidae comprising the 146 species of ducks, geese and swans.

The need for providing special reserves, in this case well described as 'wildfowl refuges', assumed practical shape in October 1955 when the Humber Wildfowl Refuge was set up – the first in Britain. Since then the interest in wildfowl refuges has grown at a phenomenal rate. Those who appear on television or talk on sound radio on wildfowl and their refuges – such as Peter Scott and James Fisher – have become some of the best known figures in our national life, and millions listen in to hear news of latest arrivals at Slimbridge, now the most famous of all the wildfowl refuges.

With the help of Peter Scott, James Fisher, and half a dozen distinguished artists, the Shell Company devoted its 1966 Calendar to the bird life of Britain, with special emphasis on the wetlands and their users. This is surely an indication of the wide interest in birds in general and wildfowl in particular. But the serious will turn to the magnificent monograph, *Wildfowl in Britain*, described as a 'survey of the winter distribution of the Anatidae and their conservation in England, Scotland and Wales' (Monographs of the Nature Conservancy no. 3, London, H.M.S.O. 1963), prepared by the Wildfowl Trust, edited by G. L. Atkinson-Willes and illustrated by Peter Scott.

In 1947 wildfowl counts were pioneered by the Wildfowl Inquiry Committee of the British Section, International Council for Bird Preservation. In 1939 and 1941 the Committee had already published two volumes on the factors influencing the status and distribution of wild geese and wild duck in Britain. The year 1954 marked a turning point in wildfowl conservation in Britain. The Protection of Birds Act became law; the Wildfowlers' Association of Great Britain and Ireland, its authority recognized, showed its readiness to take part in constructive conservation; whilst the Wildfowl Trust, founded and directed by Peter Scott, grant-aided by the Nature Conservancy, became the acknowledged centre for research on wildfowl. The Nature Conservancy had already set up a Wildfowl Conservation Committee 'to consider all matters directly affecting wildfowl and wildfowling, in particular the establishment of a National System of Wildfowl Refuges, and to advise the Nature Conservancy accordingly.'

The investigations which followed are remarkable for the cordial co-operation between the interested bodies, national and local. Ringing of ducks was undertaken at four main stations: Orielton Decoy, Pembrokeshire, from 1945; Berkeley New Decoy, Slimbridge, Gloucestershire, from 1946; Abberton Reservoir, Essex, from 1949; and Borough Fen Decoy, Peakirk, Soke of Peterborough, from 1949. Swans and geese have also been ringed. The head-quarters of the Wildfowl Trust at Slimbridge have become one of the most famous stations in the world. Here, on the estuary of the Severn, the wildfowl are concentrated in a three-mile stretch along the eastern bank. The tideway is a mile wide, mud-flats reach almost to the far shore; a strip of high salt-marsh extends inland for several hundred yards and beyond lie 1,000 acres of enclosed pasture. The whole for centuries was carefully preserved by the Berkeley estate, with only an occasional shoot, and became a natural refuge, especially the foreshore. To the north on the Frampton estate the mud-flats are similarly undisturbed, and a further sanctuary has been established in old gravel pits, now an orna-mental lake some eighty acres in extent. White-fronted geese (*Anser albifrons albifrons*) have wintered here for at least a century, and the regular flocks, numbering between 3,000 and 5,000 (the maxi-mum supportable on the pasture available is about 3,500), are half those in Britain. As James Fisher has said, there is nothing like Slimbridge anywhere else in the world. The Wildfowl Trust regularly shows here 120 or more of the world's 146 species of Anatidae, including the (lately, but fortunately not presently) near extinct ne-ne or Hawaiian goose. The 'exotics' are mostly in con-ditions of only semi-captivity in the beautiful waterfowl gardens.

The National Nature Reserve of the Nature Conservancy at Caerlaverock in Dumfriesshire was declared on 4th April 1957. It covers 13,514 acres, of which about 1,500 consist of the typical salt-marsh or saltings, known as merse, the haunt of wintering geese – flocks of pinkfeet from Iceland; barnacle geese from Spitsbergen; grey lags from Iceland and from Scotland itself. The barnacle geese (*Branta leucopsis*) may number 2,000 at winter's peak – probably the largest herd in the world. Also commonly seen are whooper swans from Iceland, and merlins – the bold little falcon from the Scottish moors – and sometimes the rare peregrine falcon which may winter here. The remainder of the Reserve, some 12,000 acres, is foreshore – sand flats covered daily by the tide and known as Blackshaw Bank.

The Reserve was established by agreement with the Duke of

Norfolk for the merse and the Crown Estate Commission for the foreshore. But the area had long been used by local and national wildfowling associations and the Nature Conservancy agreed that shooting should continue under a carefully controlled permit system. The central merse (470 acres) is shot over by wildfowlers, the shooting area being surrounded by a no-shooting zone including the whole foreshore, and the eastern merse is a wildfowl refuge (581 acres), to which access is entirely prohibited except by permit. Bird watchers have excellent viewpoints from lay-bys provided along the seven miles of B 725 from the mouth of the Nith to the mouth of Lochar Water. From these viewpoints the greatest of all Solway landmarks, the granite mass of Criffell, appears snow-sprinkled in winter.

The issue of shooting permits is controlled by a panel of three – representing the Conservancy, the owner, and wildfowling interests. In a typical year it was found that wildfowlers came from no less than forty-five counties in England, Wales and Scotland, and are a mainstay of local hotels. The birds chiefly shot are wigeon, pink-footed goose, grey lag goose, mallard, teal, pintail and legitimate waders, to a total number averaging 500 a year. Barnacle geese and certain other species are protected. The Resident Chief Warden, or one of his wardens, is always present at the morning and evening flights and often much of the midday period as well. This example of Caerlaverock is quoted in detail as a successful compromise between nature conservation and sport.

The success of Caerlaverock has certainly encouraged the Nature Conservancy to continue collaboration with the wildfowlers. A most important development took place in February 1966 when the Lindisfarne National Nature Reserve on the coast of Northumberland, established in September 1964, was extended by the addition of 5,703 acres to cover a total of 7,368 acres, or over eleven square miles. Nearly all the reserve is foreshore over which access is unrestricted, though reached by certain definite rights of way. Lindisfarne is the main refuge for migrating and wintering wildfowl in north-east England, but the traditional sport of wildfowling has long been practised. Now shooting is by permit over much of Holy Island Sands and Fenham Flats; the rest of the Reserve is a

Sanctuary area.   A leading wildfowler is chairman of a panel advising on the conservation of wildfowl; the Professor of Botany at Newcastle is Chairman of a parallel committee advising on other management matters.

Not all the wetland sites of Britain are part of this network. The bird sanctuary in St. James's Park, in the heart of London, has existed since 1536 when Henry VIII issued an order preserving partridges, pheasants and herons from the Palace of Westminster and Highgate. The exotic waterfowl date from the Restoration of Charles II to the Monarchy in 1660. Upwards of forty-five species can be seen even in mid-winter; mallard, tufted duck, and pochard breed regularly, and so may mute swan, moorhen and coot.

There is evidence to suggest that the network of wildfowl refuges has been created just in time. Wetlands are particularly vulnerable to changes which are taking place at the present time. Britain is divided between River Boards which have very wide powers. They are concerned especially to drain wet areas for conversion to agricultural land, to control rivers and prevent flooding. At the same time many coastal salt-marshes are regarded as ripe for reclamation; the large scale of machines now available makes the work economic. Gigantic schemes are afoot to throw great dykes across Solway Firth, Morecambe Bay, the Dee Estuary, the Wash, with the idea of forming huge storage reservoirs for freshwater on which sailing and boating may be encouraged, but not necessarily wild life. There may be a new pattern of inland reservoirs, but many of the valued types of habitat may disappear, unless the plans are thoughtful.

A good example of the type of clash which can occur is afforded by the little river Amble which enters the north side of the Camel estuary between Wadebridge and Padstow, Cornwall. Part of the marshy floor of the valley had been secured by local naturalists as a bird sanctuary. But the Cornwall River Authority had got to work with a dam and drainage works before the Nature Conservancy was aware of what was happening. Too late: the best that could be obtained was a promise that projected drainage works would be notified on future occasions.

CHAPTER 12

BOTANICAL GARDENS AND ZOOS

Many may read the title of this chapter with surprise and wonder what botanical gardens and zoological gardens can have to do with the conservation of nature in the wild. Not a few may say that the wholly artificial maintenance of exotic trees, shrubs and flowering plants in gardens is the very antithesis of their concept of nature conservation, others that their wish to conserve wild life is coupled with a fervent desire to abolish zoos, and to work for the day when no wild animal shall ever be seen behind bars.

In fact the issue is not so simple. Some plants need protection if they are to survive, many animals and birds certainly do. There are times when a carefully managed nature reserve may not be very different from the wilder area of a botanic garden; already several of our wildfowl refuges are largely of the nature of zoos. What is the lake in London's St. James's Park, with its forty or fifty species of wild fowl and birds – a nature reserve or a zoo?

It is indeed surprising how rare plants can be induced to thrive and spread with a little encouragement. It is quite staggering how soon animals and birds get to know the refuges where they are free from persecution and adapt their habits accordingly. It is said that African elephants and lions, happily strolling outside the bounds of their reserves, will, on hearing an approaching car, make a dash to get inside the boundary. If they are then shot, at least the onus will be on the shooter.

Let us face the first issue fairly and squarely. A large number of animals and plants now have little or no hope of survival in the wild. It is an inevitable part of the whole process of evolution that extinction overtakes those which have failed to adapt themselves to changing environments and circumstances. Also many of the niches, which would have offered chances of survival for at least a long time ahead, have been destroyed, albeit unwittingly, by man. A good

example of this is afforded by the ecosystems of oceanic islands. By
definition an oceanic island is one far removed from continental land
where such animals and plants as succeeded in reaching it have
evolved in isolation and in response to local conditions. Excellent
examples are afforded by the scattered island groups of the Pacific
and Indian Oceans, and one thinks of the Galapagos, Mauritius or
Hawaii. Recognizing the uselessness of flight, the great birds of
Mauritius became flightless with the inevitable consequence – when
the island fastness was invaded by man and conditions changed,
there was no escape and so the dodo was extinguished: indeed became so dead as to leave its main trace in the popular phrase 'as dead
as the dodo'. In Hawaii the birds nearly all became ground nesting
for, despite limited cover on the lava-covered islands, there were no
native rodents to steal eggs. With the changed circumstances of the
arrival of human beings, the only hope of suvival for some is in zoos.
It is the custom of every state of the U.S.A. to select a state wild
flower and a state animal or bird. Hawaii chose the distinctive ne-ne,
or Hawaiian goose, but alas it is now only beginning to recover from
near extinction. Half of all the Hawaiian geese in the world are at
Slimbridge Wildfowl Refuge in what may be called an open zoo. It
is not necessary to labour the point: the American bison, once the
proud possessor of the vast American prairies, survives only in such
open zoos as parts of Canada's Rocky Mountain National Parks, just
as the European bison survives in the closely protected forest park of
Bialowieza in Poland. Père David's deer of China has been demon-
strably saved from extinction in the Zoo park of the Dukes of Bedford at Woburn.

Two of the most misused and misunderstood words in the English
language are freedom and liberty. If both have undertones suggest-
ing wide open spaces, the misuse is complete. In reality freedom is
the liberty to choose, and the choice is usually, above everything
else, security: the security basically of a home, warmth, food,
together with an increasing range of self-incarcerating gadgets such
as TV. It is pleasant to have a small part of the home snug and
secure from wind and rain, but on wheels so that the scenery can
be changed, hence the family car. More and more human beings
choose to live in zoos. The world-wide phenomenon of today is not

so much the continued staggering growth of total population, as the growth of the large city, commonly associated with rural depopulation. What must a wild animal think of the human race and its passion for little boxes: the ideal holiday a thousand little boxes: exercise six times round this deck equals one mile; three times a day the move to a bigger box for feeding; every now and then a transfer to a still smaller box on wheels for 'sightseeing'. It is probably true that most human beings, who look upon themselves as nature lovers, are guilty of three cardinal errors. One is to presume that all wild animals like being wild and fail to appreciate warmth and security; a second is to think that in their attitude to freedom all animals and birds can be grouped together; the third is to attribute to animals and birds human attributes of thought and feeling.

Human beings, though they choose to live in little boxes piled together with a million others, do not like it if the windows are barred and the doors locked. They want a zoo of their own choosing. To that extent I suggest the attitude of most mammals and birds in cages is the same. This is increasingly recognized. So the old type of zoo, with its restricted pens and cages, gives place to the Whipsnades and, by easy stages, to Slimbridge or Murchison Falls and Kruger National Park. Modern developments in farming come into the picture here. Few who have watched Dartmoor sheep or cattle in driving rain can really believe they prefer the wild to a nice dry stall and food arriving regularly by conveyor belt or otherwise. There may be aspects of cruelty to be watched in factory farming, but to paraphrase an American advertisement, 'the best milk is from contented cows'.

Undoubtedly a development of fundamental importance in nature conservation is the ever-increasing symbiotic relationship between man, plants and animals. One of the earliest volumes (now out of print) in the New Naturalist series was R. S. R. Fitter's *London's Natural History*. Published first in 1945, it is a picture of war-time London now much changed, but it does afford a fascinating example of both plant and animal life fitting into a wholly man-made environment. The glorious rose bay (*Epilobium angustifolium*) in my old *Johns* described as 'rare', gave a blaze of colour on every blitzed site: the imported exotic *Buddleia* established itself likewise almost everywhere. But above all it is the bird life of London's open-space network which really affords the object lesson: the many species which have found both liberty and security.

When travelling abroad I find no creature more endearing than the cheeky Cockney sparrow. A Londoner myself, he is always a fellow Londoner. Like, it must be unfortunately admitted, many a Britisher abroad, he is supremely conscious of his superiority to the mere natives around him, and is not always on his best behaviour. In London it is a polite acceptance of crumbs on the window-sill, in Honolulu he will perch on your breakfast table and seize a selected morsel from your very own plate. But is it my imagination, or has he learnt that it is not polite to leave visiting cards on the tablecloth?

London affords an interesting example of the way in which zoos and botanic gardens, parks and commons, stately homes and gardens, waste ground and reservoirs, all fit into a nature conservation pattern. James Fisher has pointed out that the famous ravens of the Tower of London represent the relics of the Royal Menagerie, the oldest surviving zoo in the world, having been founded in, or before, 1252. The Royal Botanic Gardens at Kew, covering 300 acres, were established in 1759 and apart from some 25,000 species and varieties of plants, have a range of waterfowl on the lakes. The gardens of the Zoological Society of London in Regent's Park – London's Zoo – cover thirty-six acres and have some 1,400 species; the gardens date from 1828, with the overflow at Whipsnade in the Chilterns established in 1927, covering 567 acres arranged in vast paddocks. Many of London's parks are in effect nature reserves – notably the Inner London Parks of Hyde Park, Regent's Park, St. James's Park, Green Park, Kensington Gardens. Outstanding also are Greenwich Park, Battersea Park, Syon House, Kenwood, Richmond Park, and Osterley Park, but there are many smaller ones. The great commons in and around London are remarkable reservoirs of native vegetation – Wimbledon, Hampstead Heath, Chislehurst and St. Paul's Cray Commons, and the numerous Surrey Commons all come to mind. Nor must one forget the important role played by London's reservoirs – Ruislip, Tring, Lea

Valley and others. Epping Forest owes its preservation in large measure to the far-sighted magnanimity of the Corporation of the City of London.

As the conurbations of Britain spread, elsewhere the same pattern is building up: the local zoo, the town park, the large town garden, the urban common all become part of the open-space network vital to wild life conservation.

Perhaps a special comment is needed on aquaria with both fresh-water and saltwater plants and animals. A major advance in presentation was marked by the opening of the Aquarium at London's Zoo, the model of so many which have followed, in that viewers in the dark chamber see aquatic life as it were on equal terms. In recent years the rapid increase in possibility and popularity of skin-diving, with aqua-lung equipment, makes it possible for the young and active to go down to the hitherto private habitats of marine life. How far is man acceptable to the existing members of the ecosystem? It is becoming clear that a new problem of conservation is now with us. The intruders are resented; the fish are leaving. We already face the need for underwater nature reserves round our coasts.

The ecological wind of change has not failed to exercise a profound influence on our museums so that, both nationally and locally, they have come to play an integral and vital part in the conservation movement. Gone are the days when museums could be dismissed as enshrining only the dead and to be shunned by lovers of the living. The British Museum (Natural History) was early in the field with animals and birds realistically mounted in very large cases showing natural habitats; the Museum of Geology seized the opportunity of its removal in the 'twenties from its old cramped quarters in Jermyn Street to its spacious new building in South Kensington to introduce its world-famous series of dioramas depicting life in the past, whilst a similar idea was adopted by Sir Harry Lindsay when he took over in 1934 the old Imperial Institute Museum (now the Commonwealth Institute) to bring home to successive thousands of youngsters a vivid portrayal of life in other lands. In the country one recalls such pioneer work as that of the Haslemere Educational Museum, and how many local museums sought to vitalize their exhibition by attractive mounting and some to arouse interest in wild life by named wild flowers in season. In recent years the links between the local museums and natural history societies and county trusts have become increasingly strong. By March 1966 thirty-two museums were members of the Council for Nature – including the National Museum of Wales.

CHAPTER 13

CONSERVATION IN THE SOUTH-WEST

For a very large number of English families the very name Cornwall conjures up visions of carefree holidays basking on the golden sands of sheltered coves backed by towering cliffs. Though the actual fact may be that the car is turned homewards before the time planned when south-westerly gales and lashing rain invade the sacred holiday month of August, still they come till one feels there ought to be warning notices on all approach roads – Sorry! Cornwall full up. Though they come, and continue to come, and even come again, many do not really enjoy a Cornish holiday. Sophisticated urban amusements, 'something to do in the evening', are often conspicuous by their absence even in the larger settlements which now rely so much for their very existence on summer visitors. Often friends departing say, 'Yes, but what *do* you do in the winter?' The answer is simple: we can then begin to live. Even if one has little direct interest in wild nature, the dominant influence in the south-western peninsula is that of the natural environment modified by man to only a limited extent.

In the south-west, properly speaking, we may include the counties of Somerset, Devon and Cornwall – not forgetting the Isles of Scilly – and those parts of west Dorset which abut on Devon. On the whole the farther west the wilder and the more natural the scenery.

Yet in the farthest west stands one of the problem areas in nature conservation. The Isles of Scilly – locals object to their being called the Scilly Isles – are the higher parts of an almost submerged granite mass: the total area of the islands above the high-water mark is only a little over six square miles and only six of the islands are inhabited. In the warmest part of the British Isles frost is rare and snow almost unknown. Though strong south-westerly winds sweep across the islands there is a relatively sheltered and protected inner stretch of shallow water, and communication between the occupied islands is rarely rendered impossible. Until recently the whole was Crown property (Duchy of Cornwall) and land could only be leased. The decision to allow some of the tenants on St. Mary's to buy their land has created a class of freeholders. The lease of the island of Tresco and of all the uninhabited islands and islets is held by the Dorrien-Smith family and has been since Augustus Smith, founder of the family, became 'Governor' of the islands in 1831. On Tresco is the family mansion with its celebrated botanic gardens around the ruins of an abbey. No motor vehicle is allowed on Tresco and visitors to the fine modern hotel built and owned by Commander Dorrien-Smith enjoy a serene quiet. The Commander is an Honorary Warden of the Nature Conservancy: theoretically no one is allowed to land on any of the uninhabited islands without his permission. In particular the relatively large island of Annet is a magnificent bird sanctuary; seals breed and bask in numbers here and on the western rocks. Several of the other islands have been inhabited or grazed in the past: Samson has cromlechs and Tean remains of a farmhouse. So far so good, but the last few years have seen great changes. Early flowers sent by the *Scillonian* to Penzance for despatch by rail to London are no longer the chief source of the islands' income: summer visitors come in numbers difficult to control and to accommodate, the *Scillonian*, much improved, is supplemented since 1964 by a BEA helicopter service (replacing the two six-seater single-engined planes previously in use). It is difficult for the local boatmen to resist the £1 note slipped them for landing just for a picnic on one of the remoter islands or rocks, but wild life is seriously threatened thereby. The presence of the lighthouse men on Round Island marked the disappearance of the puffin; many other birds are now infrequently seen. The neighbouring sea floor yields fine large sea-urchins, making good souvenirs – already they are getting scarce and a new problem arises in the need for protection of the marine fauna and flora. The need for properly constituted nature reserves with resident wardens becomes imperative.

Turning to the mainland of Cornwall, the county is of course celebrated for its magnificent coastline. There are still some 200 miles of unspoiled cliff coast, about a third of the total for England.

Much has been acquired by gift or purchase by the National Trust and Enterprise Neptune was designed to secure much of the remainder. At the same time the planning authorities – headed by the County Planning Officer, Mr. H. J. W. Heck, Past-President of the Town Planning Institute – are fully alive to the necessity of coastal preservation. To date there is no National Nature Reserve in Cornwall – nor is there a National Park – but the necessity of watching the unique serpentine area of the west Lizard peninsula is very much in mind. Its geology is unique, so are its soils and resulting vegetation, its coastal scenery is superb and much of the moorland is common land. But the well-drained plateau surfaces proved attractive to the Services. Though the wartime installations in the southern Lizard Down have been swept away – more or less – the Navy is firmly entrenched farther north.

If Cornwall has no National Park and no National Nature Reserves, 360 square miles have been declared Areas of Outstanding Natural Beauty (AONB) and the re-opening of the old Coastguards' Path right along the coast was planned as one of Britain's long-distance footpaths. The truth must, however, be admitted: it is little used over large stretches and parts can no longer be traced through lack of interest. Everywhere along the coast in summer cars will be found wherever a car can possibly go (ignoring all notices), but few of their occupants depart more than a dozen yards from their home-on-wheels.

Although formed only in 1962 the Cornwall Naturalists' Trust (CNT) has been very active and there is also the older Cornwall Bird Watching and Preservation Society (CBWPS). The former has established reserves at Luckett (Stoke Climsland), Peter's Wood at Boscastle, and Hawke's Wood at Wadebridge; the latter has a Regional Wildfowl Refuge in the Walmsley Sanctuary at Wadebridge (but seriously threatened in its value and viability by drainage works), whilst the cliff haunts of the large blue butterfly have been discussed elsewhere.

Crossing the Tamar means going from Devon to Cornwall, or vice versa, since the Tamar for most of its course forms the boundary between the two counties. Many years ago, and in advance of local enterprise, the Council of Bude-Stratton Urban District secured for themselves a good water supply by building a dam across the upper part of the Tamar Valley, the water being conducted by an open aqueduct for most of the distance. Tamar Lake so formed, of seventy-five acres, is a regional wildfowl refuge, much used in winter by gulls driven in from the stormy coast.

The whole of the Dartmoor National Park lies within the county of Devon, and Devon also has part of the Exmoor National Park in the north. Dartmoor, a huge granite mass with conspicuous tors separated by sweeps of moorland, has been in particular and still is a battleground for competing interests, and has been held by many to illustrate the weakness or inadequacy of our National Parks legislation. The complex legal position (much being common land) is explained in a chapter of the New Naturalist volume on common lands. Commoners' Rights are numerous and extensively exercised. Undoubtedly large sections of Dartmoor's margins were formerly woodland, and there is pressure for reforestation both by the Forestry Commission and private interests. A large part of the Moor has long been leased to the War Office for military training and the rent is a source of income to the Commoners – much appreciated. There is the attractive Burrator reservoir from which Plymouth draws much of its water supply; there are others, and pressure to construct more. On the northern flanks Meldon Quarry has long supplied the metal or ballast for the Southern Region of British Railways: there is local pressure to keep it open. There may be metallic minerals which would be revealed by a modern survey, perhaps economic deposits of china clay. How many of these activities are compatible with the status of Dartmoor as a National Park? The Dartmoor Preservation Association, headed by the energetic and forceful Lady Sayer, says none of them: Dartmoor should be kept as the wild inaccessible moor that it now is; even improved access for visitors wishing to enjoy the scenic beauties is undesirable. Let them walk. The Nature Conservancy has three National Nature Reserves actually within the Park; these are Yarner Wood, Dendles Wood and the Bovey Valley Woodlands. The Park also includes two of Britain's thirteen Forest Nature Reserves – the famous Wistman's Wood of tortuous oaks with many epiphytes and a rich undergrowth, and Black Tor Copse.

Dartmoor is the subject of a special volume by L. A. Harvey and D. St. Leger Gordon in the New Naturalist series.

Other important conservation areas in Devon include the Exe Estuary Wildfowl refuge and the fine stretch of coastal dunes in the north, now the Braunton Barrows NNR (1964), until recently occupied for Service use. Lundy, with its handful of permanent residents, is virtually an island nature reserve of some 1,100 acres, owned by the National Trust who acquired it in 1969. The Lundy Field Society has maintained an observatory there since 1947. It is sufficiently inaccessible to be relatively safe – despite summer crowds of day visitors, weather permitting – and is famed for its puffins, fine range of other sea-birds, key migration point, and rare plants, one at least – the Lundy cabbage – being unique. In South Devon the Slapton Ley station of the Field Studies Council has within a short distance a wide range of habitats.

In the extreme east of Devon is the remarkable stretch of coast between Seaton and Lyme Regis, where greasy clays dipping gently seawards have caused huge landslips – the Dowlands Cliffs and Landslips declared a National Nature Reserve of 793 acres as early as 1955. Geologically it is a classical example of a major landslip: the whole area is unstable so that cultivation or other economic use is almost impossible. Proximity to the sea ameliorates the climate, and a wide range of habitat conditions exist. Spontaneous ashwood has colonized one of the major chasms and here one can see vegetation developing from scratch on bare rock surfaces. Except by permit, access is limited to a main footpath – from which there are attractive glimpses of the sea.

Somerset is a county of interesting contrasts. In the north-west it includes a large part of the upland mass of Exmoor, a National Park. In the north-east is the Carboniferous Limestone mass of the Mendips, with its famous Cheddar Gorge, other dry limestone valleys such as Burrington Combe, and ashwoods in the NNR of Rodney Stoke, as well as the celebrated Cheddar Caves and Wookey Hole. Early in 1966 it was made possible for the Conservancy to acquire the magnificent wooded Ebbor Gorge close to Wookey Hole, and the two reserves are now managed together. Geologically the Quantock Hills are a detached mass of Exmoor: the poor soils derived from the Devonian sandstones have never encouraged cultivation, and so the extensive areas of common land interspersed with forest and woodland constitute an AONB (since 1957) which is in effect a large natural reserve – with a herd of red deer. Between the Quantocks and the Mendips much of Somerset is occupied by the Somerset Levels, the surface standing but a few feet above sea level, and ill-drained at that. In consequence there has in the past been extensive growth of peat in raised bogs and much cutting of peat at different times. Shapwick Heath NNR is a typical section of the Somerset Levels, 546 acres situated some four miles west of Glastonbury. The Reserve has not only some of the few remaining stretches of raised bog, 15 feet above sea level, but there is much variation in the acidity of the peat elsewhere due to cutting. At different stages islands amid the bogs afforded human refuges; so that a wealth of Neolithic, Bronze Age, Iron Age and Romano-British remains have been traced even though the refuge of King Alfred from the invading Danes, when he burnt the cakes, has not been exactly identified.

Where the Somerset Levels reach the coast there are extensive salt-marshes and mud-flats, some parts cut off by tidal creeks to form islands where wildfowl and waders can feed and roost undisturbed. By agreement with the Somerset Rivers Board the Nature Conservancy holds 6,076 acres of these flats under a Nature Reserve agreement. Though the Atomic Power Station of Hinkley Point is nearby, disturbance does not seem to have been serious.

Many different regional divisions have been proposed and used for England. For purposes of the Census 'South-west England' is standard region 7 and includes also Dorset, Wiltshire and Gloucestershire. With the exception of Dorset this is also the South-west Region of the Ministry of Housing and Local Government, whereas the Nature Conservancy puts Wiltshire in its Southern Region. Gloucester includes the major part of the Cotswolds and so is linked with the Jurassic scarps of the Midlands and South-east; most of Wiltshire is essentially part of the great chalklands, whilst Dorset includes the extension of the Hampshire Tertiary basin, so each is considered with those areas rather than the South-west where conservation is concerned.

CHAPTER 14

THE SOUTH-EAST AND SOUTH

In 1964 the Ministry of Housing and Local Government issued the first of its regional studies, the South-east, covering the large section of England south-east of a line from Lyme Bay around Lyme Regis, across to the Wash. This is essentially the area dominated by the Metropolis and, unless present trends are reversed, the 17,747,000 population at the Census of 1961 may be expected to rise by three and a half million before 1981.

So far as wild life conservation is concerned, it seems natural to include as a whole south-east England as bounded by the westward or north-westward facing scarps of the chalk. The downs of Dorset, Wiltshire and Berkshire, and the Chilterns in Oxfordshire, Buckinghamshire and Hertfordshire form a natural belt bordering the whole. Within this limit lies the whole of the Hampshire and London Basins and that fascinating area of Kent, Surrey and Sussex, the Weald. Broadly this is the area covered by the South Region of the Nature Conservancy based at Oak Cottage, Brimpton, Reading, Berkshire, and the South-east Region, based on Wye, Kent. It is the region which includes most of the country used by Londoners for recreation: it is the garden of London considered as a City Region.

Geologically it is country underlain by Cretaceous and Tertiary rocks, with superficial gravels at both high and low levels, and important stretches of coastal alluvium; but the ice-sheets of the Great Ice Age only reached its northern margins, so that the greater part is free of any covering of glacial drift. Though the highest points do not touch 1,000 feet above sea level, in detail the whole region is one of surprising diversity with a consequent range of habitat conditions.

The main central area of London and its sprawl was considered in the early New Naturalist volume, *London's Natural History* by

R. S. R. Fitter, and of which some details have been included in
Chapter 12. The regional volume by S. W. Wooldridge and F.
Goldring on *The Weald* covers most of Kent, Surrey and Sussex
with a section of eastern Hampshire. J. E. Lousley in *Wild Flowers
of Chalk and Limestone* has naturally dealt with the vegetation of
the chalk lands.   The ever-fascinating area of the New Forest,
though not covered specifically by a volume of the New Naturalist
series, has a chapter in *Common Lands* and is well known.

Starting first in the west, Fyfield Down in Wiltshire, about three
miles west-north-west of Marlborough, is a National Nature Reserve
of some 612 acres, described as one of the finest remaining stretches
of unreclaimed high chalk downland in England.   It is probable
that sands of the Tertiary Reading Beds at the extreme western end
of the London Basin originally spread over the area.   Locally these
sands were cemented by percolating waters into a very hard compact sandstone, and this is the origin of the 'Sarsen stones' scattered
about the surface of the Reserve and surrounded by pockets of
locally acid soil.   The Wiltshire Trust for Nature Conservation has
also been active in the county; it has taken over Blackmore Copse
from the SPNR and has established a nature reserve at the Iron
Age hill fort of White Sheet Hill.   Though not a reserve, Savernake
Forest, through the northern part of which runs the Bath Road
(A 4), is a fine old forest with many rare insects and plants.

Loose unconsolidated sands predominate among the Tertiary
beds of the Hampshire Basin, especially towards the west, and have
resulted in sandy soils which from the farmer's point of view are
permanently 'hungry' and so have been allowed to remain in
woodland and heath.   Bands of clay, however, may often hold up
free flow of water and result in waterlogged and potentially boggy
areas.   Not infrequently sheets of river gravel overlay the Tertiary
deposits and likewise result in coarse hungry soils.   It is the combination of these physical conditions which has resulted in the
extensive heathlands of Dorset and the large tract occupied by the
New Forest and its surrounding commons.   Conveniently sited for
the study of the fascinating Dorset heaths, the Nature Conservancy
purchased a country house known as Furzebrook near Wareham
and has built on laboratories and offices. Nearby is Hartland Moor,

637 acres, with the rare Dorset heath (*Erica ciliaris*) and a number of rare bog plants. The Moor is a National Nature Reserve (restricted access) two miles south-east of Wareham; to the north of Wareham Morden Bog is also a NNR, covering 367 acres with habitats ranging from old pinewood and dry open heath to *sphagnum* and cotton-grass bog. An interesting little Reserve of nine acres is Arne, east of Wareham, with a rare transition from salt-marsh to birch-pine-oak woodland. In 1966 the neighbouring heath of Arne Peninsula, with its rare Dartford warblers, became a 680-acre Nature Reserve of the Royal Society for the Protection of Birds. In 1962 the Nature Conservancy added Studland Heath of 429 acres (58 woodland) bordering Poole Harbour. Here the problem is one of an area already much frequented by the public and where there are tracts adjoining the Reserve of great scientific interest, but where a compromise with public use has to be worked out. Actually in Poole Harbour is the fascinating Brownsea Island, for long kept as virtually an island fortress by a private owner until it passed into the hands of the National Trust. In a fruitful collaboration the Trust and the Dorset Naturalists' Trust became interested in the establishment of the area as a nature reserve with limited public access. The first opening to the public resulted in several damaging fires. The whole of Poole Harbour is a great wildfowl and wader refuge and an interesting conservation problem has arisen over Brownsea Island. Should the importation of certain exotic birds be permitted? The Nature Conservancy took the view that, while it was not generally in favour of this, Brownsea Island permitted close control.

A large part of Dorset has been declared an AONB and there are many features of interest outside the Reserves of the Nature Conservancy and the seven controlled by the County Trust. At Abbotsbury is the unique Swannery, established before 1393, when it was known to be flourishing. The 18-mile long unbroken pebble ridge of Chesil Beach is about 170 yards wide and up to 35 feet above high water: it is the finest example of its kind in Europe and links Portland Bill – a promontory built up of the famous Portland oolitic limestone – with the mainland. Portland Bill has old quarries which afford attractive hiding-places for migrating birds, studied from the Bird Observatory and Field Centre there. On the southern coast of Purbeck, Lulworth Cove is a classical example of sea erosion where beds of alternating hardness are nearly vertical. The sea, having broken through a limestone barrier, has scooped out an almost circular cove. Also in Dorset, Weymouth Corporation has taken a hand in nature conservation by making Radipole Lake a regional wildfowl refuge of 70 acres.

The Isle of Wight is one of the few parts of south-eastern England where, owing to difficulties of access to an island, there has been an almost stationary population. Apart from the towns and Parkhurst Forest, the whole is an AONB with such classical coast features as the Needles (vertical chalk).

For details of the New Forest, reference should be made to Chapter 15 of *Common Lands*. The present control of this ancient Royal Forest is in the hands of the Forestry Commission, working happily with a modernized survival from the past, the Court of Verderers. With great skill the interests of the commoners, of the public seeking facilities for walking, picnicking and camping, and of the innumerable bird-watchers and naturalists have been carefully dovetailed. Apart from certain statutory enclosures and temporary enclosures dictated by needs of good woodland management, the public has right of access to some 45,000 acres of open heath and 5,000 of unenclosed woodland. By arrangement with the Forestry Commission, the Nature Conservancy has three Forest Nature Reserves – Mark Ash of 226 acres with oak and beech; Matley and Denny of 2,577 acres, including also bogland and many famous entomological sites; and Bramshaw of 525 acres along the northern edge of the Forest with oak-beech woodland.

In the heart of Hampshire is Old Winchester Hill, some eleven miles south-east of Winchester itself, which is a National Nature Reserve of 140 acres, including about forty acres of woodland with much well-grown yew. The rest is rough chalk grassland with juniper or hawthorn scrub. Like other counties, Hampshire and the Isle of Wight now have a strong Naturalists' Trust with twelve reserves, including Catherington Down.

The three south-eastern counties of Kent, Surrey and Sussex, together with that small section of the Weald around Selborne which overlaps into Hampshire, epitomise in miniature the present-day problems of Britain's land-use in general. The immense variety of scenery and the correspondingly wide range of habitats characteristic of Britain as a whole are there seen to perfection – from the shingle desert of Dungeness and the salt-marshes of the Swale or Chichester harbour to the dry heaths and woodlands of Surrey's commons and the immensely fertile loams of North Kent's fruit belt. Surely here, more than anywhere else, is the challenge to man to fit himself into a complex ecosystem. Is it too much to suggest that each of man's requirements of land should here be correlated with the complex environmental factors and conflicts resolved? For conflicts there certainly are, and bitter ones too. North Kent is a natural battleground between heavy industry demanding a waterside location and the maintenance of wetlands; Dungeness has been the battleground between atomic energy development and conservation, the South Downs for amenity and economic overhead distribution of electric power. There is much rich land ideal for intensive vegetable and fruit production, much poor land best for housing or open space. The close intimate nature of much of the Weald renders it attractive for the wealthy resident who may well maintain the private personal nature reserves discussed in Chapter 13. But definite conservation areas are needed. Kent, Surrey and Sussex have each active Naturalists' Trusts, there are many amenity societies, the National Trust holds many properties, numerous local authorities are looking after common land, the Nature Conservancy has some important key areas.

On the South Downs we may notice first the National Nature Reserves of the Conservancy. The chalklands of the South Downs, recommended as a National Park, have been declared an AONB. Here the Nature Conservancy has Kingley Vale near Chichester – 352 acres, including magnificent yew woods and chalk grassland contrasting with acid heathland developed on high-level clay-with-flints – and Lullington Heath of 155 acres of chalk downland perhaps uncultivated since the early Britons hoed their small square fields and where shallow-rooted calciphobes mingle side by side with deep-rooted calcicoles.

The whole of the coast of the south-east, in Sussex and Kent, is within a hundred miles of the heart of London: the south coast around Brighton within sixty. A glance at any map shows how nearly continuous settlement has become: large numbers commute between the coast towns and London daily, and there is a high proportion of retired townfolk. The pressure on the remaining coastlands has become intense and the competition between competing uses is more intense here than anywhere else in Britain. The southeastern coastline is extremely varied but all types come under this pressure. In the western end of Sussex are the large tidal inlets, notably the large Chichester harbour with its numerous branches, with tidal currents sufficiently treacherous to make the management of small craft not a little exciting. Now that the possession of a boat has become an important status symbol there is severe competition for mooring sites; what is left for wild life is of restricted extent. The nearby Pagham harbour, similar in character, is in fact a local reserve. Farther east where the chalk reaches the coast are the lovely cliffs, whose sevenfold rise and fall provided the obvious name of the Seven Sisters, with the extension to Beachy Head, which were saved in the 'thirties from spoliation through bungalow development by the National Trust supported by the local authorities (notably Eastbourne Corporation). Not so the clifflands east of Brighton where the land was parcelled out into small building sites shortly after World War I, and what was first named New Anzac-on-Sea became Peacehaven. In the neighbourhood of Eastbourne it is interesting to record the activities of Eastbourne College, which has established a number of nature reserves – at Og's Wood, Polegate; the Mere, Hampden Park; and in the Cuckmere Valley.

Immediately over the border in Kent is that remarkable promontory, built up of successive ridges of shingle, known as Dungeness. Physiographically it is unique in Britain. The huge lonely isolated expanse of shingle has its own strange plant assemblage, and it is of course a famous posting point for migratory birds – 170 species a season – an obvious choice as a National Nature Reserve. But its isolation attracted attention as a site for a nuclear power station of the Central Electricity Generating Board at a time when the public, scared by the very word nuclear, sought to relegate the new power stations to coastal sites away from settlements. After a pitched battle in 1957 which the Conservancy lost, the Royal Society for the Protection of Birds and the Bird Observatory have been maintained on the still existing SSSI with the help of a warden financed by the CEGB.

The coast between Folkestone and Dover is classic ground for the geologist: type sections of the Hythe, Sandgate and Folkestone Beds (all Lower Greensand) succeeded upwards by the Gault clay teeming with fossils. This clay is very greasy when wet and dips gently seaward so that the Warren, between Folkestone and Dover, is a vast area of tumbled chalk masses, ever sliding seawards. The railway built through the Warren has been interrupted by further slips at intervals throughout its history and the land can never be rendered stable. This did not prevent the office-minded pundits of the Beeching railway-destruction era from scheduling this as one of their major routes for future improvement. Safe from housing development, it is a natural wilderness area though not scheduled as such.

Continuing round the coast, the immortal white cliffs of Dover include Shakespeare Cliff on the west and stretch eastwards to St. Margaret's Bay. The nature reserves established on these chalk downs are inland: Wye and Crundale Downs of 250 acres, of which forty-nine are scrub and woodland, are a National Nature Reserve of the Nature Conservancy occupying part of the chalk scarp between Ashford and Canterbury. The Lady, Fly and Man orchids are found here and a wealth of notable insects.

The Kent Naturalists' Trust has been very active and among more than thirty reserves are fine examples of downland and woodland as well as some of the coastal land of Sandwich Bay. Since Roman times the former sea channels between the Isle of Thanet and the mainland and between the Isle of Sheppey and the mainland have silted up, but poor drainage in places has left some interesting freshwater marshes. One such, along the Stour near Stodmarsh, has rare plants as well as wildfowl, and was made an NNR in 1968. The estuarine marshes of both the Thames and Medway are of great interest, but heavy and noxious industries such as oil refining, petrochemicals and cement which it is desirable to keep away from major settlements are competitors for this land.

The Royal Society for the Protection of Birds established a reserve (which became an NNR in 1957) at Northward Hill, High Halstow (a famous heronry), where there is adjoining estuarine marsh.

Among other Kent localities Blean Woods NNR on very heavy London Clay between Canterbury and the coast was long worked as coppice (chestnut and birch) with standards (sessile oak) and has an interesting range of insects including the heath fritillary butterfly. These coppiced woodlands contrast in several ways with the Ham Street NNR woods near Ashford. The gravel pits in the neighbourhood of Swanscombe have yielded through the years a rich assemblage of flint implements of Chellean and Acheulian types, but one site became internationally famous for the discovery in 1935-6 of the Swanscombe Skull – fragments of a human skull dating from the Paleolithic stone age, but of surprisingly modern type. An area of five acres became a National Nature Reserve but this presents a problem: the gravel slopes are soon smoothed by rain and become covered by vegetation, and there is little to be seen unless fresh excavations are undertaken.

Surrey is a county unique in many ways. It has an exceptionally large area of common land, much of it wooded; it has long been a favoured residential neighbourhood with houses in gardens large enough to serve as refuges for wild nature. The Surrey Hills have been declared an Area of Outstanding Natural Beauty, large tracts are in the protective ownership of the National Trust. A large south-west part of the county might indeed be considered as a Regional Nature Park: wild nature in Hindhead and the Devil's Punch Bowl inspired the Haslemere Educational Museum; wild nature links with artifice in the Royal Horticultural Society's gardens at Wisley and, Londonwards, the Royal Botanic Gardens at Kew; there are arboreta at Winkworth (NT) and Grayswood Hill. Outstanding 'beauty spots' include Box Hill, Leith Hill with its tower, and Newlands Corner. The Juniper Hall station of the Field Studies Council has already been mentioned.

Turning to the counties north of the Thames, although Essex has only one small National Nature Reserve at Hales Wood (oak-ash woodland on chalky boulder clay with the rare oxslip, *Primula elatior*), the Essex Naturalists' Trust has ten reserves. The Essex

County Council (Hadleigh Marshes), several local authorities (notably Benfleet, Southend-on-Sea, and Rochford) have shown great public spirit in promoting conservation areas; Hatfield Forest is in effect a nature reserve of the National Trust as Epping Forest is of the City of London Corporation. Abberton Reservoir has been described as the most active duck-ringing station in Britain; at Stansted the Wildlife Reserve is showing exotic birds in almost natural surroundings.

The Lea Valley presents an interesting problem and an exciting possibility. The working of the valley gravels for the raw material so much in demand for building and road-making has left a waste of tip heaps and water-filled abandoned pits. The once important glasshouse industry, producing tomatoes, flowers, etc., has largely moved away without clearing up all its debris. Imaginative proposals are being put into effect to make the whole into a recreational area with plenty of facilities for water-based recreation and sports, but also with rough areas where wild nature can have a place. This is an important example of nature conservation by *creating* appropriate areas rather than *preserving* what is there. Many of the canals, so important in the pre-railway era, are no longer of any importance in the transport system of the country: very many have been abandoned and just lost. But many now have an exceptional amenity value and as nature reserves. Near Tring in Hertfordshire reservoirs were constructed to maintain the water supply to the Grand Junction Canal and were on the sites of old marshes. Today as a National Nature Reserve of forty-nine acres the Tring Reservoirs are classic ground with remnants of marsh flora and fauna, an interesting entomological assemblage and numerous breeding and migrating birds. This has another lesson for the present day when branch railways are being abandoned in quick succession: railway cuttings and embankments are often very rich floristically having been for so long protected from public access.

In some respects Hertfordshire and the neighbouring parts of Bedfordshire (Woburn, Whipsnade) and of the Chilterns in Buckinghamshire resemble Surrey in the large extent of open land attached to large residences, or in common land. There is still considerable room for wild nature and the Chilterns were declared an

AONB in 1965. Similarly in Oxfordshire where the A 40 descends the Chalk scarp are magnificent beechwoods. Nearby in Oxfordshire the Nature Conservancy holds 258 acres (115 in woodland) in the Aston Rowant NNR with chalk scrub of different types and nearby some finely grown lofty beech trees on Beacon Hill (by agreement with the Forestry Commission), very different from the hangers of the North Downs. Bedfordshire chalk lands provide the Nature Conservancy with the Knocking Hoe NNR – close-grazed downland turf.

Berkshire has only one small NNR in the north – a four-acre swamp (the Ruskin Reserve at Cothill), but the Berkshire, Buckinghamshire and Oxfordshire Naturalists' Trust has eight reserves in the county. In the east, Windsor Forest and Park date from medieval times, and forty-five acres of High Standing Hill in the part of the Forest not open to the public form a Forest Nature Reserve of the Forestry Commission and Nature Conservancy and perhaps the best surviving example of beech-oak in Britain, with natural regeneration. The Windsor Estate as a whole affords an interesting example of multiple use: due in large measure to the generous attitude of the Royal Family, the bulk is open to the public, but restricted access in a few parts helps greatly in wild life conservation.

CHAPTER 15

CONSERVATION IN EAST ANGLIA

Strictly East Anglia may be confined to Norfolk and Suffolk – the old Kingdom of East Anglia divided between the North Folk and the South Folk with an undisputed regional capital at Norwich. But the waste of waters and fens which once separated this island from the rest of England is now the fertile farmland of Cambridgeshire with the Isle of Ely, and to some extent Cambridge is a more convenient capital of the region. The Nature Conservancy for their East Anglia Region have added Lincolnshire, Huntingdonshire-Peterborough, Bedfordshire and Essex with offices at Norwich, and the important Research Station at Monks Wood near Huntingdon. Such a unit is perhaps better called Eastern England.

Certainly it was early in the field with modern concepts of conservation. The movement owes much to the influence of members of the University of Cambridge. Sir Arthur Tansley was at Cambridge during the formative period of his work in laying the foundation of ecology and though he became Sherardian Professor of Botany at Oxford he continued to live on the margins of Cambridge at Grantchester. Cambridge botanists had a special interest in the Fens and realized the importance of securing for posterity a typical section of the old reed fenland; the curious sandy wastes of Breckland were also near at hand and unique; the Broads and the Norfolk coast attracted attention too. Norfolk was the first county to establish a Naturalists' Trust (1926) and Professor J. A. Steers, whose name will always be associated with the study of the physiography of the Norfolk coast and all the conservation work which emanated therefrom, edited and published the first volume on Scolt Head as early as 1934. It is not surprising that National Nature Reserves are numerous as well as extremely important in East Anglia.

First, the coast. Scolt Head National Nature Reserve covers

1,821 acres of coastal sand-dunes and associated hollows and salt-marshes, cut off by a considerable creek from Brancaster Staithe, where the charming Dial House is the residence of the Warden. The Staithes are the permanent home of large numbers of pleasure craft and even with assistant wardens it is difficult to keep picnic parties off the breeding colonies of terns (access is restricted in May, June and July). The whole area has been intensively studied. Along the coast, between Scolt Head Island and Salthouse is also an extremely interesting area of coastland: indeed it is not too much to say that the whole of the north Norfolk coast of about forty-four square miles ought to be considered as a National Nature Park with integrated recreational and conservation interests, to include Wells Marshes, Blakeney Point (NT and NNT), Cley Marshes (NT, NNT) and the famous coast sections in Pleistocene of the Weybourne area. Along the coast Winterton Dunes (eight miles north of Yarmouth) of 259 acres have been a NNR of the Nature Conservancy since 1956. Within the dunes are 'slacks' or depressions with a wet heath or bog vegetation.

Along the coast of Suffolk there is an extensive belt of light sandy land over which spread the east Suffolk heathlands. Much has been reclaimed for agriculture, some has been afforested, some is used for defence purposes. A good surviving example of the acid heathland with heather, bracken and birch and a wide range of bird life has been made into the NNR of Westleton Heath (see Chapter 20), two miles south-west of Dunwich. In 1948 the Royal Society for the Protection of Birds purchased Havergate Island and continue to own and manage it under a Nature Reserve Agreement. It has become famous in recent years as the site to which the avocet has returned. Also in the reserve, totalling 514 acres, is Orfordness shingle spit, classic ground now for the study of coastal physiography. Another coastal site of great interest is the Blyth estuary which is a natural waterfowl and wader refuge: a ringing station has been established at Walberswick. Though not a reserve, Shingle Street has great physiographical and botanical interest.

It was Constable who made famous Flatford Mill, in the midst of the Constable country of the Suffolk-Essex border. It is fitting that it should have been preserved as a Centre of the Field Studies

16 *Above*: a tree hide in the Minsmere Nature Reserve. *Opposite*: Woodwalton Fen — Gordon Mason standing by a muslin-covered cage in which Large Copper larvae are reared on a great water dock

17 Eglwyseg Mountain, near Llangollen, Denbighshire. A scarp of Carboniferous Limestone. Listed as a Site of Special Scientific Interest

Council, though problems have arisen regarding the maintenance of an adequate flow of water – demanded by commercial interests higher up the River Stour.

Returning to Norfolk, roughly between Norwich and the North Sea is the fascinating area of the Broads or Broadland, the subject of a recent regional volume of the New Naturalist series. For long the origin of these wide stretches of shallow water bordering two or three main rivers was under investigation and discussion: it is now clear that they occupy the flooded sites of early medieval peat workings. There are, then, the main river channels connected in places with these large shallow lakes which are fringed with marsh and bog. They constitute the greatest reservoir of wetland flora and fauna in Britain, with many rarities and relict species. Broadland has been made the subject of a special study by a group of over twenty interested parties organized by the Nature Conservancy, for the problems of competing claims are numerous. Not many years ago shooting, especially of duck, was the main occupation, and one learns the nauseating details of the vast numbers driven over to fall victims to the guns of sportsmen comfortably entrenched in protected redoubts. The time is not far distant when the highest in the land counted their prowess by the size of their bag. Then came the tremendous growth of the tourist industry, with ten thousand craft of many types. The area was considered for demarcation as a National Park, also as a National Nature and Recreation Park, but an overall plan has still to be worked out. The Nature Conservancy manages as an NNR jointly with the Norfolk Naturalists' Trust, Hickling Broad (1,204 acres) and also Bure Marshes with Decoy, Cockshoot and Ranworth Broads (1,019 acres), and Horsey Mere is a Nature Reserve of the National Trust. Although these reserve areas to some extent lack the scenic attraction and the many little havens and waterside hostelries which characterize the Broads most favoured by holiday visitors, those who prefer solitude make their way into them by water despite warning notices, with serious consequent effects on wild life. The question in crowded England inevitably arises: which should have priority, humans or birds? So popular is boating there have been serious discussions regarding the possibilities of actually making other broads: it must be admitted that the range of bird species is narrower than it was with the added difficulty that it is the bolder, commoner species, not unappreciative of food left by human visitors, which have increased in numbers to the detriment of the rarer.

There are other wetland sites in the two eastern counties. James Fisher has described Minsmere, 'this glorious Suffolk marsh', managed by the RSPB, as one of Britain's – indeed Europe's – wetland treasures. It is Britain's headquarters for the marsh harrier, now reduced to a handful of pairs, and the bearded tit which is here on the very edge of its world range and barely survives the severer winters. Access to Minsmere is by permit from the RSPB; hidden board walks and trails bring visitors to one or other of the eight built-in hides strategically placed round the freshwater lagoon and marsh.

The University of Cambridge established its Botanic Garden in 1761 and it has played its part in the stimulation of a wide range of studies, not least under its present Director, John Gilmour. Biologists associated with the University of Cambridge have long had a special interest in two types of habitat within easy reach. Cambridge was once on the margin of the great watery wastes of the Fens, with Ely Cathedral crowning its little island in the midst, and the fight has been, after the great medieval work of draining the Fens, to preserve at least a representative area or two. The most famous is Wicken Fen, now an area of 320 acres, owned by the National Trust. It has been intensively studied for many years and a comparison of careful maps made in 1923-4 with those only ten years later, 1934, demonstrated the rapidity with which the whole was being invaded by bush and passing into carr-woodland. This showed beyond doubt that there could be no conservation without active management. This has been undertaken by the University with clearance of woody vegetation, the regular cutting of reeds (*Phragmites*) as in the past, and even the creation of an artificial mere. A somewhat different area is the valley fen of Chippenham, three miles north of Newmarket, a NNR of 193 acres (40 acres of woodland). It has a rich insect fauna.

A quite different area near and dear to Cambridge is Breckland, a large area partly in Suffolk and partly in Norfolk, of very light sandy soil. The origin of the sands, which are of considerable thickness and rest ultimately on Chalk, has been a matter of much dispute, but it would appear they are glacial, but from them all lime has been leached away. It is possible that the vegetation was a relic of the *Steppen-heide* widespread over continental Europe after the retreat of the ice-sheets. Neglected by early and medieval farmers because of its hungry character, the whole area was a vast grass-heath dominated by species of *Agrostis* and *Festuca* with patches of bracken, heather and *Carex*. Where overgrazing – including that by the vast rabbit population – destroyed the natural sod, 'blow-outs' or wind-erosion hollows were liable to occur. It was found, however, that some areas could be reclaimed and farmed with such light land crops as carrots and a 'breck' is an intake made for this purpose. The land, however, is excellent for afforestation especially with Scots pine, and Thetford Chase established by the Forestry Commission is now one of the largest forests in the country. Following extensive and large-scale research it has been found that certain systems of light land farming can yield excellent results. Consequently there is considerable pressure on the area and a need to conserve some representative sections of the old heath. A special Conservation Committee was set up by the Nature Conservancy in 1958 jointly with the Royal Society for the Protection of Birds, the Norfolk Naturalists' Trust, the Forestry Commission, the Breckland Research Committee, and other interests. On Thetford Heath is a NNR of 243 acres; on Weeting Heath another of 338 acres (both owned by the Norfolk Naturalists' Trust) and on Cavenham Heath in the south a third of 337 acres. Thetford and Weeting in particular are famed for their birds – including stone curlews and wheatears.

In the west of the Nature Conservancy's East Anglian Region the new county of Huntingdon-Peterborough is included. The Castor Hanglands constitute a NNR of 221 acres (113 woodland) five miles north-west of Peterborough with a mixture of habitats on Jurassic limestones and clays. In Huntingdon is the really important group of reserves, sufficiently close together to be usable as an open-air laboratory of Monks Wood. The three National Nature Reserves are first Holme Fen, 640 acres of woodland which adjoins the site of

Whittlesey Mere, drained in 1851. The famous Holme Fen post is an iron pillar showing the remarkable shrinkage of the peat since drainage began. Woodwalton Fen was acquired in 1919 by the Society for the Promotion of Nature Reserves and extensive work has been undertaken to maintain a high-water table throughout the year and so to keep the old fen conditions. It covers 514 acres. Monks Wood is typical oak-ash woodland of the heavy Oxford Clay of the English Midlands: part has been worked as coppice with standards and it has a rare and rich insect fauna. Of the total area of 387 acres 370 are woodland. The Monks Wood Research Station of the Nature Conservancy is the first to be specially built as such. It is an interesting modern building with residential and conference facilities and a range of well-equipped laboratories, all under the direction of Dr. Kenneth Mellanby. Here is focused the important work of the Conservancy on toxic chemicals. Being only some twenty-five miles from Cambridge, the staff can keep in close touch and the Biological Records Centre was recently moved from Cambridge to Monks Wood. At the same time there is space for outdoor experiments: one such is an attempt to find out the influence of different types of hedges and the effect on hedgerow flora and fauna.

There is a Lincolnshire Trust for Nature Conservation which now has more than twenty reserves in the county. Gibraltar Point was the first Local Nature Reserve to be declared in England (1952) – declared as such by the Lindsey County Council. Its thousand acres of dunes and salt-marshes south of Skegness are important as a sanctuary for migrant and wintering birds as well as in many other ways. Lindsey County Council has shown itself the leading local authority in this country on matters of nature conservation not only in its pioneering acquisition of Gibraltar Point but also in its continuing collaboration with the Lincolnshire Trust in management. In 1968 the Nature Conservancy declared as an NNR 1,088 acres of foreshore, sandhills and marshes at Saltfleetby-Theddlethorpe, stretching along four and a half miles of the Lincolnshire coast.

CHAPTER 16

CONSERVATION IN THE MIDLANDS

The Midlands Region of the Nature Conservancy comprises eleven counties of which only one – Cheshire – reaches the coast, the others being the shires of Stafford, Derby, Nottingham, Salop, Hereford, Warwick, Worcester, Northampton, Leicester and Rutland. Most of these counties have in common the existence of industrial areas, frequently with the problem of extensive waste land, yet set in a fertile agricultural countryside. Wild nature has a special difficulty in survival: the reserves are consequently small and scattered, but very precious. Looked at geographically the Midlands stretch westwards to the edge of the Welsh massif; southeastwards across the Jurassic scarps with their extensive open-cast iron ore workings to the foot of the chalk scarp. Penetrating from the north into the centre is the broad and varied upland of the Southern Pennines. A large part of the latter is now the Peak District National Park, the subject of one of the regional volumes of the New Naturalist series, edited by Professor K. C. Edwards. The Peak District is perhaps the most used of our National Parks because it is flanked by great industrial regions on either side and to the south – reservoirs of urban people, young people in particular, who seek the quiet of the countryside and are often intensely interested in nature. This Park has been outstanding in the provision of a large keen warden service, and it is this which has helped to make the whole a huge reserve. Many of the Midland counties have keen County Trusts and we may mention especially the West Midland Trust, and the Staffordshire and Worcestershire Trusts with local conservation corps and a special interest in the integration of recreation and conservation.

The Midland offices of the Nature Conservancy are in the fine Georgian mansion of Attingham Park near Shrewsbury, which the Shropshire County Council has developed as an adult college housing frequent conferences and a range of courses. Conveniently near too is the Preston Montford Centre of the Field Studies Council. Among the direct activities of the Nature Conservancy may be mentioned the current work with Telford new town. This is an area of old small coal-workings and there are exciting possibilities of fitting in little wild areas, many with ponds due to subsidence, within the confines of a modern planned town. In the Midlands, notably at Coalbrookdale, there are electricity generating stations of the Central Electricity Generating Board (CEGB) producing large quantities of inert 'fly ash' which can be used to build up useful agricultural areas or to fill old unwanted mineral workings. The old Black Country, the coals exhausted, became a depressing area of abandoned works and grimy tip heaps till work was undertaken to help Nature in colonizing and reclothing the dereliction caused by man, with the result that today a new clean landscape is embellished with many exciting little Switzerlands. The same is true of the remarkable Wren's Nest at Dudley – an inlier of Silurian limestone honeycombed with old workings, now a National Nature Reserve of seventy-four acres where the richly fossiliferous Wenlock limestone may be studied still in the shade of fine ash and other trees.

The Nature Conservancy has in fact only four National Nature Reserves in its Midland Region. Apart from Wren's Nest there are three mosses or meres. When the ice-sheets of the Great Ice Age retreated, shallow glacial lakes were left in many parts of the boulder clay plain. These have gradually dried up: in some cases a lake of diminished size remained, probably with fen or bog round the margins, in other cases a thickness of *sphagnum* bog has been formed and there is no open water. Many such bogs have been drained and may afford fine agricultural land. The three areas which have been made National Nature Reserves are Wybunbury Moss, Cheshire, three miles south of Crewe, Chartley Moss, Staffordshire, seven miles north-east of Stafford, and Rostherne Mere, Cheshire, three miles north of Knutsford. Wybunbury Moss consists of the centre of a raft of *sphagnum* peat ten to twenty feet thick and floating on water as much as 45 feet deep. This is the *Schwingmoor* of the Germans, or quaking bog, and the first to be described in England. Towards the margins the peat rests on glacial sands and passes into a *Pinus* woodland and other types, so that woodland covers ten of the twenty-six acres. Chartley Moss is somewhat similar but the basin is a steep-sided rocky one some fifty feet deep.

As James Fisher has commented, 'Ever since civilized bird watching began, the Cheshire meres have attracted naturalists from neighbouring towns. Some meres like Rostherne and Marbury have become sanctuaries; others like Pick Mere, Tatton Mere and Redes Mere, are places of public recreation; others like Hatchmere are easier to watch from public roads; yet others like Lymm Dam and the Flashes at Northwich are not strictly meres but man-made waters and freely accessible. Rostherne, the finest mere of all, became a National Nature Reserve in 1961 through the generosity of the Egerton Estate executors. Because of its biological importance, access is limited.' In Rostherne Mere the open water is nearly three-quarters of a mile long and over a quarter of a mile wide and round the margins are reed beds (*Phragmites*), willow and mixed woodland. It is a main inland refuge for wildfowl of which mallard and teal may number 5,000 in winter, whilst 20,000 gulls may roost on the water at night in autumn and winter. There is a bird observatory erected in 1962 in honour of the Cheshire naturalist, A. W. Boyd.

Although the Nature Conservancy has only these four actual reserves, nature conservation is very active in the Midlands. There is much activity, too, on the education front; Attingham Park accommodates the Conservancy's Education Advisory Section as well as its Midland Regional Office. The University of Birmingham has carried out a West Midland Survey of Inland Waters in which recreation and physical education are linked with the planned use of the waters. The Chartley Moss reserve was the first to include a length of abandoned railway line and in Warwickshire the National Trust has taken over a stretch of the Stratford-on-Avon Canal. Leicestershire's Trust for Nature Conservation has also placed special emphasis on amenity and educational interests and is much concerned with the use of abandoned canals; it has established twelve reserves, including two in the delightful Charnwood

Forest area of woodland and rough grazing much used for picnics. Shropshire has a Conservation Trust which has established a reserve on Pontesford and Earl's Hills, while 300 square miles of the Shropshire Hills form an AONB. Geologically much of Shropshire is classic ground: special interest attaches to the Wrekin, Wenlock Edge, the Clee Hills and the large moor-covered upland of the Longmynd.

On the borders of Worcester, Hereford and Gloucester is the conspicuous north-south ridge of the Malvern Hills with some large associated commons on the flanks; the whole is an AONB.

Although outside the Midland counties under most groupings, the natural boundary with the south-east as a major region is the chalk scarp. Thus much of Oxfordshire may be regarded as Midland and includes the 647 acres of the NNR of Wychwood – one of the few remaining stands of old English oakwood but with many other species and a rich ground flora. The Berkshire, Buckinghamshire and Oxfordshire Naturalists' Trust has several reserves in the county, including Chinnor Hill.

Through the centuries the University of Oxford has played a major part in the development of studies basic to conservation. The Oxford Botanic Garden, founded in 1621, is the oldest surviving botanic garden in Britain and has a fine collection. The alluvial meadows around Oxford, especially the 400 acres of Port Meadow continuously pastured by horses and cattle (not sheep) at least since Domesday (1085) and others mown annually for hay for at least two centuries, have been described as the most intensely studied grasslands of their type in the world. The semi-feral deer of Magdalen Meadow may be described as the most urban-oriented deer in the world. In more recent years Oxford scientists have pioneered in the study of animal population (Bureau of Animal Population), work which will always be associated with the name of C. S. Elton. Intensive studies in forest entomology have a fundamental scientific importance vital in the management of reserves and those who have been trained in the School of Forestry at Oxford under such distinguished Directors as Sir Harry G. Champion have laid the foundations of good forest conservation all over the world.

If Gloucestershire is included with the Midlands, the Gloucestershire Trust for Nature Conservation has twenty reserves and note should be taken of the arboreta of Hidcote Manor (National Trust), Westonbirt (Forestry Commission since 1956, 116 acres), and Batsford Park. Across the Severn estuary, but still in Gloucestershire, is the Forest of Dean, situated on a coalfield which is structurally and geologically a miniature edition of the South Wales coalfield. The Forest of Dean is well described in the Forestry Commission booklet and there is a chapter on it in *Common Lands* which records the increase in the range of birds and also in other forms of life consequent upon the introduction of conifers. For the Wildfowl Trust at Slimbridge, see Chapter 11.

An important aspect of conservation in the Midlands, still far from fully explored, is the treatment of waste areas of different types. Apart from the examples already mentioned of the Wren's Nest and areas of the Black Country, the old coalfield workings, spread tips of various types, and also subsidence hollows which become shallow lakes or 'flashes', are often prominent. It is the general practice now to restore opencast workings of iron ore to other purposes but some large 'deserts' on the ridges of waste material (hill and dale) still remain. Fortunately the land is not poisoned as it was in some of the older industrial areas, and hence may be of importance in nature conservation. The Gloucestershire Trust has developed local conservation corps work more than any other Trust.

CHAPTER 17

CONSERVATION IN THE NORTH

Merlewood at Grange-over-Sands on the coast of Morecambe Bay was acquired by the Nature Conservancy as a Research Station and northern headquarters, and opened in July 1952. The Conservancy had already come into possession of Moor House in 1951 – 10,000 acres of bleak upland moor mostly above the 2,000-foot contour in the north-east of Westmorland – and the farmhouse proved convertible into a field research station. To a major extent the northern region of the Conservancy is concerned with highland problems, but not exclusively so.

The north of England can be considered as comprising a broad north-south upland sometimes called the 'backbone of England', otherwise the Pennine Upland. Structurally it is an asymmetrical anticline of Carboniferous rocks, the coarse sandstones of the Millstone Grit predominating, but with the hard Carboniferous Limestone once, significantly, called Mountain Limestone, exposed in places and occasionally even ancient Silurian rocks. There is usually a steep, sometimes faulted, face to the west, a long gentle dip slope towards the east. The Pennines are sufficiently elevated to be for the most part above the tree-line, and the wet windswept heights are clothed with cotton grass and wet grass moors with frequent boggy stretches. Only on lower ground, eastwards, are heather moors to be found.

Flanking the Pennine Upland on the north-west and joined to it by Shap Fell is the roughly circular hill mass of the Lake District with its finger lakes radiating from a centre near Keswick almost like the spokes of a wheel. The core is of older Palaeozoic rocks with abundant ancient volcanics, so that many of the peaks are rugged and famous for the rock climbs they afford. As the core gives place to lower ground there are hills of Carboniferous Limestone in the south and of other rocks in the north. On the wet, western side of Britain the Lake District has some of the highest recorded rainfalls in the country – over 200 inches certainly fall on central peaks. The Lake District is the most obvious choice for one of Britain's National Parks, and has good claims to be considered the finest – it is the largest, covering 866 square miles. The heart is moorland, only two per cent is improved farm land in the valleys. Afforestation is a disputed subject in the Lakes, and by agreement between the Forestry Commission and the amenity societies is restricted to certain valley areas. Here and there are some older woodlands and some fine stands of trees, including the exotic *Pinus nobilis*. Still more hotly disputed is the use of Lakeland water for the supply of distant urban centres. At an early date Manchester acquired Thirlmere and certainly did nothing to please public opinion by blanketing it with a plantation of conifers and prohibiting all public access to its shores. Manchester has sought since to acquire rights to Ullswater and other lakes, and though defeated in Parliament returns to the contest. The Lake District is full of anomalies: it lies in three counties (Westmorland, Cumberland and the northern part of Lancashire), so that planning control is complex. A large part in the centre is in the Lakes *Urban* District Council, which has the effect of automatically making a large extent of common land open to public access by law. There is great doubt as to the status of much of the remainder.

The whole National Park may be regarded as a nature reserve: it has a great variety of habitats and some fine geological sites with a wide range of birds of all types. There is a Lake District Naturalists' Trust with nine reserves (including part of Walney Island) – and the Nature Conservancy has four NNR in the south. The first of these is Blelham Bog, two and a half miles south-south-west of Ambleside, covering only five acres but representing an intermediate stage from the conditions found in North Fen, the second NNR of four acres of open woodland nearby, and the third which is Rusland Moss of 58 acres in the Rusland Valley. This is a 'raised bog' which originated in a lake. Another NNR is Roudsea Wood, a natural outdoor laboratory for the Merlewood Research Station nearby. It owes its very varied character over its 287 acres to the underlying geology, including both slate and limestone.

Within the Lake District England's highest mountain, 3,210 feet, is Sca Fell Pike, belonging to the National Trust, which also owns part of Great Gable. The Forestry Commission has made Hardknott a National Forest Park and has also opened parts of Thornthwaite. Manchester Corporation, perhaps in atonement for the past, has arranged Nature Trails along The Swirls and Launchy Gill, Thirlmere. Many critics have regretted that the boundary of the Lake District National Park was not drawn so as to include some of the fascinating coastlands. Along Solway Firth forty-one square miles have been declared an AONB and this includes Rockcliffe Marsh, an important winter refuge for wildfowl. There is a bird-ringing station at Skinburness. St. Bees Head, of fine red Permian sandstone, has sea-bird colonies including fulmars. Farther south the Ravenglass and Drigg Dunes covering 583 acres were declared a Local Nature Reserve by the Cumberland County Council in 1954, and include the largest black-headed gullery in England and a flourishing strictly protected ternery. Much farther south on the coasts of the Lancashire plain the Nature Conservancy declared Ainsdale Dunes a NNR in 1965.

In recent years projects have been discussed in connection both with Solway Firth and Morecambe Bay where there are huge stretches of mud and sand uncovered at low tide. Earlier plans were concerned with land reclamation on the Dutch model; latterly attention has been given to the construction of barrages and large freshwater lakes where storage for urban supplies might be combined with pleasure boating. There are obvious consequent effects on the conditions and wild life of the surrounding areas and conservationists need to be on the alert. It may be noted that the original station of the Freshwater Biological Station was at Wray Castle on Windermere – now at Ferry House.

Turning to the Pennines, the Nature Conservancy is fortunate in having acquired the attractive little Ling Gill Reserve which is a small wooded ravine cut into Carboniferous Limestone near the source of the River Ribble in the Craven area. But the great reserve on the Pennines is farther north.

Moor House deserves separate consideration. An excellent monograph on the geology by G. A. L. Johnson and K. C. Dunham was published for the Nature Conservancy by H.M.S.O. in 1963. The Reserve comprises some 10,000 acres of high moorland and fell country in Upper Teesdale and the Westmorland Pennines just to the south of Cross Fell (2,930 feet O.D.), the highest point of the Pennines. Moor House Field Station is on the eastern side of the Reserve and is reached by track from Garrigill, a small village not too far from the market town of Alston. Within the confines of the Reserve there is exposed the almost complete stratigraphical succession of the Lower Carboniferous rocks of the northern Pennines where the massive Carboniferous limestones of the south are beginning to pass into the Scottish type of interbedded limestones and sandstones. The intrusive Great Whin Sill of quartz dolerite is also exposed in the Reserve and also some of the Ordovician slates of the famous Cross Fell inlier. Prior to the year 1951 the area of the Moor House Reserve was a grouse moor and part of the Appleby Castle Estates. The whole region is uninhabited though in previous times lead, zinc and barytes have been mined, a little coal, and limestone in large quarries. Sheep grazing – but only at a stocking of one animal per acre – takes place over the entire Reserve, but it is a severe climate. The annual rainfall at Moor House is 76 inches, average summer temperature is 55° F and winter 29° F, whilst strong winds are common. The dominants in the vegetation are cotton grass (*Eriophorum*), *sphagnum* and heather (*Calluna*). It is a challenging situation where some of the thirty different research projects in progress may yield results of far-reaching importance. Is it possible to re-establish the high-level woodland which grew on the drier soils before sheep grazing began? Is it possible to use modern developments of paring and burning, to benefit from local availability of limestone, to control peat erosion and bog growth? What are the really significant factors in this high-altitude climate and how can they be overcome?

The Moor House Reserve extends on the east over the Pennine water divide into the Tees basin and there adjoins the National Nature Reserve of Upper Teesdale, Yorkshire, of 6,500 acres including fifteen of woodland. This reserve is nowhere below 1,000 feet and rises to 2,591 feet at the summit of Mickle Fell. Much of the reserve consists of typical western moorland vegetation with *sphagnum* bogs and heather moor, but where the rocks of the Carboniferous Limestone sequence reach the surface more unusual plant communities occur. Without doubt this is one of the most exciting and scientifically important areas in Britain, probably including more rare plants than any comparable tract in Britain, and exhibiting many features which are unique. Among the species present are arctic-alpine, continental and southern elements not found growing together elsewhere. Some of the assemblages are on flood plains or on unstable flushes, but special interest attaches to the coarsely granular 'sugar' limestone, again unique.

Probably more than any other area in the whole country, this is the locality most sacrosanct for conservation and where scientific results are most likely to be of far-reaching importance. Yet this is the one threatened by reservoir construction—and where the reservoir can only provide water for a few years as a temporary palliative to impending shortage. Although the Select Committee of the House of Commons decided on May 27 1966 that the reservoir project could proceed, important safeguards to protect the famous Teesdale flora were inserted into the Tees Valley and Cleveland Water Act of March, 1967.

Amenity interests are also threatened because the Whin Sill is spectacularly exposed at High Force and depends for its attraction on the maintenance of the flow of water.

On the eastern side of the Pennines, the Yorkshire Naturalists' Trust has done valiant work in several parts of the country. It was instrumental in safeguarding and managing the famous promontory of Spurn Head in the East Riding where there is a Bird Observatory at a key migration point not far from the Humber Wildfowl Refuge (see Chapter 11). In the West Riding a Local Nature Reserve of 618 acres has been in existence since 1957 when it was declared by the West Riding County Council. This is Fairburn Ings, twelve miles south-east of Leeds, and is a large expanse of open water created by coal-mining subsidence. The fringing reedland offers an excellent habitat to many water-loving birds. In the North Riding the County Council declared 2,500 acres in Farndale, seventeen miles south-west of Whitby, as a reserve to protect the wild daffodils growing on either side of the River Dove. Yorkshire now has the National Park of the North York Moors: some protest at the afforestation and also the rather conspicuous Fylingdales Early Warning Station. The Forestry Commission has lately opened three Nature Trails in its forests in the National Park.

Yorkshire also has the Yorkshire Dales National Park and within its borders is the Malham Tarn Centre of the Field Studies Council. Northwards Durham County Council in agreement with the Easington Rural District Council and the Peterlee Development Corporation established a Local Nature Reserve of 517 acres over the Castle Eden Denes – a region of steep-sided wooded valleys running down to the sea and with numerous rare plants and insects.

The Universities of Durham and Newcastle-upon-Tyne, both before and after their recent separation, have maintained a lively interest in conservation and, in particular, their initiative in establishing courses in ecology, conservation and town and country planning is noteworthy as well as the broadly based surveys associated with the name of Professor G. H. J. Daysh, Professor of Geography and Deputy Vice-Chancellor.

Northumberland has both a National Park and a National Forest Park on its border, but interest focuses on the Farne Islands and the neighbouring coastal tract, now the National Nature Reserve of Lindisfarne extended in February 1966 to cover 7,368 acres. The conservation tradition of Holy Island and the Farnes goes back to St. Cuthbert in the seventh century: the Farne Islands as a whole passed into the possession of the National Trust and are administered by a local committee. They comprise some fifteen or twenty islands, marking the coastal extension of the dolerite of the Whin Sill, and the huge population of sea-birds is visited by seven or eight thousand people every year. The Farnes are an important staging post for migrants also; over 200 species have been recorded. Guillemots, kittiwakes, shag, razorbill and terns are especially noteworthy. The larger islands are open to the public but the smaller are out-of-bounds. The control of the large population of grey seals has been discussed in Chapter 7 as one of the most controversial questions of nature conservation. The coastal reserve of Lindisfarne consists of sands and mud-flats, the main refuge in north-east England for migrating and wintering wildfowl (see Chapter 11).

The active Northumberland and Durham Naturalists' Trust has been much concerned with the various problems – Teesdale and the grey seals in particular – and also with the development of educational sites. It owns one of the best of the denes, Hawthorn Dene.

18 Nature Conservancy staff and students studying the stabilising of scree, Crib Coch, N. Wales

19 The Highland Boundary Fault across Loch Lomond. This remarkable air view is taken looking north-eastwards and shows the wooded islands which constitute the main part of the National Nature Reserve. The two main islands are bounded by the Boundary Fault on the south, and its continuance beyond is very striking

CHAPTER 18

WILD WALES

Regarded geographically Wales, or more correctly the Welsh massif, is that detached section of highland Britain lying west of a north-south line from the estuary of the Dee to the estuary of the Severn. Built up for the most part of slow-weathering Palaeozoic slates and sandstones, with an abundance of contemporary volcanic rocks in the north and passing southwards into large areas of Old Red Sandstone with the great coal basin of South Wales, the whole massif can be described as a core of rolling moorland in the centre, giving place to valleys and small plains round the margins. Largely due to the outcrop of resistant volcanic rocks, the most rugged country is in the north, culminating in Snowdon. This is the core of the Snowdonia National Park where the grand scenery, of forms moulded by ice-caps and valley glaciers of the Great Ice Age, is out of proportion to the modest height of the mountains judged by world standards. The former isolation of Welsh valleys, leading away from the central core, is so well known as to be proverbial: to a not inconsiderable extent the lonely caches of human habitation are matched by isolated caches of interesting vegetation. It follows almost automatically that the nature reserves of Wales fall into three groups: representative sections of the mountain core, sand-dunes, bogs and marshes of the coastal fringe and some bordering islands difficult of access and so constituting natural refuges for wild life.

The former West Wales Field Society, now the West Wales Naturalists' Trust, pioneered in safeguarding these offshore islands as nature reserves and for a long time, from the 'thirties, was the only body in Wales which undertook practical conservation.

Wales has no natural capital: the function of capital is shared between Cardiff, Swansea, Aberystwyth and Bangor, each of which has a section of the University of Wales. The National Museum is

at Cardiff and has been an active promoter of conservation. The
Keeper of Geology, Dr. F. J. North, was a principal author of the
first regional volume of the New Naturalist series, *Snowdonia* (now
out of print). Swansea is the natural gateway and guardian to that
exciting peninsula, the Gower, and beyond lies the curious National
Park of the Pembrokeshire coast with the deep, sheltered inlet of
Milford Haven, almost forced by its physical advantages to become
a leading harbour for import of crude oil and where, in consequence,
conservation, recreation and industry are liable to clash. Aberystwyth will always be associated with the pioneer work of Sir
George Stapledon when he was there as head of the Welsh Plant-
breeding Station and showed what could be done by scientific
management of the hill moorlands. The Nature Conservancy chose
Aberystwyth as their branch office for the southern half of Wales,
their main centre being at Bangor. The Welsh Committee of the
Conservancy was established early – in 1953 – and the office at
Bangor opened the same year. In due course a fine, if modest,
Research Station was built on the outskirts of Bangor and opened in
1960 under the direction of Dr. R. Elfyn Hughes and with Dr.
R. J. Elliot as Conservation Officer.

Of the twenty-nine National Nature Reserves in Wales no less
than fifteen are within the Snowdonia National Park and after
some years of negotiation include Snowdon itself. The NNR
known as Y Wyddfa-Snowdon covers 4,145 acres and has a wide
range of habitats. This is indeed a test case for the blending of
conservation and recreational interests. The first reserve to be
declared in Wales was the valley famous for its moraines, known as
Cwm Idwal, 984 acres, five miles west of Capel Curig. The varied
Ordovician volcanic rocks give some interesting local variations in
soil and the arctic-alpine flora is one which has survived from
immediately after the retreat of the ice. An allied flora descends
over lime-rich volcanic ash soils in the small reserve of Cwm Glas in
Grafnant. North Wales has an interesting series of reserves which
comprise sections of relict wood-lands; there is Coed Dolgarrog,
relatively dry oakwood of the Conway Valley; Coed Gorswen, also
oakwood, in the same valley at a lower level; Coed Tremadoc,
oakwood, which clothes precipitous cliffs and screes near Portmadoc.

These are all in Caernarvon; in Merioneth are Coed y Rhygen on the western shore of Trawsfynydd Lake, oakwood growing under very wet conditions; Coed Camlyn, Coed Cymerau and Coed Ganllwyd, each with different types of ground flora. Most of these reserves have interesting geological features, but it is that glorious mountain Cader Idris, rising in a majestic scarp to the south of Dolgellau, which is classic ground for the student of the Ordovician sequence and its associated vulcanicity. The NNR covers 969 acres (fifty under woodland) and is a southern extension of the arctic-alpine vegetation. The NNR of Rhinog (991 acres) east of Harlech is also rugged mountain terrain.

There is a North Wales Naturalists' Trust which has a number of properties including an important marsh in Anglesey. Farther south in Cardigan are other wooded reserves – Coed Rheidol in a wet gorge-like valley, ten miles east of Aberystwyth – oakwood with a rich flora and fauna. Not far away is Cors Tregaron, a raised bog, perhaps the finest in the country.

On the Old Red Sandstone, largely in Brecon, are large expanses of uninhabited, forbidding moorland, large parts of which lie in the Brecon Beacons National Park. The Carnegie U.K. Trust with the Brecon Beacons Park Joint Advisory Committee and the Breconshire Park Planning Committee have built a fine observation post. The NNR of Craig Cerrig Gleisiad has sandstone crags with the southernmost occurrence of Britain's arctic-alpine flora. The NNR Cwm Clydach is semi-natural beechwood with lime-rich soils from the Carboniferous Limestone of the coalfield rim; Craig y Cilau, also in Brecon, is likewise a Carboniferous Limestone outcrop overlooking the Usk valley with a famous series of caves and passages extending a dozen miles underground. Nant Irfon, in north Brecon, five miles north of Llanwrtyd Wells has oakwood which is a breeding ground for the pied flycatcher, and open high-level acidic grassland with red grouse.

Turning to the coastlands of Wales, perhaps pride of place should be given to the magnificent stretch of sand-dunes on the south-western coast of the isle of Anglesey known as Newborough Warren. The Reserve covers 1,566 acres and the view of the whole line of the Snowdon range is superb. The Reserve has perhaps the finest

stretch of sand-dunes in Britain with every stage of plant colonization, and there are salt-marsh estuarine areas together with a ridge
of pre-Cambrian volcanic rocks (Ynys Llanddwyn) with a classical
exposure of pillow lavas. Ornithologists have known the area for a
long time: its famous tern colonies have been watched and guarded
for years and its migrants counted. At Malltreath Pool a fine selection of feeding waders can be seen, as James Fisher notes, without
leaving the car and including godwits, redshank, greenshank, little
stint, ruff, knot and curlew sandpiper. There are other sand-dune
areas on the Welsh coast. The NNR of Morfa Dyffryn, Merioneth
(500 acres), is within the National Park and particular interest
attaches to the vegetation of the wet 'slacks' between the dunes.
Morfa Harlech, 1,214 acres, is a NNR north-west of Harlech
mainly of salt-marsh.

But the area of really major interest is the great Borth Bog where
the West Wales Trust and the Nature Conservancy have battled
hard to conserve at least a major section. Here the fight is with
drainage engineers and agricultural interests, and the problem is
that drainage in any one part is likely to lower the water table over
the whole and so to alter completely its ecological interest.

The Gower is a peninsula of unique interest in South Wales. The
whole has been declared an AONB. Its fine Carboniferous Limestone cliffs separating delightful little bays render the whole a
natural recreational and holiday area. The Glamorgan Trust has
played an important part on conservation in Gower, and the Nature
Conservancy has secured three National Nature Reserves on the
Gower Coast along the south where steep south-facing limestone
slopes have long been known to botanists for the rich flora and
many rare species. Many sea-birds breed on the cliffs and ledges
of Worm's Head. The caves of the mainland have also yielded
remains of early man and a Pleistocene fauna. Second, the NNR
of Oxwich (542 acres), also on the south coast, has a wide variety
of habitats in a small area – foreshore, dunes, salt-marsh, reed
swamp, fen with freshwater pools, scrub oak and alder woodland;
the wildfowl are particularly interesting. Third, there is the NNR
of Whiteford, 1,933 acres, on the remote part of the north coast of
Gower, an extensive salt-marsh which borders the 8,952-acre Burry

Estuary National Wildfowl Refuge, one of the most important of the wintering stations for wildfowl in South Wales.

From the point of view of the wild life perhaps the best of all nature reserves are islands, uninhabited by man but not too far from mainland food supplies, inaccessible or difficult of access and so rarely disturbed. Fortunately there are a number of such islands off the coast of Wales. Cardigan Island is a reserve of the WWNT, Grassholm (Pembroke), the remotest, is a reserve of the RSPB with one of the four largest gannet-breeding grounds in the world (over 15,000 occupied nests). Skokholm is also a bird observatory of the Field Studies Council and the WWNT with about 20,000 breeding pairs of Manx shearwaters and numerous puffin. The Field Studies Council, it may be noted, has a fine station at Dale Fort and the surrounding area is now well documented through papers published in the annual volumes of *Field Studies*. The Council has also taken over Orielton, well known for the duck-ringing carried out in its own decoy.

But pride of place must go to Skomer island, a National Nature Reserve since 1959 of the Nature Conservancy, but wardened and managed under lease by the WWNT which charges a landing fee. It covers 759 acres and has been farmed. Its claims to fame are numerous. It gives its name to a distinctive type of volcanic rock, Skomerite, and can be classed geologically as a classic locality. There is a strong breeding colony of the grey seal; the unique and remarkably tame Skomer vole, apparently evolved on the island, differs from the common bank vole in its larger size and brighter colour. Among the great number of sea-birds which breed on Skomer may be noted the Manx shearwater (25,000 pairs), puffin, guillemot, razorbill, cormorant, fulmar and chough.

The Nature Conservancy has no reserves on the Isle of Man, but perhaps this is the appropriate place to mention the 616-acre cliff-bound rugged island off the south-west corner of the Isle of Man and known as The Calf of Man. Since it was presented to the National Trust in 1937 it has become in effect a major bird sanctuary. Since 1952 it has been managed by the Manx Museum in conjunction with what is now the Manx National Trust, and since 1959 has been run as a bird sanctuary with over 150 species observed and over fifty which have nested. The island was formerly farmed and it is interesting to record that since farming ceased the number of nesting species has decreased, though others have come back.

The Isle of Man has its own National Trust – the Manx National Trust, whose headquarters are the Manx Museum in Douglas. The Trust owns Maughold Head famed for its fine views, prehistoric remains and bird colonies. There are botanical and entomological interests at the sand-dune and pasture area of The Ayres and a wildlife park was opened in 1963 at The Curraghs.

CHAPTER 19

CONSERVATION IN SCOTLAND

The story of the conservation movement in Scotland has been somewhat different from that in England. Two-thirds of the country is upland and moorland and Scottish thought has been directed more towards the need to maintain a viable economic existence for the people of the 'crofter counties' of the north than towards the reservation of areas for wild nature when wild nature already seems to control so much of the country. In the Victorian and Edwardian era Highland Scotland derived much of its income from the letting of shooting and fishing rights and the necessary accommodation in shooting lodges or Highland hotels. The preservation of game – the deer of the deer forests, the grouse of the heather moors, the salmon of the rivers – was important work and Big Business so that nature conservation with certain definite ends in view was widely practised. The whole social organization in Scotland, first with the specialized clan system with clan territories, then with the great landlords owning vast acreages and the crofter settlements, is not matched south of the Border. The Barlow Commission was not concerned with Scotland, neither was the Scott Committee nor, in due course, was there any common land in Scotland to concern the Royal Commission. An investigation into National Parks in Scotland was undertaken and definite proposals were made for Parks in Wester Ross, Glen Affric, Glencoe and around Loch Lomond (including what is now the Queen Elizabeth Forest Park – see Chapter 10). But Scotland decided against their creation and so Scotland still has no National Parks. Fortunately when the Nature Conservancy was granted its Royal Charter in 1949 Scotland was included but with a semi-autonomous Scottish Committee and an Edinburgh office right from the start.

In Scotland, as a result, conservation has depended much more on the efforts of the Nature Conservancy than in England and but little on interest at county level. Scottish landowners, however, have shown themselves very ready to enter into Nature Reserve agreements. By mid-1969 the Nature Conservancy had thirty-seven declared National Reserves extending to 182,536 acres in Scotland, the bulk covered by agreements with the owners, whilst a further eight were proposed (to extend over more than 20,000 acres). The Scottish reserves, speaking generally, are covered by carefully worked out Management Plans and Scotland, under the Director, Dr. J. Berry, has carried out a notable research programme. Research has been closely linked with the traditional Scottish interest in sport and has been concerned with red deer, red grouse, mammal and bird predators, voles and grey seals, and with the Highland vegetation. The Conservancy has published a magnificent monograph, *Plant Communities of the Scottish Highlands*, in which the authors D. N. McVean and D. A. Ratcliffe developed some concepts first advanced by continental European botanists and promoted in Britain by Professor Duncan Poore, now Director of the Nature Conservancy.

To a considerable extent the large nature reserves established by the Nature Conservancy have taken on some of the characters of National Parks and their function is somewhat different from the English or Welsh reserves. The National Trust established for England and Wales in 1895 does not function in Scotland, but in 1931 a few prominent and public-spirited Scots set up the National Trust for Scotland. By 1965 it had become an influential body having in its care some sixty properties covering 70,000 acres. As with the National Trust in England and Wales, many tracts of beautiful scenery and haunts of wild nature are thereby secured.

For purposes of administration Scotland has been divided by the Nature Conservancy into three regions but each is based on the Edinburgh office. Research is carried out by a mountain and moorlands team and a wetlands team; the former work from Banchory and the latter from Edinburgh, making use of Loch Leven as a major research site. On the island of Rhum and elsewhere important experiments in the rehabilitation of overstocked pastures and other urgent Scottish problems are in hand.

The great Cairngorm National Nature Reserve covers 64,118

acres (2,152 acres of woodland) and is easily the largest in Britain: indeed it is one of the largest in Europe. The greater part lies in Inverness-shire, but includes also a large section of Aberdeenshire. It is in fact the heart of the part of the Scottish Highlands lying to the east of the Great Glen: the massif often called the Grampians. A large part was doubtless once forested – with native Scots pine, juniper, and birch, but little now remains except in the Rothie-murchus forest though fine specimen trees of great age are found in many of the valleys. The area is dominantly moorland with interesting assemblages of arctic-alpine plants at highest levels where the slow-growing *Rhacomitrium* may be dominant. In places there are precipitous cliffs and deep gullies, numerous corries and screes so that there is no lack of variety in habitat. The larger animals include the red deer and roe deer; the rarely seen untameable wild cat is present whilst birds include ptarmigan, dotterel, greenshank, peregrine, merlin and snow bunting. But it is the golden eagle which excites the birdwatcher on the high cliffs, the huge capercaillie on lower ground. The celebrated osprey nest is outside the Reserve to the north, at Loch Garten.

A clash of interests in this large area is almost inevitable. There has been a sudden upsurge of what is loosely being called tourism and winter sports, both very much encouraged by the construction of a ski-lift in two sections east of the main road and railway at Aviemore. Indeed, the story of the ski-lift is an interesting one. It was an altruistic private venture designed to tempt the youth of Scotland's crowded industrial towns, Glasgow in particular, to learn to appreciate the open air and an exhilarating sport by bring-ing the joys of ski-ing within their reach both physically and financially. Indeed any suitable day, especially over the week-end, will find a dozen or two coaches – together with two or three hundred cars – in the car park. There are nursery slopes and instructors, competitions with classes starting with the under-fives, a spacious refreshment hut half-way. A ski-lift is not something to put up in a week-end: machinery has to be efficient and safe, so that £100,000 does not go very far. But no doubt this venture marks a turning point in Scottish Highland development. Apart from the refurbishing of local hotels, two luxury hotels with student accommodation attached and backed by leading financial interests were opened in 1966. And it is to be an all-the-year-round season, for the ski-lifts are as popular in summer as in winter with the superb views all the more appreciated when weather allows.

It may be noted that the Nature Conservancy also has west of Aviemore the Craigellachie NNR, covering an expanse of birch-woods passing up into moorland with a remarkable insect fauna.

This Cairngorm development has been noted because it is destined to have a marked effect on nature conservation. First, the heights previously only attainable by considerable effort and energy are now accessible to all with the minimum of personal exertion; thousands of feet tramp over previously almost unused upland trails. What the effect on arctic-alpine vegetation may be is yet to be determined; it is learnt that some upland vegetation, including the important *Rhacomitrium*, is slow to recover. There is certain to be a comparable effect on animal and bird life. Second, this increased accessibility will necessitate more exact management in the reserves, probably the creation and guarding of wilderness areas. Third will come the call for better access, opening up by motor roads, which are also demanded by forestry interests. Fourth there will almost certainly be the demand for week-end or summer cottages. Having seen developments in North America I am confident that the remoter parts of Scotland will soon be facing the helicopter menace – surface transport becomes unimportant and the remotest lochan may be invaded by humans and all the evidence is that helicopters are particularly disturbing to wild life. It is my belief that access by air will affect the Western Highlands and Islands in particular.

Reference has already been made to the pioneer work of the Smith brothers and Marcel Hardy in mapping the vegetation of the Scottish Highlands. Some years ago (1945) I was privileged to examine a number of unpublished field maps and with the help of Dr. Arthur Geddes of the University of Edinburgh, I prepared a Vegetation Map of Scotland. This was published as one of the National Planning Series on the scale of 1:625,000 with an explanatory booklet. We distinguished among the moorland or highland vegetation seven types – arctic-alpine vegetation, alpine

moors, peat moors, mosses and bogs (Sphagneta and Eriophore-
ta), wet grass moors (Molinieta), dry grass moors (Nardeta),
heather moors (Calluneta) and mountain pastures proper
(*Agrostis-Festuca*). Our map was reproduced on a small scale as
Fig. 90 of my *Land of Britain: Its Use and Misuse*. What one notices
especially from this map is the distribution of heather moor:
dominant in the drier east, including the Cairngorms massif, but
replaced in the wetter west by grass moors.

So we turn to the other great Nature Reserves of Scotland in the
wetter north-west Highlands. Beinn Eighe (Ross and Cromarty) of
10,507 acres, of which 330 are woodland, lies forty-five miles west-
north-west of Inverness and was the first National Nature Reserve
to be declared in Britain, to some extent coincident with the proposed Wester Ross National Park. It was acquired primarily for
the preservation and study of a fairly large remnant of Caledonian
pinewood and with great geological, physiographical and ecological interest in the mountain slopes of Beinn Eighe. Pine martens
still occur. The small NNR of Rassal, near the head of Loch Kishorn,
also in Wester Ross, is a remnant of natural ashwood growing on
limestone.

The great NNR of Inverpolly in Ross and Cromarty, near the
Sutherland border, covers 26,827 acres of almost uninhabited but
exciting country of the north-west coast. On the east boundary is
Knockan cliff with its exposure of the Moine Thrust zone, westwards
there are three summits over 2,000 feet including the spectacular
Torridonian Sandstone mass of Stac Polly. In consequence there is
a great range of habitats including a large relic of birch-hazel
woodland, the whole of Loch Sionscaig and some long-deserted
crofting land. Animals include wild cats, pine martens, red and
roe deer as well as golden eagles.

Over the Sutherland border the NNR of Inchnadamph (3,200
acres) includes not only famous exposures of the Cambrian Durness
Limestone with karst phenomena such as sink holes, caverns, underground streams and limestone pavements (and an accompanying
calcicole flora), but also exposures of the Glencoul and Ben More
Thrust plane and the Moine Thrust plane in or near the reserve.
In north Sutherland the Invernaver NNR of 1,363 acres lies near

the mouth of the Naver and so within a short compass has the plant assemblages of northernmost Scotland, and those attempting to colonize blown sand. Strathy Bog also in Sutherland is low-lying blanket bog with a rich assemblage of bog plants and part covered with parallel furrows, apparently due to the whole bog starting to slide downhill.

From the mainland it is natural to go to the islands and interest centres on Rhum, the whole of whose 26,400 acres is a National Nature Reserve. It is geologically of great interest as a Tertiary volcanic complex with a suite of basic and ultrabasic rocks and physiographically the existence of three peaks over 2,500 feet gives a great range of conditions. The island was formerly farmed and indeed overgrazed. It would also seem that burning was carried out to excess so that there are major problems of land restoration and the relationship of the grazing to a large herd of red deer. Rhum illustrates some of the many problems still facing conservation. A careful management plan has been drawn up and the island is administered from Edinburgh by the Regional Officer for West Scotland. There is the old farmhouse accommodation: should a research station be built or is the area too small, too specialized, or too remote? It is difficult to visualize successful experiments without a considerable degree of control, including limitation of public access. There is, however, considerable opposition to restriction of access, which at present is limited to the Loch Scresort area.

The special case of St. Kilda has already been noted (Chapter 5). North Rona and Sula Sgeir NNR are two islands situated out in the wild Atlantic some forty-four miles north-west of Cape Wrath. There is a large breeding colony of grey seals and the rare Leach's storm petrel is another resident. One might think that the very remoteness of the islands would accord all necessary protection to wild nature, but the very remoteness makes supervision and policing very difficult quite apart from the traditional annual harvesting, long practised and legally authorized, by the men of Ness on the large colony of gannets on Sula Sgeir.

The NNR of Noss, Shetland, covers 774 acres four miles east of Lerwick. Noss, with its great cliffs of Old Red Sandstone there splitting into huge flagstone masses, affords a wonderful breeding ground for many sea-birds – gannets, guillemots, shags, kittiwakes, puffins and several gulls, whilst great skuas and arctic skuas nest on the moorland of what has been described as the most spectacular island in Europe. Hermaness, the northernmost island of Shetland, has another NNR covering 2,383 acres, where great skuas and arctic skuas breed and many other birds nest on the cliffs. The small uninhabited island of Haaf Gruney is also a NNR.

Fair Isle is very different in character. It is remote, but linked by a regular twice-weekly steamer service with the mainland of Shetland. Perhaps the description 'the most isolated inhabited island in Britain' is a reasonable one. It has been owned by the National Trust for Scotland since 1954 and many improvements have been undertaken to stem the tide of depopulation – such as the provision of piped water, electricity and radio-telephone. It is not a Nature Reserve but has a famous bird observatory (with accommodation at the hostel) and an extraordinary total of 300 species has been logged.

Far to the south in the Firth of Forth lies the Isle of May, also with a bird observatory and field station set up by a joint committee which manages this NNR of 140 acres on behalf of the Nature Conservancy.

Returning to the western islands of Scotland, the Conservancy has a NNR at Loch Druidibeg, South Uist, of 4,145 acres with a small hostel. Here the grey lag goose breeds.

On that favourite holiday Isle of Arran the Conservancy has a small reserve in the steep-sided gorge of Glen Diomhan with woodland of two rare whitebeams. On the familiar steamer trip from Glasgow millions must have seen this Reserve, but few set foot on it. The same is, fortunately, true of the islands of Loch Lomond, five in number, which, together with part of the marshy shore of the loch, constitute a National Nature Reserve. The islands are largely covered with oak woodland in striking contrast to the bare moorland flanking so much of Loch Lomond and perhaps suggest how well-wooded much of moorland Scotland may have been in the past.

There are some other interesting reserves in mainland Scotland north of the latitude of Edinburgh. They include a stretch of 3,704 acres of Rannoch Moor on the Perth-Argyll border – a shallow blanket bog at a height of over 1,000 feet, and the cliffs and ledges of Dalradian rocks at Meall nan Tarmachan in Perthshire. On the borders of Perthshire and Argyll, Ben Lui, reaching 3,708 feet and with a rich montane flora, is now a National Nature Reserve of 925 acres. The Dalradian rocks which make up the mountain have calcareous mica-schists with bands of impure limestone, sufficient to introduce a variety and luxuriance into the vegetation. The higher levels of the mountain are snow-covered much of the year. The large reserve of Caenlochan (8,991 acres) has similar varied soils. The Reserve is a resort of red deer, ptarmigan and golden eagle. The coastal sand-dunes, marsh and pasture of St Cyrus, five miles north of Montrose, the equally varied Sands of Forvie (1,774 acres) on the coast of Aberdeenshire, the Morton Lochs – artificial lochs (59 acres) on a main wildfowl migration route in Fife, and not far from Tentsmuir Point (1,249 acres), seven miles north of St. Andrews, are other NNR.

A landmark in the development of nature conservation in Scotland was undoubtedly the completion of negotiations in 1964 to constitute Loch Leven in Kinross a National Nature Reserve of 3,946 acres including 125 acres of woodland. In the plain of Kinross, midway between the Firths of Tay and Forth, the loch is world famous for its trout fishing and is also the most important freshwater area in Britain for migratory and breeding wildfowl. In autumn thousands of pink-footed geese and hundreds of grey lag geese arrive at Loch Leven and later disperse for destinations all over Scotland. Thousands of duck winter on the loch and those which breed include mallard, tufted duck, gadwall, teal and shoveler. Clearly most careful byelaws had to be negotiated to maintain fishing rights and to continue public access to Castle Island and to three points on the loch shore. The loch is of course very near the main road and but a few miles from the new Forth Road Bridge and hence readily accessible from Edinburgh.

Apart from the wonderful Caerlaverock (see Chapter 11), southern Scotland has a number of localities of major interest. The NNR of Silver Flowe (472 acres), some twelve miles north-north-west of

New Galloway, is a unique series of seven raised bogs, undrained and virtually undisturbed by human interference. The Kirkconnell Flow in Kirkcudbright is an NNR of 383 acres covering a remnant of an estuarine peat moss near the mouth of the River Nith where bog passes into birch scrub and pinewoods. The Tynron juniper wood in Dumfriesshire has a dozen acres of tall juniper which apparently played an important part in primitive woodland but has practically disappeared from most of northern Britain. Dumfriesshire also has a Local Nature Reserve covering the two lochs, Castle Loch and High-tae Loch, 339 acres, seven miles north-east of Dumfries. They are excellent examples of rich or eutropic lowland lochs and the Reserve was established in 1962 by the County Council under agreement with the owners. The first local nature reserve to be declared in Scotland, Aberlady Bay in East Lothian (1952), has already been noted. It consists largely of an intertidal stretch of mud, sand and rock with some associated salt- and freshwater marsh.

It would not be right to terminate any chapter on conservation in Scotland without calling attention to the pioneer studies of Scottish naturalists, amateur and professional alike. Professor James Ritchie (1920) wrote his book on the *Influence of Man on Animal Life in Scotland* in advance of his time: it includes much which is of the highest value today. Another aspect of conservation in Scotland is the important work of the Forestry Commission, discussed in Chapter 10, and the National Forest Parks created by the Commission. The Royal Society for the Protection of Birds has, among many, a reserve on Horse Island, Ayrshire, and the Scottish Society for the Protection of Birds one on Lady Isle in the same county. The latter has also Possil Marsh, Lanark.

Among the treasures of the National Trust for Scotland may be noted Brodick Castle and Goat Fell, Arran; Culzean Castle, Ayr; Ben Lawers in Perthshire and Dollar Glen in Clackmannan. In Ross and Cromarty the National Trust for Scotland has established two vast recreational parks: one of 8,000 acres (Balmacara) and the other at Kintail, 15,000 acres along the traditional 'road to the isles'. Glencoe (12,000 acres) is another recreation park of the NTS.

That bold spectacular island rock, Ailsa Craig, so well known by those who approach the Clyde and Glasgow by sea, is a private nature reserve whose seabird community includes one of the largest gannet colonies in the world. On the other side of Scotland Bass Rock in the Firth of Forth is also a private reserve.

In a sense the great deer forests of Scotland are automatically nature reserves. A well-known one is Black Mount of 80,000 acres in Argyll.

This very brief account of nature conservation in Scotland will have made clear that the position there is very different from that in England. There is an *embarras de richesses*. But such is the pressure of tourism and the urge to get away from the strain and stress of city life that it would be most unwise to be lulled into a false sense of security. It will not be long before modern roads will be driven across the Cairngorms, and the roads to the West Coast relying at present on crossing places every few hundred yards will be deemed inadequate, before helicopters will descend on the remotest points. Those animals and birds which do not take kindly to co-existence with *Homo sapiens* will leave unless adequate seclusion is assured them.

20 Guillemots on The Pinnacles, Farne Islands, with kittiwakes on the ledges

21 Golden Eagle and young

CHAPTER 20

THE MANAGEMENT OF RESERVES

A National Nature Reserve is established by purchase, lease or by concluding a Nature Reserve Agreement (of which details are given at the end of this chapter) with the owner. According to the position of the Reserve the actual negotiations are in the hands of the Conservancy's Land Agent for England, Wales or Scotland, as the case may be. The Reserve is then added to the County Schedule and notified to the Planning and other authorities.

The preceding pages have made clear the necessity for the proper management of reserves so that, at an early stage, there must come the preparation of a Management Plan. These are substantial documents and may run into 50,000 words or more in the case of larger reserves, and include appropriate maps which are often the results of original surveys. In due course they are submitted for approval to headquarters and passed by the appropriate regional committee and finally by the Conservancy. The preparation or supervision of these Management Plans is a primary duty of the Regional Officer who may, and usually does, delegate the actual work. Owing to restrictions of space it is impossible to reproduce an example of one of these Management Plans, but the standard list of contents gives a guide to the coverage:

General Table of Contents
of a
NNR Management Plan

Introduction

I Name and General Information

II Reasons for Establishment
   (a) Primary Interests
   (b) Additional Interests

III   Description of Reserve
     1) Topography
     2) Geology
     3) Climate
     4) Soils
     5) Vegetation
     6) Fauna
     7) Land Use History
     8) Archaeology
     9) Public Interest

IV   Objects of Management

V   Research and Management Programme
     1) Subdivision of Reserve
     2) Conservation Management
     3) Research
     4) Estate Management

VI   Public Access

VII   Wardening

VIII   Priorities, Time Schedule and Finance

IX   Division of Responsibilities

X   Progress Reports and Revision

Authorship

Bibliography

Appendix   I Particulars of Property
       "   II Habitat Classification Chart

When such a Management Plan has been approved it becomes the basis of operations and an annual report is rendered to the Conservancy. In due course it may become necessary to amend the original Plan and this has been done in a number of cases. Looking at a typical, fairly brief Plan before me as I write – the

Plan for Westleton Heath NNR in East Suffolk – the Introduction
lays down concisely that 'the primary object of management in this
Reserve is to conserve the flora and fauna of a representative East
Suffolk Sandlings heath; this will be reconciled with a secondary
educational objective by zoning. A large-scale programme of
experimental management will be carried out in a Conservation
and Research Zone of approximately 103 acres to determine which
techniques will best satisfy the ecological requirements of the plants
and animals characteristic of the Sandlings. The chief problems
will be to contain the spread of scrub, to promote an uneven-aged
stand of ericaceous heath and restore the habitats of such indicator-
species as Stone Curlew (*Buhrinus oedicnemus*), Woodlark (*Lullula
arborea*) and Wheatear (*Oenanthe oenanthe*). Research on all aspects
of heathland ecology will be encouraged.

'A small Public and Educational Zone, demonstrating the value
of the Conservancy's local work, is thought to be a necessary com-
plement to the Conservation and Research Zone in this Reserve.'

The Plan is signed by D. A. White, Warden Naturalist, and goes
on to give general details of the extent, history, flora and fauna of
the light-land district of East Suffolk known as the Sandlings.
Reference is made to the area and site of the Reserve, maps, air
photos and other material, and where available. After details of the
relief, geology, climate (inferred from the records of the nearest
stations available) and soils, the vegetation is described in some
detail. It is divided into ericaceous heath, grass heath, bracken
heath, gorse-broom scrub and birch scrub. Under fauna, pro-
visional lists are given including a season's list of thirty-one breeding
birds. The nine or ten mammals include red deer (*Cervus elaphus*).
Old maps have been examined to try and determine previous use –
for the most part heathland of long standing. In this Reserve no
features of archaeological interest are noted; public interest is
mainly in four rights of way, but it is then noted that 'it will not be
possible to carry out any effective conservation management or
research work on this relatively small Reserve (117 acres) unless
the mounting public pressure on the area is brought under control.
To this end it has been decided to sub-divide the Reserve into two
main zones: one of these will be set aside for conservation and

research work, while the other will be made available for public and educational uses.' Already, when the Management Plan was written, some plot-experiments were in progress and an account is given of research projected. Under Estate management come such items as signs, fencing, gates, realignment of footpaths, agreement on existing shooting rights. In this Reserve wardening duties were being carried out by one part-time warden, resident nearby, and three honorary wardens: the Plan lays down the duties of all concerned. Attached to the Plan is a bibliography of works consulted. Appendix I notes that the land was purchased from the Ministry of Agriculture, Fisheries and Food 30 March, 1953, at a cost of £467 for 116.746 acres subject to a right of way of the Forestry Commission and certain sporting rights. A printed Chart of Animal Habitats is standard to all the Plans; in this Plan maps include a general location map, a map showing the Reserve relative to surrounding heaths; a detailed map of vegetation, 1 : 2,500; a map of management areas and another of management proposals.

Looking at another Management Plan for a nearby area, the Orfordness-Havergate National Nature Reserve, signed by Dr. Martin George, Deputy Regional Officer,* it is noted that the Reserve consists of the distal end of the Orfordness Shingle Spit, known usually as Orford Beach, which is long-leased from the War Department, and Havergate Island managed under a Nature Reserve Agreement with its owners the Royal Society for the Protection of Birds. The primary interest of this Reserve lies in its breeding-birds population, notably its colony of avocets (*Recurvirostra avosetta*). The description of the two somewhat contrasted parts follows closely that given above but much greater detail is available so that the Plan runs to some 30,000 words and details are given of no less than 193 birds.

Naturally Management Plans vary greatly from one part of the country to another, but these two examples may serve to indicate their general character and scope. Obviously the preparation of these Plans is a major part of conservation work. Where reserves are acquired by County Trusts the necessary surveys depend mainly on leisure time available to volunteer amateurs.

* Now Regional Officer.

A Nature Reserve agreement between an owner and the Natural Environment Research Council (formerly with the Nature Conservancy) has the usual somewhat complex wording common to legal documents in general. There is a standard form which may be varied but the owner is usually left responsible for general estate management but in accordance with an agreed management policy. The Council are 'empowered to carry out scientific observation investigation research experiment and other work' and are given 'full and free right of access'. The owner normally transfers sporting rights but retains the ownership of timber and other produce. The owner continues to pay charges necessitated by estate management, the Council the costs of any work in connection with Conservation and the Council commonly pays an annual rent for privileges enjoyed. The agreed 'management policy' is a separate document and may allow either that 'the land shall permanently remain so far as practicable in its present uncultivated state' or in the case of woodland 'shall be managed silviculturally in accordance with the Silvicultural Plan annexed.'

A very important part in Nature Conservation is that of the 'Nature Trail'. A nature trail may be briefly defined as a path cut or laid out in such a way that it is made to pass near points of major interest – typical trees, habitats, rock exposures and the like – which are indicated by discreet signs or may be left to be pointed out by a warden-guide. Clearly there is a high educational value in such a walk whether for parties of juniors or the interested adult. At the same time visitors by following the trail will be led away from areas where protection and quiet are essential to the maintenance of rare species. Because the public are afforded this access to the most interesting spots, there is less likelihood of resentment when certain parts of a reserve are prohibited. During National Nature Week of April 1966 Nature Trails were available at a dozen of the Nature Conservancy's reserves – over the sand-dunes of Studland, the woodlands of Dartmoor, Cwm Idwal, Snowdonia, Newborough Warren, Loch an Eilean in the Cairngorms, Kingley Vale, and Tring Reservoirs, to name some of the varied ones made available.

CHAPTER 21

SURVEY AND RESEARCH

For the sake of completeness it seemed desirable to have a chapter with a heading including 'Research' if only as a reminder that conservation is utterly dependent upon the acquisition of further knowledge and understanding. If by survey one means the actual recording and mapping of data in the field, then there is a special obligation on the conservationist. I have often said that it is frequently possible to analyse a body of data in two ways. One is the statistical analysis which now implies the use of a range of specialist apparatus such as punch cards, tabulating machines and computers as well as the techniques devised by the statistician. The other is the cartographical analysis which involves plotting on maps. In conservation work several types of maps are involved – at the one end the background maps giving the overall picture of Britain as a country, at the other the detailed plotting and mapping within an individual reserve. Between the two lies a range of maps and cartograms both general and specialized.

To proceed from the particular to the general, Britain has been well served by the official Ordnance Survey so that maps on the scale of six inches to one mile (1: 10,560) are available for the whole country and on the scale of twenty-five inches to the mile (more precisely 1: 2,500) for all inhabited areas. Financial stringency imposed on the Survey from time to time (as after the disastrous 'Geddes Axe' of the 'twenties) has delayed the process of revision so that some of these large-scale maps are seriously out-of-date and, by virtue of their interest in the wilder remoter areas, conservationists are often concerned with those very areas where revision has fallen behind. However, most reserves can be demarcated on the 1: 2,500 maps and outline maps on this scale are commonly used for the recording of the details required for Management Plans.

Nature reserves must fit into the overall pattern of land-use in the country. As pointed out in Chapter 1, our statistics of land-use other than for agriculture and forestry and a few specialized uses are woefully inadequate, nor have we maps to show the distribution of the various categories of land-use. When I organized the Land Utilisation Survey of Britain in the 'thirties (most of the mapping relates to 1931-3) it was to show the then-existing use or non-use of the whole surface of England, Wales and Scotland. The maps used in the field were the six-inch maps and the record was made on the 15,000 sheets involved. The categories used were relatively simple – arable, permanent grass, rough grazing, forest and wood-land (with sub-divisions), orchards, nurseries, gardens, land agri-culturally unproductive. After checking and editing, the field sheets were reduced to the scale of one inch to one mile (1 : 63,360) and on that scale the maps were published for the whole of England and Wales and for the more populous parts of Scotland. Manuscript maps for the remainder of Scotland were prepared and copies deposited in certain central libraries. A calculation was made of the areas covered by the several categories which became the only complete land-use statistics for the whole country. But that was thirty-five years ago and changes have been considerable. A Second Land Utilisation Survey has accordingly been organized by Miss Alice Coleman, Reader in Geography at King's College, London. The classification of land is more elaborate than that of the first survey and publication is being made on the scale of 1 : 25,000 (2½ inches to the mile). The calculation of areas concerned will give, when the survey is complete, full statistics of land-use. We shall at last know the areas which are available between competing users. Clearly such a survey is basic to the work of nature con-servation and has appropriately been supported as a research pro-ject by the Nature Conservancy.

When the Labour Government was returned to power in October 1964 one of the first acts of the Cabinet was to set up a Ministry of Land and Natural Resources. When I was asked to act as the Chairman of the Advisory Committee to the Minister, set up in consultation with his colleagues in Scotland and Wales, I fully endorsed the official view that an overall look at land-use and an assessment of land resources were vital and overdue. After examining all possible alternatives the Ministry came to the conclusion that the completion of the Coleman survey would give much of the information so badly needed.

Most of the land in which conservationists are interested comes into the category of 'heathland, moorland, commons and rough pasture' of the first Land Utilisation Survey – the land coloured yellow on the published maps. There was at the time much abandoned farmland which came into that category and by comparison with the Second Land Use Survey it is possible to trace the major changes. Indeed the history of land-use is of great interest and importance in conservation and in the Management Plans of the NNR efforts are made to trace the previous history of the area. Some information is usually available from earlier editions of the OS maps; for many parts of the country there are records collected by the Tithe Redemption Commission about 1840-5 and not infrequently county maps or, better still, estate maps of the eighteenth century or earlier. Sometimes these reveal previous attempts at cultivation of land later abandoned but on the whole it is the overriding strength of the physical factors which is emphasized. Land which it did not pay to cultivate in the Middle Ages and which was left as rough pasture has often remained so through the ages. On the other hand many of our best farmlands were already known to our Anglo-Saxon forebears and have remained in cultivation through the intervening years despite economic vicissitudes and political upheavals. The maximum of change is in land which is, agriculturally, intermediate in quality – lands which it has paid to plough when agricultural prices have been high and which now, with modern techniques, are again productive.

Since the special interest of nature conservation is in the moorland and rough grazing, there is a particular need for a survey of the plant communities differentiating the many types involved. Reference has already been made to the pioneer surveys of Scotland and to the habitat types early distinguished by Tansley and still in general use. During the last war Sir George Stapledon and Mr. William Davies carried out a reconnaissance 'grassland survey' of England and Wales with the severely practical objective of instructing the County War Agricultural Executive Committee in each county, and through them the farmers, of the best means to be adopted to improve the carrying capacity of their grazing lands. The 'Grassland Map' so produced was published as one of the National Planning Series (1 : 625,000). It serves as a very rough guide to the broad distribution of the main types of heathland, moorland and rough pasture as well as lowland pastures classified into eight groups. But something much more detailed is needed and the completion of a vegetation survey, covering the non-agricultural lands, seems to me an urgent necessity.

This brings me on to the question of research. Broadly speaking all research in ecology and very much in pure botany and zoology is relevant to conservation. That this is recognized is clear from the grants-in-aid for research given by the Nature Conservancy: it is equally clear from the range of publications emanating year by year from members of the staff of the Conservancy. Every nature reserve is an actual or potential open-air laboratory and it almost seems as if every investigation, whatever the results, throws up new problems for study. The Conservancy does receive annual reports of research in progress on its reserves. Perhaps the range of work in the Nature Conservancy's own research stations can be taken as an index of work regarded as urgent or fundamental to conservation and which is not being covered, or not covered fully, in the universities or elsewhere.

The Report covering the period 1960-5 being the first five years of its existence of the Monks Wood Experimental Station, under the direction of Dr. Kenneth Mellanby, may serve as an illustration. In 1963 the Station took over the responsibilities for the management of the adjoining Monks Wood NNR and the nearby Woodwalton Fen. Certain activities of the Station are under the immediate supervision of the Director – the meteorological station, experiments on the effect of fallowing on soil fauna, effects of grazing by goats, moles studied in their original woodland habitat. Otherwise the work at the Station is divided into four Divisions: Lowland Grasslands, Woodland Management, Toxic Chemicals and Wildlife, and Biological Records. Special interest attaches to the Division on Toxic Chemicals and Wildlife which, incidentally, was started in February 1960 two years before the publication of Rachel Carson's

Silent Spring. At that time the principal hazards seemed to be to wild plants from the increasing use of herbicides on roadside verges and to wild birds and mammals from direct poisoning by organo-chlorine insecticide seed-dressings. It was soon realized by Dr. N. W. Moore that pesticides affected whole ecosystems and their effects needed to be studied ecologically. To kill is one thing, but actually sublethal effects may in the long run be far more serious. Again we are reminded of thalidomide and human babies. So organochlorine compounds, such as Dieldrin, had to be followed into a wide range of habitats – into hedgerows and rivers and ponds only to reveal the ever-increasing complexities of the problem. Far away in the mountain fastnesses of the western Scottish Highlands the golden eagle seemed unable in 1961 and 1962 to hatch eggs; all round the country the peregrine seemed to be disappearing. The organochlorine insecticides had come to rest in their eggs and sterility resulted. But it was also found in the eggs of the fish-eating heron and great crested grebe. Then the discovery of the build-up in the head and tail sections of salmon and the shadow of unknown dangers ahead fell on the human population – even when, as a Scotsman protested, he only ate the middle cut of the salmon.

This one investigation of one section of one research station of one organization in the field of nature conservation should be sufficient to show how far man, as a member of the ecosystem, cannot separate himself from the whole complex of wild nature by which he is surrounded.

Many important nature reserves are along our coasts where shingle spits and bars, sand-dunes and tidal flats or, elsewhere, cliffs and landslips afford just those refuges needed by wild life. It is there that pioneer plants come in to colonize and create new habitats. The physical geologist is concerned with coastal erosion and accretion but the interaction of plant and animal life with the changing physical environment has been a neglected field of study. In the reserves of the Norfolk coast in particular the Nature Conservancy is in possession of such classic ground as Scolt Head; it is appropriate that the Conservancy should have a Physiographic Unit for the study especially of coastal phenomena. This was located temporarily at Furzebrook – near to some famous stretches of coastline in the Isle of Purbeck and Chesil Beach – and the need for a full-scale Earth Sciences Research Station is widely recognized.

An interesting example of co-operative research is that carried out by the Unit of Grouse and Moorland Ecology jointly by the Nature Conservancy and the University of Aberdeen based on a field station at Blackhall, Banchory, Kincardineshire. Work on the red grouse has there produced some most interesting results. Each moor has its own grouse population and few birds move from one area to colonize another. Breeding depends upon a pair of birds obtaining their own 'territory'. If they fail to secure a territory they usually die before they are a year old. The 'carrying capacity' of a moor depends upon heather management and growth which is in turn closely related to the underlying rocks and chemical composition of the soil. There is usually a surplus population each year which, if it is not shot or does not fall victim to predators, dies of starvation. It would seem therefore that, strange as it may seem, shooting does no harm to the red grouse population: it is a kinder death than starvation.

Important research is carried out by the mountain and moorland ecology research team; this unit was formerly run jointly by the Conservancy and the University of Aberdeen and is based on a research station at Banchory in Kincardineshire. The strength of the movement through the length and breadth of the land still lies in their hands: the active members of the County Trusts and the many supporters of natural history societies are drawn from a very wide range of society. Important contributions have always been made by those with a professional interest – biologists in our universities and teachers of biology in our schools, for example – but there has always been needed something in addition to a professional training. That something has been an instinctive appreciation of what our Victorian ancestors would have called the wonders of nature which were for them so often linked with the mystery of creation and the hand of God. The great amateurs of the past turned from their daily tasks to the study of nature as a relaxation. Happily millions still do and they still, as in the past, can and do add to the sum total of knowledge by their observations.

But a major change has taken place. Coincident with the development already discussed whereby nature conservation has passed from being the hobby interest of a few to the vital concern of nations and their governments, nature conservation has become a profession which offers a career – one might say a variety of careers – and a new avenue for the school-leaver.

In May 1968 the staff of the Nature Conservancy alone was 521. Within that number may be found a wide range from the almost pure administrator in the office through the heads and leaders of research and conservation and the lawyers and the land-agents to the white-coated scientists in the research laboratories and the regional staff, the scientific officers, the naturalists, and so to the wardens and assistant wardens on the ground in the reserves.

Viewed as a career, what is the training needed? What are the personal and professional qualifications required?

I would put first, unhesitatingly, the love of nature and the countryside. Nature conservation is a vocation, not a job. It is my belief that a sense of vocation is vital for success in many walks of life – medicine, teaching, the Church, music and the arts to name but a few – and I am sure it is for nature conservation.

But in this organized modern world love of nature is far from being enough and the question arises, what is the educational approach to a career in conservation?

We are in Britain perhaps liable to be misled by the American position. Stemming at least in part from the great depression of the 'thirties which not only rendered millions virtually penniless but shook American confidence to its very foundations, came the realization that natural resources were a national endowment to be systematically studied and carefully developed, not exploited, for the national good. Hence the development of many courses in conservation in American universities. In these Nature Conservation may play a role, but rather an incidental one. For example, in the well-known American text entitled *Conservation of Natural Resources* (New York: Wiley, 1950; 2nd ed. 1958), to which a number of authors contribute and which is edited by Guy-Harold Smith, Professor of Geography at the State University of Ohio, Columbus, one chapter of twenty pages out of a total of twenty-three chapters and 450 pages is devoted to Wild Life. We have always had, in the small space of Britain, to look at our resources intensively and there has scarcely been the need to develop studies on American lines in our Universities. As a profession, Nature Conservation is new, and special provision in our educational system is only just beginning. One may claim that the establishment (encouraged by the Nature Conservancy) by University College, London, under Dr. P. J. Newbould,* of a post-graduate conservation course leading to a diploma marked the beginning of University recognition of the need.

Nature Conservation is essentially applied ecology and ecology is the study of plants, animals (and man) in relation to the environment. One can say that the essential basic knowledge must therefore be botany, starting from the plants, or zoology, starting from the animals, or better the two combined in biology. But what of the environment? It is legitimate to argue that the basic study is geology with geomorphology, pedology and climatology. So many have come into conservation having done biology at school, with degrees or other training in botany, zoology and to a much less extent in geology, possibly in agriculture. But I should not be true to my own training and interests if I failed to argue that the ideal training is a university course in geography, especially if taken in the faculty of science with biology as a subsidiary, and with such of the special scientific options as biogeography which are features of many of our university courses. Geography has been variously defined: by some it is equated with human ecology, by others as the study of the complex man-land relationship, by others as the science of space relations. But in any case the viewpoint is essentially that of the ecologist in bridging the gulf between the biological sciences and the earth sciences.

Given that fundamental love of nature I would urge a thorough grounding in geography and biology at school and a degree in geography with the specialisms mentioned as the best general training at present available.

The position is changing and several universities are now offering or considering undergraduate courses leading to a first degree in nature conservation. The University of Edinburgh has pioneered

*Now Professor of Biology, the New University of Ulster.

in this field at the same time as its old-established Department of Forestry became a Department of Natural Resources under a leading agriculturalist, Professor Black, as head. To a man who has devoted three or four years to getting a good first degree to spend another year or two for a diploma is not very attractive, so that the University of London is now offering an M.Sc. in Conservation to follow an appropriate first degree.

Clearly nature conservation as a profession will increase in importance and the spread of the movement all over the world gives it an international interest.

CHAPTER 22

THE PROBLEM OF INTRODUCTIONS

In a fascinating volume which I edited a few years ago for the United Nations Educational Scientific and Cultural Organization (UNESCO) under the title *A History of Land Use in Arid Lands*, successive authors are at pains to show the delicacy of balance of nature which exists in those parts of the earth's surface which suffer from a deficiency of moisture. The plants which, by various modifications, have adjusted themselves to the particular conditions of a difficult environment together with the fauna likewise closely attuned constitute an ecosystem which is very easily upset by the introduction, deliberate or accidental, of aliens whether in the plant or animal kingdom.

The supreme example, of course, is Australia, so long isolated from other land masses as to have developed a biota of unique character. The immigrants, whether plant or animal, in so many cases found life easy: away from the competition of strong rivals present in their country of origin, they often found but light resistance in their new homes. The disastrous spread of the prickly pear (*Opuntia*), which refused to confine itself to the arid lands where it was intended to form a new source of fodder but spread over good farmland, is well known. So too is the spread of the rabbit, which despite annual expenditure running into millions of pounds could not be kept under control until myxomatosis arrived.

In nearly all oceanic islands, those far removed from neighbouring land, the story is the same – the development of a delicate balance of plants and animals which have evolved in long-continued isolation till upset by the arrival of man. Even in continental islands such as Britain, only recently in geological terms cut off from the continent, there has developed a major island ecosystem to be described as basically well balanced. In such climatic conditions of adequate moisture and range of temperature as exist in Britain,

plants and animals have a good hold on life and the balance which
has been established is much firmer or more secure than in arid
lands and so less easily upset.

In Britain it is broadly true to say that among plants few immigrants have succeeded in establishing themselves in competition
with the existing vegetation without strong human support.   Sir
Edward Salisbury has dealt with this topic in his *Weeds and Aliens*
in this series. One of the most successful on its own was the Canadian
water-weed, *Elodea canadensis*, which took advantage of our canal
system in the middle of the last century to become, very quickly, a
menace to navigation, though tending to diminish naturally after
the first flush of victory. *Spartina* is the grass which has colonized
saltwater mud-flats very freely round much of the coast; the
Oxford ragwort (*Senecio squalidus*) is a waste-land plant which
spread from Oxford, a botanic garden escape, very largely along
railway lines. Despite the immense number of aliens introduced into
our gardens it is difficult to point to any which have escaped and so
multiplied as to form a menace to existing vegetation. On the contrary, when a garden is neglected native weeds soon take over.

The situation is more dangerous in the animal kingdom. In my
book *Man and the Land* in this series I pointed out how many of our
animal plagues had been introduced.   The rabbit (*Oryctolagus
cuniculus*) was probably introduced by or at the time of the Norman
invasion and for a very long time spread but slowly: probably it
was the war of the British gamekeeper against 'predators' which led
to its rapid and disastrous spread last century. The grey squirrel is
an alien from eastern North America (*Sciurus carolinensis*) and
although it may have escaped from zoos as early as 1830 it was
deliberately released, notably at Woburn, from 1889. It is an om-
nivorous feeder and consumes with avidity the young main shoots of
valuable trees and the eggs and young of many birds. In recent years
as many as 50,000 a year have been destroyed in State forests alone
but still it spreads – driving out the little native red squirrel. The
black rat (*Rattus rattus*) which brought plague to Europe probably
came in the ships of the returning Crusaders; the brown rat (*Rattus
norvegicus*) from western Europe did not reach Britain till about
1728 or 1729 but within forty years had so overrun the country as

22 The Red Grouse investigation. The upper picture shows tracks in the snow left by two cock red grouse having a boundary dispute where their territories met.

Before the photograph was taken the birds had paraded along threatening each other about three to four feet apart

23 Grey Squirrel (*Sciurus carolinensis*)

to make the trade or profession of rat catcher, now known as rodent operative, a thriving one.

In more recent times the story of the North American muskrat or musquash (*Ondatra zibethica*) is an interesting one. For many years three-quarters of all the furs entering the great Canadian fur trade were of this animal, so it is not surprising that 'fur farms' were established in Britain. But the animal is a great burrower and wanderer: escapes were inevitable and are known to have taken place in Scotland in 1927 and England in 1929. Each female will produce six or seven litters of eight – say fifty young – each season and within a few years there were reports of canal and river banks undermined, low-lying meadows flooded, streams blocked by fallen trees and the water spreading into extensive marshes. The keeping of muskrats was entirely forbidden in 1932 and an intensive campaign undertaken (under the Destructive Imported Animals Act, 1932) by the Department of Agriculture for Scotland and the Ministry of Agriculture and Fisheries for the elimination of the muskrat. In the winter of 1933-4 a thousand were caught in Scotland alone (together with 7,000 innocent and unintended victims in the traps) and many more in England and Wales. By 1939 the muskrat was extinct in Britain, but not till a very expensive campaign had demonstrated the danger and folly of animal introductions.

Another very large rat is the two-foot long South American coypu (*Myocastor coypus*) whose fur is the nutria of commerce. Colonies have been established on river banks in Norfolk and elsewhere and damage is considerable. A much more serious escapee is the North American mink, an incredibly savage and untameable little animal which has escaped and is still spreading throughout Britain. It is particularly dangerous because it has few if any enemies in Britain as powerful as itself excepting only man himself, and is not only a deadly enemy of many birds, including wildfowl we seek to conserve, but will also eat fish such as trout and salmon. It is said too to kill for the love of killing and will even jump on the back of a deer and effect a kill. Legend or humour has it that the mink imparts some of its character to those who wear its skins.

There seems less danger in the introduction of deer. There are native and introduced strains of both fallow and roe deer. There are now six or seven other species of deer which have escaped or been released and have become feral in Britain. The most interesting is the Government-sponsored introduction of reindeer into Scotland on which the Nature Conservancy was invited to express an opinion.

Mr. Brunsdon Yapp of Birmingham University started a considerable argument by an article he published in *Wildlife and the Countryside* in June 1966. He advocated the reintroduction of certain extinct species of the British fauna, naming specifically the wolf into the Highlands to serve as a predator on red deer and the lynx as a predator on roe deer. He further advocated the introduction of the American black bear (rather than the dangerous ex-native brown bear) as a tourist attraction in State Forests.

So far as birds are concerned, the majority being capable of flight, 'introductions' are more a matter of encouragement to come and remain, to winter, or to breed. This has been discussed in Chapter 10 in connection with Slimbridge. In other cases the Nature Conservancy is, on the whole, against importations. In 1965 the question arose of two proposed importations to Brownsea Island, Poole Harbour. There Mr. Philip Wayre, the Honorary Director of The Ornamental Pheasant Trust, with the agreement of the National Trust and the Dorset Naturalists' Trust, proposed to establish six pairs of Swinhoe's pheasant (*Lophura swinhoei*) and six pairs of blue eared pheasant (*Crossoptilon auritum*), both threatened with extinction in their native habitats. To this the Conservancy agreed, the site on Brownsea Island being one easy to control.

An interesting example of a recent natural invader is the collared dove. It has spread with remarkable rapidity, nests indiscriminately in a variety of trees, swoops in crowds on chicken runs at feeding time and (some believe, though it is early to judge) threatens to become a worse plague than the woodpigeon.

Turning to creatures of lower orders, various cockroaches were introduced into Britain in the Middle Ages and the bed bug, which became a major plague in the slums of London and elsewhere, in the sixteenth century. The dreaded Colorado beetle, attacking potatoes, reached France about 1922 and strenuous efforts have been made to keep it out of England. From time to time specimens have been reported and some discovered colonies eliminated: the public is appraised of its handsome striped thorax on widely displayed advertisements asking for notification by anyone seeing this dangerous intruder. From time to time various butterflies and moths have been introduced or re-introduced. Some rare native species have been bred and released, but the general tendency of the conservation movement is to conserve what we have and not to risk new introductions.

CHAPTER 23

OPPOSITION TO CONSERVATION, AND THE FUTURE

Because the concept of nature conservation has gained wide acceptance in recent years, it would be foolish to deny or to overlook that
there is still widespread and deep-seated opposition, silent rather
than vocal. It is very important that conservationists should build
up a good public image of themselves and their objectives.

In the first place the varied sections of the great British public
have each their own particular ideas of liberty, but a general
opposition to infringement of liberty. The very word 'reserve'
implies a restriction of right of access; 'National Nature Reserve'
to many suggests by the word 'national' interference from White-
hall. It has been made clear in the preceding pages that nature
conservation *does* involve a certain amount of prohibition of access,
a certain amount of enclosure, and it is clearly necessary to let the
aims of nature conservation be widely known so as to get public
approval and backing. Two examples, at different levels, may be
quoted to illustrate the dangers of the present position. When the
Cornwall Naturalists' Trust established a reserve over a small section
of the Luckett woods in the Tamar valley, it was marked by a notice-
board and a light wire fence. When visited a little later the fence
had been torn up, the notice-board pulled up (a considerable
effort must have been needed) and a large number of empty
cartridge cases scattered round as a gesture of defiance. When
the island of Rhum was acquired as a National Nature Reserve
a not inconsiderable local press campaign was organized against
the 'infringement' of public rights in controlling access.

At times the national press enters the discussion. On Saturday,
30 April, 1966, at the end of the National Nature Week, the *Daily
Mail* carried an article entitled 'I'll Give 'em Nature Week.' The
writer, Vincent Mulchrone, is widely known as one of Fleet Street's

ablest journalists. Broadly, as a 'townie' he objects to the 'broad-sides from the National Trust, Nature Conservancy, the Forestry Commission, County Naturalists' Trusts, the National Parks Commission, and many more capital-lettered fusspots' as well as country-men and farmers in general with 'their obvious wealth, their out-landish clothes, their strident voices, their overbearing manners' when they come to town. His objection is to restrictions such as notices, being confined to 'nature trails' and 'hides'.

The language used suggests a very biased and prejudiced view, but he comes up with the right solution. 'It is for the great urban centres to copy the Civic Trust's imaginative Lea Valley scheme to reclaim a huge area of derelict land for wooded camping grounds, walking, golf, sailing and water ski-ing so that such *handy* play-grounds will 'drain the countryside of unwelcome hordes and satisfy the townie.'

In the second place there is the long-standing feud between the hunting and shooting tradition, deeply entrenched in Britain, on the one hand and such bodies as the League against Cruel Sports on the other. I have been at pains to point out the degree of mutual collaboration which has been established between the Nature Con-servancy and the Wildfowlers' Association because this is obviously important. There is also the realization that the controls needed to maintain a balance of wild life are not very different from those used by the more enlightened sportsmen and their gamekeepers. There is, however, a real danger that the conservationist may find himself regarded as an enemy by both sides, a danger which has been realized by the RSPCA in relation to fox-hunting. As far as fox-hunting and stag-hunting are concerned, the conservationist realizes that the sportsmen concerned have a major interest in maintaining the existence of the animals and take positive steps to secure their survival. The huntsman may be regarded as one form of agent in maintaining the balance of nature. This will not please those who take what is sometimes called the 'sentimental' view of conservation which is equated with a refusal to take life – except of such creatures as fail to arouse human sentiment on their behalf. To these people there should never be any taking of life on a nature reserve.

The conservationist is in real difficulty when such a major control operation is in question as the culling of grey seal pups. The Nature Conservancy was wise to allow the Ministry of Agriculture, Fisheries and Food to assume the burden of making the main decision. It is still difficult to educate the public to a full understanding that the cruellest course of all may be to 'leave things to Nature'. Though well-known to naturalists, the case of the Eskimo and the reindeer is worth remembering. A small number of reindeer were introduced on to a North American island to serve as a ready supply of protein to the small group of Eskimo residents. The Eskimo went on using their fish diets and eventually migrated elsewhere. The reindeer multiplied exceedingly, fought savagely for a dwindling food supply, became emaciated and disease-ridden. Eventually the few which survived had to be shot to end their misery. The same story can be told of hippopotami and elephants in Africa. Elephants, for example, need an *average* of 300-400 lb. of green fodder per day; with the savanna lands of Uganda this means that any area with more than one elephant per sixty acres, *even if there were no other herbivorous animals*, would be overstocked and the elephants in danger of starvation. There are plenty of examples of trends in the same direction with certain species of birds in this country. If a strong species multiplies to excess it can only be to the detriment and possible extinction of the weaker.

It would be foolish to deny that there is often a conflict between farming and wild life conservation. It is twenty-five years since one aspect of this conflict was epitomized on the variety stage by the hit song of the time:

> Run rabbit, run rabbit, run, run, run.
> Don't give the farmer his fun, fun, fun.
> He'll get by without his rabbit pie;
> So run rabbit, run rabbit, run, run, run.

This was of course before the arrival of the rabbit plague, myxomatosis. It was estimated that immediately before this happened the rabbit population in Britain was of the order of fifty (perhaps a hundred) million, or more than the human population, and that the annual consumption of rabbits was of a comparable number. Farmers were aware, if not fully aware, of the toll on growing crops and corn taken by the rabbit population, but many a small farmer, especially in the West Country, found his chief pleasure in life in going out on a slack afternoon with a gun under his arm to pot at rabbits. Agricultural economists were able to show that many an owner-occupier of a small family farm was making less than the minimum wage laid down for a hired farm worker. But the gun under the arm was a status symbol of independence. Myxomatosis is a horrible disease and although it was clearly the effective means of controlling the rabbit plague, most countries hesitated to intro-duce it deliberately. It was introduced into Britain accidentally. Probably farmer and conservationist might agree that the small remaining rabbit population of Britain is a reasonable one: official policy is the extermination of the wild rabbit entirely.

Almost inevitably the major clash between agriculture and con-servation is over the use of sprays and dustings for the control of pests, diseases and weeds. The situation is that the farmer has now powerful aids in the increase of yields, elimination of waste, and so the maintenance of efficient and economic farm production. Taking the world as a whole, this is the only solution to the food problem. On the other side is the toll of wild life. Both sides are aware of the dangers of the situation with the known and suspected dangers of using powerful poisons without full knowledge, as yet impossible, of long-term and side-effects. But the modern 'clean' arable fields and high quality grassland and pest-free orchards must mean to the conservationist the necessity of retaining definite reserves else-where.

The landowner is apt to be in something of a quandary when faced with the problems of conservation. Whilst almost every owner of rural land is aware of the necessity of maintaining a balance of nature, he may feel that knowing local conditions he is better able to manage this aspect of life on his estates than anyone from out-side. On the whole – Scotland is a good example – landowners have been willing to enter into Nature Reserve Agreements and thus to allow appropriate areas of their estates to be managed in the national interests of conservation. Others may still feel that this is an intrusion on privacy and personal liberty. With increasing pressure on the land, especially by the townsman for recreation, protection is afforded to the landowner by collaboration with such a national statutory body as the Nature Conservancy.

Naturalists may well be the enemies of naturalists. The old tradition was that of the collector-naturalist and in the past the pride was always in the rare species – of birds, of eggs, of pressed flowers – in the collection. The collector, especially the wealthy collector, is a danger, even a menace. There is a modern aspect of collecting which is harmless, or nearly so: photography, including colour photography. Even then the enthusiast may do harm by frightening away, in the case of birds and mammals, the timid rarity.

Perhaps the greatest obstacle to conservation still to be overcome is public behaviour – much harm inevitably results from carelessness such as the leaving of litter, especially bottles and tins, much from thoughtlessness in country behaviour, some from ignorance, some from deliberate vandalism. There is still a curious attitude towards public property illustrated by a true story from the days of the last war. The owner of a requisitioned mansion returned unexpectedly one day to find a squad of half a dozen men under a sergeant hacking down a famed rhododendron hedge bordering the drive so as to widen the approach. He remonstrated vehemently and the sergeant was profuse in his apologies. 'We didn't know it was yours, sir, we thought it was only the Government's!' The lowering of standards of public behaviour on national property is a curious but at the same time difficult problem of conservation.

What is the way ahead for nature conservation in Britain? Great progress has been made in recent years and the task is to build on the foundations already laid. First there is education in the broadest sense. From being the hobby-interest of a privileged few, conservation has become the concern of all. The spread of field studies in school, college and university, together with the proper facilities, will take care of the generations to come, but to educate the adult general public there is work for TV, Radio, publicity through such means as National Nature Week, conferences such as The Countryside in 1970, and the many specialist meetings designed to bring together those faced with practical problems but seeing them from different viewpoints. Among the last we may note such as the Conference on Education held at the University of Keele in March

1965 under the auspices of 'The Countryside in 1970', or the conference sponsored by the Midlands Region of the Central Electricity Generating Board, on Power in the Midlands at Attingham Park, October 1965.

The latter conference strikes the essential note for the future, which is co-operation based on mutual understanding and respect. I come now in full circle to the point emphasized in my first chapter: Britain is a small and very crowded country with only one acre per head of land of all sorts to serve all purposes. Some have advocated a 'land budget' and the allocation of land between competing users; it has also been urged that there should be an overall plan of land-use. I suggest the essential is a continuing and continuous collaboration in which nature conservation has the double role to play: that of providing the scientific guidance relative to man's place in the ecosystem, his position against the background of his natural environment, coupled with the special task of fostering the national pride of the British public in the native fauna and flora and so of making due provision for their conservation.

BIBLIOGRAPHY

Official Documents

ACTS OF PARLIAMENT
Game Act 1831
The Destructive Imported Animals Act 1932
Agriculture Act 1947
Town and Country Planning Act 1947
Town and Country Planning Act 1953
National Parks and Access to the Countryside Act 1949
North Wales Hydro-electricity Act 1952
Protection of Birds Act 1954
Protection of Birds Act 1967
Countryside (Scotland) Act 1967
Countryside Act 1968

REPORTS
Report of the Royal Commission on the Location of the Industrial Population, H.M.S.O. Cmd. 6153, 1940 (Barlow Report)
Report of the Committee on Land Utilisation in Rural Areas, H.M.S.O. Cmd. 6378, 1942 (reprinted 1962) (Scott Report)
Report of the Expert Committee on Compensation and Betterment, H.M.S.O. Cmd. 6386, 1942 (Uthwatt Report)
National Parks in England and Wales, H.M.S.O. Cmd. 6628, 1945 (Dower Report)
Report of the National Parks Committee, H.M.S.O. Cmd. 7121, 1947
Conservation of Nature in England and Wales, H.M.S.O. Cmd. 7122, 1947
Report of the Committee on National Parks and Conservation of Nature in Scotland, H.M.S.O. Cmd. 7235, 1947
Forestry, Agriculture and Marginal Land. A Report of the Natural Resources Technical Committee, H.M.S.O., 1957 (Zuckerman Report)
Report of the Royal Commission on Common Land 1955–1958, H.M.S.O. Cmd. 462, 1958
Forestry, Agriculture and the Multiple Use of Rural Land, H.M.S.O., 1966 (Ellison Report)

Publications of Official and Other Bodies

NATURE CONSERVANCY, 19-20 Belgrave Square, London, s.w.1
    Annual Reports: First Report 1949–52 published December 1953, subsequently annual volumes
    The First Ten Years 1949–1959. 1959
    Monograph No. 1   D. N. McVean and D. A. Ratcliffe. *Plant Communities of the Scottish Highlands.* 1962

Monograph No. 2   A. L. Johnson and K. C. Dunham.   *The Geology of Moor House.*   1963
Monograph No. 3   G. L. Atkinson-Willes and Peter Scott.   *Wildfowl in Britain.*   1963
Report on Broadland, 1965
Grey Seals and Fisheries, H.M.S.O., 1963
Countryside in 1970, First Conference, 1963;   *Proceedings*
Countryside in 1970, Second Conference, 1965;   *Proceedings*
Science Out of Doors.   Longmans, 1963

NATIONAL PARKS (now COUNTRYSIDE) COMMISSION, 1 Cambridge Gate, London, N.W.1
Annual Reports
National Park Guides from No. 1, Dartmoor 1957–

NATIONAL TRUST, 42 Queen Anne's Gate, London, S.W.1
Annual Reports
List of Properties (periodically revised)

NATIONAL TRUST FOR SCOTLAND, 5 Charlotte Square, Edinburgh, 2
Seeing Scotland, 1965 (published jointly with The Scottish Tourist Board); also many guides to individual areas

FIELD STUDIES COUNCIL (formerly Council for the Promotion of Field Studies), 9 Devereux Court, Strand, London, W.C.2
Annual Reports
Field Studies *Vol. I,* No. 1 (May 1959) then in annual parts;
    Vol. II, No. 1 (December 1964)

FORESTRY COMMISSION, 25 Savile Row, London, W.1
Annual Reports
National Forest Park Guides: Argyll, Glen More, Glen Trool, Hardknott, Queen Elizabeth, Snowdonia, New Forest, etc.; also booklets on each of the main forests
Hedgerow and Park Timber and Woods under Five Acres, 1951.   H.M.S.O., 1953
Camping in the National Forest Parks

COUNCIL FOR NATURE, c/o Zoological Society of London, Regent's Park, London, N.W.1
Habitat (cyclostyled, bi-monthly)

MINISTRY OF AGRICULTURE, FISHERIES AND FOOD
Agricultural Statistics, Part I.   H.M.S.O. (annual)
Bulletins.   A long series, with many of importance

SCOTTISH DEPARTMENT OF AGRICULTURE
Agricultural Statistics (annual)

BOARD OF AGRICULTURE (1793 onwards)
A General View of the Agriculture, published for most counties 1793–1815

HER MAJESTY'S STATIONERY OFFICE (general)
Annual Abstract of Statistics

SOCIETY FOR THE PROMOTION OF NATURE RESERVES (S.P.N.R.)
Handbook (annual). Includes details of County Trusts

COUNCILS FOR THE PRESERVATION OF RURAL ENGLAND (C.P.R.E.), 4
Hobart Place, London, S.W.1 and PROTECTION OF RURAL WALES
(C.P.R.W.), Meifod, Montgomeryshire
Annual Reports (for England and for Wales; also of local branches)
Monthly Bulletin

WILDFOWLERS' ASSOCIATION OF GREAT BRITAIN AND IRELAND
Grosvenor House, 104 Watergate Street, Chester
Annual Report and Yearbook

ROYAL SOCIETY FOR THE PROTECTION OF BIRDS
The Lodge, Sandy, Beds.

BRITISH ORNITHOLOGISTS' UNION
British Museum (Natural History), London, S.W.7
Ibis (Journal)

UNITED NATIONS, New York, U.S.A.
Demographic Yearbook (annual)

UNESCO, Paris, France
A History of Land Use in Arid Lands, Paris, 1961

BRITISH ECOLOGICAL SOCIETY
See *Journal of Ecology, Journal of Animal Ecology, Journal of applied Ecology*
also *Memorandum on Nature Conservation and Nature Reserves*, 1943

FAUNA PRESERVATION SOCIETY, c/o Zoological Society, London, N.W.1
Oryx (Journal)

The New Naturalist Series

All the books in the New Naturalist series have a relevance in Nature Conservation, but of special significance may be noted:

BACKGROUND VOLUMES
4   *Britain's Structure and Scenery*. L. Dudley Stamp
31 *Man and the Land*. L. Dudley Stamp
25 *The Sea Coast*. J. A. Steers
35 *The World of the Soil*. E. John Russell
10 *British Plant Life*. W. B. Turrill
22 *Climate and the British Scene*. Gordon Manley

45   *The Common Lands of England and Wales.* W. G. Hoskins and L. Dudley Stamp

HABITAT VOLUMES

11   *Mountains and Moorlands.* W. H. Pearsall
12   *The Sea Shore.* C. M. Yonge
15   *Life in Lakes and Rivers.* T. T. Macan and E. B. Worthington
16   *Wild Flowers of Chalk and Limestone.* J. E. Lousley
17   *Birds and Men.* E. M. Nicholson
24   *Flowers of the Coast.* Ian Hepburn
28   *Sea-birds.* James Fisher and R. M. Lockley
32   *Trees, Woods and Man.* H. L. Edlin
33   *Mountain Flowers.* John Raven and Max Walters
43   *Weeds and Aliens.* Edward Salisbury

REGIONAL VOLUMES

3   *London's Natural History.* R. S. R. Fitter
6   (2nd Ed.) *The Highlands and Islands.* Fraser F. Darling and J. M. Boyd
26   *The Weald.* S. W. Wooldridge and F. Goldring
27   *Dartmoor.* L. A. Harvey and D. St. Leger-Gordon
44   *The Peak District.* K. C. Edwards
46   *The Broads.* E. A. Ellis
47   *Snowdonia National Park.* W. M. Condry

BIOLOGICAL GROUPS

1   *Butterflies.* E. B. Ford
2   *British Game.* Brian Vesey-Fitzgerald
5   *Wild Flowers.* John Gilmour and Max Walters
7   *Mushrooms and Toadstools.* John Ramsbottom
8   *Insect Natural History.* A. D. Imms
19   *Wild Orchids of Britain.* V. S. Summerhayes
20   *British Amphibians and Reptiles.* Malcolm Smith
21   *British Mammals.* L. Harrison Matthews
30   *Moths.* E. B. Ford
36   *Insect Migration.* C. B. Williams
48   *Grass and Grasslands.* I. Moore

Important also are the *Monographs* in the New Naturalist series. Volumes have been published covering the Badger, Squirrel, Rabbit, Redstart, Wren, Greenshank, Fulmar, Herring Gull, Heron, Hawfinch, House Sparrow, Salmon and Woodpigeon

General Works

Carson, Rachel. *Silent Spring.* Cambridge, Mass: Riverside Press, 1962
Clements, F. E. and Shelford, V. E. *Bio-ecology.* New York: Wiley, 1939
Dansereau, Pierre. *Biogeography: An Ecological Perspective.* New York: Ronald Press, 1957

Elgood, L. A. (Chairman). *Natural Resources in Scotland*. Symposium Scottish Council, 1961

Elton, Charles S. *The Ecology of Animals*. London: Methuen, 1933
The Ecology of Invasions by Animals and Plants. London: Methuen, 1958

Johns, C. A. *Flowers of the Field*. London: Routledge. Numerous edns.

Ritchie, James. *The Influence of Man on Animal Life in Scotland*. C.U.P., 1920

Schimper, A. F. W. *Plant Geography upon a Physiological Basis* (trans. W. R. Fisher). Oxford: Clarendon Press, 1903

Smith, Guy-Harold (ed.). *Conservation of Natural Resources*. New York: Wiley, 1950. 2nd ed. 1958

Stamp, L. Dudley. *Our Developing World*. London: Faber, 1960
(ed.) *The Land of Britain*. 92 County Parts. Bude: Geographical Publications, 1936–46
The Land of Britain: Its Use and Misuse. London: Longmans. 3rd ed., 1962
Land Use Statistics of the Countries of Europe. World Land Use Survey Occasional Paper 3, 1965. Bude
and Beaver, S. H. *The British Isles*. London: Longmans. 5th ed., 1963
The Geography of Life and Death. London: Collins, 1964

Stapledon, R. G. *The Land Now and Tomorrow*. London: Faber, 1935
A Survey of the Agricultural and Waste Lands of Wales. London: Faber, 1936
The Way of the Land. London: Faber, 1943

Steers, J. A. *Scolt Head* 2nd ed. Heffer, 1960
The Coastline of England and Wales. C.U.P., 1946
The Coast of England and Wales in Pictures. C.U.P., 1960

Tansley, Arthur G. *Types of British Vegetation*. C.U.P., 1911
Introduction to Plant Ecology. London: Allen and Unwin, 1947
The British Islands and their Vegetation. C.U.P., 1st ed. 1939
Our Heritage of Wild Nature. C.U.P., 1946
and Chipp, T. F. (editors). *Aims and Methods in the Study of Vegetation*. London: Crown Agents, 1926

Thomas, W. L. (ed.). *Man's Role in Changing the Face of the Earth*. University of Chicago Press, 1956

White, Gilbert. *Natural History of Selborne*. Various editions

Scientific Periodicals

Among the more important in the field may be noted:

Journal of Ecology, from 1912 ⎫ Published by Blackwell Scientific Pub-
Journal of Animal Ecology, from 1932 ⎬ lications Ltd., Oxford, on behalf of the
Journal of Applied Ecology, from 1964 ⎭ British Ecological Society

The Advancement of Science, British Association, 20 Great Smith Street, London, s.w.1

New Scientist, Cromwell House, High Holborn, London, w.c.1

Among periodicals which carry articles of interest to conservationists may be noted:

Country Life, The Field, Scottish Field, Countryman, Animals, Illustrated London News, Geographical Magazine, Birds, Ibis

Atlases and Maps

Atlas of Britain. Oxford Clarendon Press 1963 (with many distribution maps)

Complete Atlas of the British Isles. The Reader's Digest 1965 (distribution maps of all main mammals, birds, reptiles, amphibians, insects and wild flowers, with illustrations)

Atlas of British Flora and *Critical Supplement.* Nelson, 1962 and 1968

Stanford's Geological Atlas of Great Britain. London: Stanford 1964 (maps on small scale, black and white only)

Ordnance Survey: Agents: Edward Stanford Ltd., 12-14 Long Acre, London, w.c.2

    Large-scale maps   1 : 2,500 covering most of the country

                          1 : 10,560 (six inches to one mile), whole country

                          1 : 25,000

    Small-scale maps   1 : 63,360 (one inch to one mile), now show National Trust properties

                          1 : 253,440 (4 miles to one inch)

Geological Survey: same agents

    Colour-printed maps, scale one inch to one mile, cover part of the country only. Some in both solid and drift editions. Scale 4 miles to 1 inch, whole country. General map in two sheets, 1 : 625,000

Soil Survey: same agents

    Small number of sheets, scale 1 inch to 1 mile; each with memoir (see also Soil Survey of Great Britain; annual reports)

Land Utilisation Survey 1931–1945: same agents

    Colour-printed maps, scale 1 inch to 1 mile, cover the whole of England and Wales, also populous parts of Scotland, but many out of print. Also County Reports

Second Land Utilisation Survey 1960–; same agents, or King's College, London, w.c.2

    Colour-printed maps, scale 1 : 25,000. In progress

National Planning Series (Ministry of Housing and Local Government): same agents

    Scale 1 : 625,000 (approximately 10 miles to one inch) in two sheets. Include Relief, Geology, Vegetation, Land-use, Land Classification, Types of Farming and others. Some with explanatory text

APPENDIX I

Council for Nature

Patron: H.R.H. The Duke of Edinburgh, K.G.
Chairman: Sir Landsborough Thomson, C.B., O.B.E., D.SC., LL.D.

Vice-Chairmen:
{
Christopher Cadbury, M.A.
Sir Charles Connell, W.S., J.P.
Stanley Cramp, M.A.
Professor H. R. Hewer, O.B.E., M.SC., D.I.S., F.L.S.
E. Milne-Redhead, T.D., M.A., F.L.S.
Peter Scott, C.B.E., D.SC., LL.D.
}
Hon. Treasurer: R. S. R. Fitter
Hon. Secretaries: { Bruce Campbell, PH.D.
John Coleman-Cooke
Acting Secretaries: { Peter Conder
A. E. Smith, O.B.E., M.A.
Information Officer: Timothy Sands

Chairmen of Standing Committees:
Youth Committee Chairman: P. J. Prosser, B.SC.
Vice-Chairman: A. S. D. Pierssene, M.A.
Natural History Societies Committee Chairman: Professor H. R. Hewer, O.B.E., M.SC., D.I.C., F.L.S.
Vice-Chairman: Mrs. Grace Hickling, M.A.

The Council for Nature held its Inaugural Meeting in July 1958. In the revised constitution which came into force on 1st June 1968 it was stated that: the function of the Council shall be to co-ordinate the views and information of the voluntary bodies in the United Kingdom concerned with the conservation of nature and the study of natural history; on behalf or these bodies collectively, to make representations to H.M. Government and other authorities whenever necessary and to act in a central consultative capacity as required; both on particular questions and in general, to keep the need for nature conservation constantly before the public; and increasingly to interest young people in safeguarding the country's natural beauty and wild life.

The Council consists of the Chairman, Honorary Secretaries and Treasurer and representatives of the following affiliated and dependent bodies;

The Royal Society for the Protection of Birds
The Society for the Promotion of Nature Reserves and its County Naturalists' Trusts Committee
The Natural History Societies Committee
The Fauna Preservation Society
The Scottish Wildlife Trust
The Scottish Natural History Societies, as a Group

The Wildfowl Trust
The Field Studies Council
The Linnean Society of London
The Zoological Society of London
The Botanical Society of the British Isles
The Geological Society
The Royal Entomological Society
The Museums Association

The Council for Nature has around 400 constituent and affiliated bodies, which includes over 50 national societies, and over 1,200 individual associates and subscribers.

Minimum annual subscription payable by affiliated organisations is:

(i) for those with up to 50 members, £2;
(ii) for those with 51-100 members, £3;
(iii) for those with over 100 members, £5.

Organisations which are not suitable for affiliation can become associate members of the Council. Individual supporters may be enrolled as associates by subscribing £5 per annum or over, or as subscribers by paying £1 to £5 per annum.

In 1963 and again in 1966 the Council organised National Nature Weeks; the first national publicity campaign for natural history which led to the setting up of the *Countryside in 1970* Conference held in 1963 and 1965.

The Council is active in supporting (or approving where necessary) legislation affecting wildlife and its conservation.

The Council produces information sheets on subjects ranging from careers in natural history to natural history films. It organises exhibitions, film shows and competitions.

PUBLICATIONS:

Habitat at present published bi-monthly,which keeps naturalists and secretaries of naturalists' societies informed of the latest news and views on natural history and conservation. Items from *Habitat* also reach the general public as they are often taken up by the press, radio and TV.

Working for Nature, its annual report.

A Handbook for Naturalists, edited by Winwood Reade and R. M. Stuttard, published by Evans Brothers Ltd. in association with the Council, 12s. 6d.

Advice for young Naturalists, 1s.

Wildlife in Britain, by Richard Fitter, published for the Council by Penguin Books Ltd., 7s. 6d.

Predatory Mammals in Britain, a code of practice for their management, 5s.

Wildlife and the Countryside, magazine published nine times a year in association with the Council by the Countryman Ltd., 16s.

Conservation Corps

Chairman of the Management Committee: John Coleman-Cooke
Field Director: Richard Jennings
Address: Zoological Gardens, Regent's Park, London, N.W.1.
Telephone: 01-722 7111

Administered by a joint Management Committee composed of the Council for Nature and Soil Association members.

The Corps organises parties of volunteers (aged 16-25) to carry out conservation tasks (residential and weekend) in any part of Britain. Principal functions are scrub clearance, tree planting, salt marsh reclamation, hedgerow maintenance, laying nature trails and constructing footpaths. Field staff and senior volunteers include qualified scientists in all the earth sciences. Over the past 10 years about 50,000 man-days have been worked, and about 10,000 young people have taken part in the work. Grants to cover overheads, educational facilities, transport, etc., have been given by the Department of Education and Science, Soil Association, World Wildlife Fund, Dulverton Trust, Ernest Cook Trust and others. Future plans include the setting up of the Corps as an independent charity trust, formation of new branches to cover areas not at present well served, and general expansion to meet the growing need for conservation of the natural environment and the increasing numbers of young people who wish to volunteer for this work. Anyone wishing to subscribe to the Corps or to volunteer for work should write to the Field Director.

Society for the Promotion of Nature Reserves

As detailed in Chapter 2, the Society was founded in 1912 and received its Royal Charter in 1916 and owes much of its early success to the generous support of the Hon. Charles Rothschild. Its early work was concerned largely with the collection of information regarding areas suitable for conservation as nature reserves – in the United Kingdom or elsewhere in the Commonwealth – and to prepare schemes accordingly, but it also had powers to acquire reserves by gift, purchase, lease or agreement and further to transfer such interests as it might require to suitable trusts, including the National Trust, and local bodies. It has thus become the father of the county trusts which have come to exercise such wide influence, especially in England and Wales. It has a County Naturalists' Trusts' Committee with a Principal Advisory Officer (Mr. A. E. Smith). By the end of 1965 the number of County Trusts had increased from 8 in 1960 to 36 with a membership approaching 20,000. These trusts had 237 reserves (73 freehold, 65 leasehold, 93 managed or protected by agreement, and 6 statutory reserves) with a total acreage of over 21,000.

SOCIETY FOR THE PROMOTION OF NATURE RESERVES
President: J. Christopher Cadbury, M.A.
Hon. Treasurer: N. D. Riley, C.B.E.
Hon. Secretary: A. E. Smith, O.B.E., M.A., The Manor House, Alford, Lincs.
Principal Advisory Officer: A. E. Smith, O.B.E., M.A., The Manor House, Alford, Lincs.

Lists of County Naturalists' Trusts and their Secretaries

No attempt is made here to give the location or extent of the Trusts' reserves or the Trusts' interest in them. Those which the Trusts themselves like to draw attention to (by no means all!) have been carefully selected for mention in James

Fisher's Appendix IV (p. 221). Some are owned, some leased and others managed jointly in agreement with landowners, local authorities or other bodies, or established in collaboration. In all cases application for access and other details of reserves should be made to the secretary of the Trust concerned.

N.N.R.=National Nature Reserve. L.N.R.=Local (Statutory) Nature Reserve

BEDFORDSHIRE AND HUNTINGDONSHIRE NATURALISTS' TRUST, LTD.
Mrs. E. Lea, Riverside, New Road, Great Barford, Bedford

BERKSHIRE, BUCKINGHAMSHIRE AND OXFORDSHIRE NATURALISTS' TRUST LTD.
Captain Sir Thomas Barlow, R.N. (rtd.), Pednor Close, Pednor, Chesham, Bucks.

BRECKNOCK COUNTY NATURALISTS' TRUST LTD.
H. M. Bugden, The Byddwm, Llanhamlach, Brecon

CAMBRIDGE AND ISLE OF ELY NATURALISTS' TRUST LTD.
Robert S. Payne, No. 1 Brookside, Cambridge

CHESHIRE CONSERVATION TRUST, LTD.
Dr. R. E. Thomas, Haresclough, Whitegate, Northwich, Cheshire

CORNWALL NATURALISTS' TRUST, LTD.
J. K. Williams, Mount Pleasant, Tehidy, Camborne, Cornwall

DERBYSHIRE NATURALISTS' TRUST, LTD.
W. H. Wilcockson, 5 Newbould Lane, Sheffield 10

DEVON TRUST FOR NATURE CONSERVATION, LTD.
K. Watkins, Butterbrook, Harford, Ivybridge, Devon

DORSET NATURALISTS' TRUST, LTD.
Miss H. A. J. Brotherton, O.B.E., J.P., Island View, 58 Pearce Avenue, Parkstone, Poole, Dorset BH14 8EH

ESSEX NATURALISTS' TRUST, LTD.
S. T. Jermyn, 9 Buryfields, Felsted, Dunmow, Essex

GLAMORGAN COUNTY NATURALISTS' TRUST, LTD.
Group Capt. E. F. Campbell-Smith, 12 Caswell Drive, Mumbles, Swansea

GLOUCESTERSHIRE TRUST FOR NATURE CONSERVATION, LTD.
R. A. Wilkinson, O.B.E., The Woodlands, St. Briavels, Lydney, Glos. GL15 6QG

HAMPSHIRE AND ISLE OF WIGHT NATURALISTS' TRUST, LTD.
Col. V. W. Tregear, 17 Bell Street, Romsey, Hampshire

HEREFORDSHIRE AND RADNORSHIRE NATURE TRUST, LTD.
R. H. Bennett, Community House, 25 Castle Street, Hereford

HERTFORDSHIRE AND MIDDLESEX TRUST FOR NATURE CONSERVATION, LTD.
Mrs. O. W. Gray, 178 Tower Road, Ware, Hertfordshire

KENT NATURALISTS' TRUST, LTD.
A. P. Brown, Beech Hill, Cryals Road, Matfield, Tonbridge, Kent

LAKE DISTRICT NATURALISTS' TRUST,
W. Annis, Bleak House, Windermere, Westmorland

LANCASHIRE NATURALISTS' TRUST, LTD.
P. G. Garlick, 21 Hamilton Square, Birkenhead, Cheshire

LEICESTERSHIRE TRUST FOR NATURE CONSERVATION, LTD.
M. Walpole, 68 Outwoods Road, Loughborough, Leics.

LINCOLNSHIRE TRUST FOR NATURE CONSERVATION, LTD.
The Manor House, Alford, Lincolnshire

MONMOUTHSHIRE NATURALISTS' TRUST, LTD.
A. T. Sawyer, 40 Melbourne Way, Newport, Mon. NPT 3RF

NORFOLK NATURALISTS' TRUST, LTD.
Group Captain G. R. Montgomery, C.B.E., 4 The Close, Norwich, NOR 16 P

NORTHAMPTONSHIRE NATURALISTS' TRUST, LTD.
Mrs. M. E. L. Nobles, 2 Stanfield Road, Duston, Northampton

NORTHUMBERLAND AND DURHAM NATURALISTS' TRUST, LTD.
A. M. Tynan, The Hancock Museum, Newcastle-upon-Tyne NE2 4PT

NORTH WALES NATURALISTS' TRUST, LTD.
Dr. W. S. Lacey, School of Plant Biology, University College of N. Wales, Bangor, Caerns.

NOTTINGHAMSHIRE TRUST FOR NATURE CONSERVATION, LTD.
G. Boylin, 30 High Pavement, Nottingham NG1 1HR

SHROPSHIRE CONSERVATION TRUST, LTD.
C. L. Russell, Primrose Cottage, Sweeney Mountain, Oswestry, Shropshire

SOMERSET TRUST FOR NATURE CONSERVATION, LTD.
A. C. M. Hingley, Strangmans, Heale, Curry Rivel, Langport

STAFFORDSHIRE NATURE CONSERVATION TRUST, LTD.
Mrs. M. Castellan, The Old House, Wolsely Bridge, Stafford

SUFFOLK NATURALISTS' TRUST, LTD.
M. J. L. Taylor, County Hall, Ipswich, Suffolk

SURREY NATURALISTS' TRUST, LTD.
P. Sowan, 1 Chaucer Cottages, Pilgrims Way, Croham Road, S. Croydon

SUSSEX NATURALISTS' TRUST, LTD.
Woods Mill, Henfield

WEST MIDLANDS TRUST FOR NATURE CONSERVATION, LTD.
J. F. Benett, 59 Selly Park Road, Birmingham, 29

WEST WALES NATURALISTS' TRUST, LTD.
Dillwyn Miles, 4 Victoria Place, Haverfordwest, Pembrokeshire

WILTSHIRE TRUST FOR NATURE CONSERVATION, LTD.
J. C. C. Oliver, Tyning Wood, Gare Hill, Frome, Somerset

WORCESTERSHIRE NATURE CONSERVATION TRUST, LTD.
A. W. Wells, Foxhill, Ullenhall, Henley-in-Arden, Warwickshire

YORKSHIRE NATURALISTS' TRUST, LTD.
Clifford Chambers, Clifford Street, York

SCOTTISH WILDLIFE TRUST, LTD.
8 Dublin Street, Edinburgh 3

APPENDIX II

The Nature Conservancy

19-20 Belgrave Square, London, s.w.1

Note. The story of the work of the Nature Conservancy 1949-65 is told in Chapter 5. In 1965, with the creation of the Natural Environment Research Council, the Nature Conservancy surrendered its Royal Charter and became a committee of the Council, though its work continued as before. Dr. E. B. Worthington resigned as Scientific Director at the end of 1965 and Dr. Max Nicholson retired on 31st March 1966 as Director-General. The constitution as from May 1969 was as follows:

THE NATURE CONSERVANCY

Lord Howick of Glendale, G.C.M.G., K.C.V.O. (Chairman)
Sir Henry Beresford-Peirse, Bt., C.B.
Professor J. N. Black, D.SC., F.R.S.E.
Professor G. E. Blackman, F.R.S.
Professor R. Ogilvie Buchanan, PH.D.
Professor A. R. Clapham, F.R.S.
Sir Charles G. Connell, W.S., F.R.S.E., J.P.
Professor M. McG. Cooper, C.B.E., F.R.S.E.
The Earl of Cranbrook, C.B.E., D.L., J.P.
Dr. F. Fraser Darling, LL.D., F.R.S.E.
Professor T. Neville George, F.R.S., F.R.S.E.
Professor H. Godwin, F.R.S.
Professor P. Hall
D. W. Jones-Williams, M.C., T.D., LL.B.
A. E. Smith, O.B.E., M.A.
Dr. J. Eric Smith, F.R.S.
R. B. Verney, D.L., J.P.
Baroness Wootton of Abinger

The Scottish Committee: Sir Charles G. Connell, W.S., F.R.S.E. J.P. (Chairman)
Scientific Policy Committee: Chairman: Professor A. R. Clapham, F.R.S.
Committee for England: Chairman: R. B. Verney, D.L., J.P.
Committee for Wales: Chairman: D. W. Jones-Williams, M.C., T.D., LL.B.
Advisory Committee on Photography: Chairman: Eric Hosking, F.R.P.S., M.B.O.U.
Wildfowl Conservation Committee: Chairman: Peter Scott, C.B.E., D.S.C.

London Headquarters
Director: Duncan Poore, PH.D.
Deputies: R. E. Boote, B.SC.(ECON.); Martin Holdgate, PH.D.
Interpretive Branch: J. F. D. Frazer, M.A., D.M., PH.D.

Biometrics Section, Head: J. G. Skellam, M.A., F.I.BIOL.
Conservation Officer, England: B. Forman, PH.D.
Land Agent: J. V. Johnstone, A.R.I.C.S.
Merlewood Research Station: Director: J. N. R. Jeffers, F.I.S.
Furzebrook Research Station: Officer in Charge: M. V. Brian, M.A., D.SC.
Monks Wood Experimental Station: Director: K. Mellanby, C.B.E., SC.D., F.I.BIOL.
Coastal Ecology Research Station: Officer in Charge: D. S. Ranwell, PH.D.
Mountain and Moorland Ecology Station: Officer in Charge: A. Watson, PH.D.

Scotland Headquarters
12 Hope Terrace, Edinburgh EH9 2AS
Director: W. J. Eggeling, B.SC., PH.D., F.R.S.E.
Conservation Officer: J. Morton Boyd, PH.D., D.SC.
Land Agent: P. A. Hardie, A.R.I.C.S., A.L.A.S.

Wales Headquarters
Penrhos Road, Bangor, Caernarvonshire
Director: R. Elfyn Hughes, M.A., PH.D.
Assistant Director: T. O. Pritchard, B.SC., PH.D.

Regional Officers

England	North	Miss H. M. T. Frankland, B.SC., PH.D.	Merlewood
„	Midland	J. A. Thompson, B.SC.	Attingham Park
,	East Anglia	M. George, B.SC., PH.D.	Bracondale, Norwich
„	South-West	P. A. Gay, B.SC., PH.D.	Taunton
„	South	M. J. Williams, B.SC.	Brimpton, Berks.
⇀„	South-East	P. A. Gay, B.SC., PH.D.	Wye
Scotland	East	J. G. Roger, B.SC.	⎱ 12 Hope Terrace
„	West	R. N. Campbell, B.SC.	⎰ Edinburgh
„	South	J. McCarthy. B.SC.	
Wales	North	B. F. T. Ducker, B.SC.	Bangor
„	South	P. Walters Davies, B.SC.	Buarth Mawr, Aberystwyth

Summary of position as at September 1969

EXISTING NATIONAL NATURE RESERVES

	No. of Reserves	Acreage owned	Acreage leased	Under NRA	Total
England	62	15,567	20,641	22,476	58,684
Scotland	37	48,824	5,291	128,421	182,536
Wales	28	2,686	9,912	8,733	21,331
Total	127	67,077	35,844	159,630	262,551

THE NATURE RESERVES REVIEW 1968-69

The selection of N.N.R.'s of biological importance has always been based on the principle that they should form a series of areas representative of all the significant ecological systems in Britain and, as far as possible, of the range of variation within each. As new scientific knowledge is acquired and changes occur to areas not yet adequately safeguarded by the Conservancy, or it proves impossible to negotiate the inclusion of selected areas within the series, a review of reserve acquisition becomes necessary. Such a review seemed appropriate when the Conservancy became a component body of N.E.R.C. in 1965, particularly in view of increasing public concern about the growing demands on Britain's limited resources of land and water.

Dr. D. Ratcliffe is the Scientific Assessor of the Review and hopes to complete his work during the summer of 1969.

APPENDIX III

Field Studies Council

The Council for the Promotion of Field Studies, inspired and founded by F. H. C. Butler, had its inaugural meeting on 10 December, 1943, and Professor A. G. Tansley was elected as first President. Its object was to provide field centres for undergraduate students especially in geography, geology, botany and zoology for whom field courses are compulsory. Later facilities were extended to schools, especially sixth forms. In the early years it was difficult to obtain funds, but the first centre was opened at Dale Fort near Haverfordwest, Pembrokeshire, followed by Juniper Hall, Mickleham, Surrey, which was offered to the Council in 1946 and opened to students at Easter 1948. Other centres were added later and the Council changed its name to Field Studies Council in 1955 when Canon C. E. Raven, the second President, was in office, and Professor S. W. Wooldridge was Chairman of the Executive. Funds are derived from student fees (a hidden subsidy from Local Education Authorities), grants from universities (notably London), membership dues and some special grants, notably from the Drapers' Company. The Annual Reports include details from the Centres and until 1956-7 scientific papers. In May 1959 appeared the first number of *Field Studies*, a volume of research papers especially related to the areas around the centres and since published annually.

Officers 1966

President: Lord Hurcomb, G.C.E., K.B.E.
Vice-Presidents: The Earl of Cranbrook, Professor Sir Dudley Stamp
Chairman of Executive: Professor A. R. Clapham
Chairman of Finance and Administrative Committee: Professor W. F. Grimes
Secretary and Treasurer: R. S. Chapman, F.C.A., 9 Devereux Court, Strand
London, W.C.2

Field Centres

Dale Fort, nr. Haverfordwest, Pembrokeshire. Warden: J. H. Barrett, M.A.
Flatford Mill, East Bergholt, Suffolk. Warden: F. J. Bingley, M.A.
Juniper Hall, Mickleham, Surrey. Warden: J. H. P. Sankey, B.SC.
Malham Tarn, nr. Settle, Yorkshire. Warden: D. Bremner, B.SC.
Preston Montford, nr. Shrewsbury, Shropshire. Warden: C. A. Sinker, M.A.
Slapton Ley, Kingsbridge, Devon. Warden: I. D. Mercer, B.A.
Orielton, Pembroke. Warden: E. B. Cowell, B.SC.
Rhyd-y-Creua, nr. Bettws-y-Coed, North Wales (March 1967)
Nettlecombe Court, nr. Williton, Somerset (March 1967)

APPENDIX IV

Conservation and allied areas

in England, Wales and Scotland, by counties

Based on details to 1966 assembled by James Fisher, M.A., with acknowledgements to *Shell Nature Lover's Atlas* (London: Ebury Press and Michael Joseph) and to the help of Dr. Eric Duffey of the Nature Conservancy. Map references are to the National Grid.

BEDFORDSHIRE

Bedfordshire and Huntingdon-shire Naturalists' Trust has 8 reserves.

Sandy (TL1848, 1847). The Lodge is a Nature Reserve of the Royal Society for the Protection of Birds, and the headquarters of this, the largest conservation organization in the kingdom. Estate, 102 a., is perched on a wooded hill, with abundant birds.

Woburn Park (SP9632). Zoo. Magnificent vast park containing menagerie founded *c.* 1838; animals roam in liberty or in spacious paddocks. Fine birds, the world's greatest herd of Père David's deer and other extremely rare mammals. Admission fee.

Knocking Hoe (TL1132). National Nature Reserve since 1958, 22 a. Small relict of close-grazed chalk downland turf with rich flora. By permit only.

Totternhoe Knolls (SP9822). Nature Reserve of B.H.N.T.

Whipsnade Zoo (TL0017). Whipsnade Zoological Park, of the Zoological Society of London, founded 1927, 567 a. The spacious country satellite of the London Zoo, with about 240 species of animals suitable for vast paddocks. World rarities in collection, interesting exotic birds, wild bird sanctuary. Admission fee.

BEDFORDSHIRE - HERTFORDSHIRE - BUCKINGHAMSHIRE - OXFORDSHIRE

Chilterns (N-E-S-W TL 0531 + 1331 – 1628 — SU6775 – 5980 + 5984). Area of Outstanding Natural Beauty confirmed 1965, embracing 309 sq. mi. of these classic chalk downlands from Luton to Goring.

BERKSHIRE

Berkshire, Buckinghamshire and Oxfordshire Naturalists' Trust has 36 reserves in the three counties.

Cothill (SU4599). National Nature Reserve since 1956, 4 a., of National Trust and Nature Conservancy. The Ruskin Reserve. Rich botanical swamp; by permit only.

BERKSHIRE and SURREY

Windsor Forest and Great Park (SU9176–9872). A vast royal nature reserve, in effect; and deer park. Interesting waterfowl around Virginia Water. Part of the Forest, at High Standing Hill, Berks (9374), is a 45 a. Forest Nature Reserve since 1956.

221

BUCKINGHAMSHIRE

B.B.O.N.T., *see* Berkshire.

Ascott, Wing (SP8922). National Trust. Arboretum (fine conifers and flowering trees), garden, lake. Access seasonal; admission fee.

Boarstall (SP6215). Duck decoy. Ringing Station of Wildfowlers' Association of Great Britain and Ireland.

Dancer's End (SP9009). Nature Reserve of the Society for the Promotion of Nature Reserves, 76 a.; typical Chiltern woodland.

Coombe Hill (SP8406). Nature Reserve, in effect, of National Trust. Interesting heath and scrub ecology; fine views.

Church Wood, Hedgerley (SU9787). Nature Reserve of the Royal Society for the Protection of Birds, 40 a.

Dropmore House (SU9286). Fine arboretum, dating from 1795, lake and natural bird sanctuary. Private.

Cliveden (SU9185). National Trust, in effect Nature Reserve in beautiful gardens and woodland. Access seasonal; admission fee.

Burnham Beeches (SU9585). Large Nature Reserve, in effect, of the City of London Corporation; good woodland birds and insects.

CAMBRIDGESHIRE

Cambridge and Isle of Ely Naturalists' Trust has 10 reserves and one nature trail.

Wicken Fen (TL5570). Nature Reserve of the National Trust, 320 a.; a classic relict of old East Anglian fenland with a remarkable community of plants and insects, many very rare, deeply studied for years. A Regional Wildfowl Refuge since 1957.

Chippenham Fen (TL6469). National Nature Reserve since 1963, 193 a. Another fen relict, this one of valley type and peaty. Very rare plants and insects. By permit off footpaths.

University Botanic Gardens, Cambridge (TL4557). Though founded later (1761), a rival in comprehensiveness to that at Oxford, with magnificent alpines and winter-flowering plants. Free admission.

Wandlebury (TL4953). Iron Age hill fort and Nature Trail of C.I.E.N.T. and Cambridge Preservation Society.

CHESHIRE

Cheshire Conservation Trust has 5 reserves

East Wood, Stalybridge (SJ9797). Nature Reserve of the Royal Society for the Protection of Birds, 12 a. By permit only.

Hilbre Islands (SJ1887). Nature Reserve of Hoylake Urban District Council; a great refuge for waders on passage.

Harrock Wood, Irby (SJ2684). Nature Reserve of the National Trust.

Rostherne Mere (SJ7484). National Nature Reserve since 1961, 327 a. Finest of the famous Cheshire Meres, and notable for its water fauna. Also a National Wildfowl Refuge, studied from A. W. Boyd Memorial Observatory, the only custom-built, architect-designed 'hide' in the business. By permit only.

Peak District National Park. A strip of this great recreational area, averaging about 2½ miles wide, lies in Cheshire (SJ9684 – 9363) from Park Moor through Macclesfield Forest to the Minns. *See* Derbyshire.

Cotterill Clough (SJ8083). Nature Reserve (T. A. Coward Memorial), 13½ a., of C.C.T. and Society for the Promotion of Nature Reserves.

Lyme Park (SJ9682). Fine gardens and park of 1320 a., with red deer. Access seasonal; admission fee.

Weston Marsh, Runcorn (SJ5180). Nature Reserve of the Merseyside Naturalists' Association.

Tatton Park and Mere (around SJ 7580). Vast public park with fine trees and many wildfowl on passage and in winter.

Marbury or **Budworth Mere** (SJ 6576). Within this unofficial wildfowl refuge Marbury Reedbed, Nature Reserve (T. A. Coward Memorial), 6 a., of the C.C.T. and S.P.N.R.

Ness (SJ 3075). Botanic Gardens of Liverpool University, based on a previous comprehensive private collection.

Burton Wood (SJ3174). Nature Reserve of the National Trust.

Chester Zoo (SJ4170). Gardens of the North of England Zoological Society since 1930, 150 a. Magnificent flowers and an imaginatively housed collection of c. 550 species of animals, including gorillas, rare rhinos, fine elephants. Admission fee.

Wybunbury Moss (SJ6950). National Nature Reserve since 1955, 26 a. A *schwingmoor* or floating raft of 6 to 10 ft., *Sphagnum* with a most interesting plant community growing on it. By permit only.

CORNWALL

Cornwall. Areas of Outstanding Natural Beauty confirmed 1959, 360 sq. mi.; march with N. and S. Devon A.O.N.B.s. Virtually the whole coast from N. and S. Devon boundaries except urbanized stretches and the Newquay coast. Also Bodmin Moor.

Cornwall Naturalists' Trust has 7 reserves.

Millook Haven (SS1800). Geology; interesting zigzag-folded Culm measures.

Peter's Wood, Boscastle (SX1190). Nature Reserve of National Trust and C.N.T., 25 a.

Pentire Point (SW9280 – 9680). Geology; fine cliff section showing Devonian pillow lavas.

Trebetherick Point (SW9277). Geology; Pleistocene shore deposits.

Walmsley Sanctuary, Wadebridge (SX0074). Regional Wildfowl Refuge since 1948, 42 a., accessible fully to members of Cornwall Bird Watching and Preservation Society only. Good passage waders and winter wildfowl.

Trethias Island (SW8573). Nature Reserve of the C.B.W.P.S.

The Cheesewring (SX2572). Geology; quarry shows typical Bodmin granite, with erosion; a topaz locality.

Luckett, Stoke Climsland (SX3972). Nature Reserve of Cornwall Naturalists' Trust, 19 a. Partially cleared woodland with rare insects and plants.

Hawke's Wood, Wadebridge (SW 9871). Nature Reserve of C.N.T. c. 9 a.

Lanhydrock House (SX0863). Fine garden. Public access seasonal; admission fee. National Trust.

Clicker Tor Quarry, Menheniot (SX2861). Geology; Clicker Tor picrite; distinctive igneous rock and boulders.

Roche Rock (SW9959). Geology; a classic granite outcrop. Also ancient chapel.

Tregargus Quarry, St. Stephen (SW 9454). Geology; a classic china-stone deposit.

St John's Lake, The Hamoaze, Torpoint (SX4254). Big area of tidal mudflats, with passage and wintering waterfowl and waders.

Cligga Head and St. Agnes (SW7353 – 7050). At Cligga Head interesting mineral geology at junction of killas and granite (7353). At St Agnes Pits (7251) Pliocene deposits. Good views from National Trust's St Agnes Beacon (7050).

Trewithen, Probus (SW9147). Fine garden. Public access seasonal; admission fee.

River Fal and Trelissick (SW8540, 8439). Estuary (birds) and fine garden and woodlands (National Trust). Public access seasonal; admission fee.

Dodman Point (SW9940 – SX0039). Fine headland, views, Bronze Age fort; beach and cove at Hemmick (National Trust).

Zennor and Zennor Quoit (SW4439 – 4638). Fine headland (National Trust) and cromlech.

Hayle Estuary (SW5437). Private nature sanctuary, with accommodation; apply Mr. and Mrs. Woolfrey, Woodcote, Lelant.

St. Erth (SW5535). Geology; sand pits, Pliocene deposits.

Trengwainton House (SW4431). Fine shrub and woodland gardens (National Trust). Public access seasonal, free.

Penjerrick (SW7730). Fine subtropical gardens; great variety. Public access seasonal, free.

Helford River and Glendurgan (SW 7026 – 7727). Fine wooded river scenery; estuary birds. At Glendurgan (7727) fine valley garden (National Trust); public access seasonal, free.

The Loe (SW6424). Fine wood-sided lagoon: a natural waterfowl refuge.

Lowland Point (SW8019). Geology; Ice Age raised beach; views of the Manacles, etc. (National Trust).

Lizard (SW6813). National Trust. Geology, botany, views and bird migration watch point.

Scilly. Almost the whole archipelago deserves some national status, perhaps as a National Nature Park. The islands have a very interesting ecology with rare plants and animals, many at the edge of their range and represented by island forms and races.

Tresco Abbey, Scilly (SV8914). Unique subtropical gardens open weekdays; admission fee.

Annet, Scilly (SV 8608). Bird Sanctuary; access controlled.

St. Agnes, Scilly (SV8808). Bird Observatory.

CUMBERLAND – NORTH-UMBERLAND
The Border Forests and Border National Forest Park, see Scotland, Dumfries.

CUMBERLAND – WESTMOR-LAND – LANCASHIRE
Lake District Naturalists' Trust has 9 reserves.

Lake District National Park (N-E-S-W NY3141 – 5609 – SD4377 – NY 0314). Largest of our National Parks, 866 sq. mi., and second to be confirmed, 1951. Wordsworth's dream of 150 years ago come true. The glories of the compact and thrilling lakes, and highest mountains of England. Most of the Cumberland places that follow are within this galaxy of scenic waters, dales and hills.

CUMBERLAND
Border Forests and Border National Forest Park, see Dumfries, Scotland.

Butterburn Flow, Gilsland (NY 6774). Forestry Commission; a *Sphagnum* bog complex of great ecological interest.

Solway Coast (N-E-SW NY3365 – 3560 – 0336). Area of Outstanding Natural Beauty confirmed 1965, 41 sq. mi. Includes Rockcliffe Marsh (NY 3464 – 3062), great winter wildfowl haunt.

Grune Point, Skinburness (NY 1456). Bird migration key point and ringing station.

Thornthwaite Forest (N-E-S-W NY 2033 – 2527 – 1922 – 1432). State Forest of the Forestry Commission

since 1920, 4875 a., of rather scattered forest and moorland.
The Swirls and Launchy Gill, Thirlmere (NY3116, 3015). Nature Trails of the Manchester Corporation.
St. Bee's Head (NX9413). Sea-bird colonies, including fulmars.
Kirk and Wasdale Fells (NY1810 – 2109). National Trust. Mountains include part of the climbers' paradise of Great Gable.
Sca Fell (NY2209 – 2004). National Trust. Hills embrace Sca Fell Pike, 3210 ft., England's highest mountain.
Hardknott (N-E-S-W NY2308 – 2703 – SD2297 – NY2000). National Forest Park of the Forestry Commission; a park within a park. One woodland in Lancashire.
Drigg Dunes and Ravenglass (SD 0497 – 0795). Local Nature Reserve of the Cumberland County Council and Nature Conservancy since 1954, 583 a. Interesting plant ecology and largest black-headed gullery in the kingdom. By permit only.

DERBYSHIRE
Castleton Caves (SK1383 – 1680). At least five fossil exploration sites, which have disclosed much human history and many animal bones from the Upper Pleistocene to the Bronze Age.
Wye Valley Caves, Buxton (SK0877, 0472). Important sites of Pleistocene fossil fauna.
Nottinghamshire Border Caves (SK 5374 – 5165). Cresswell, Langwith Bassett, Pleasley Vale; very important Pleistocene and Old Stone Age fossil sites.
Chatsworth (SK2670). Great Park with superb gardens and fine trees. Access seasonal; admission fee.
Pan's Garden, Ashover (SK3463). Zoo, founded 1955, 2 a. About 180 species; admission fee.

Brassington – Bradbourne Caves (SK2455 – 1950). Hoe Grange, Harboro (Giant's), Rain's and Ravencliff; sites of human artefacts and fossil fauna from Pleistocene to Roman times.
Trent College, Long Eaton (SK 4833). Arboretum; perhaps the best in the Midlands.
Melbourne Hill (SK3825). Magnificent formal garden with fine trees. Access seasonal; admission fee.

DERBYSHIRE – CHESHIRE – YORKSHIRE – STAFFORDSHIRE
Peak District National Park (N-E-S-W SE0711 – SK3267 – 1848 + 1248 – SJ9266). The first of our National Parks to be confirmed (17 April 1951), 542 sq. mi. The great hill country of the southern end of the Pennine Chain, England's backbone, highest point Kinder Scout (2,088 ft.); a recreational and intellectual paradise tenderly cared for by a forward-looking Planning Board. Many reserves and sites of interest lie within its bounds. Only a few groups of caves are cited.

DEVON – CORNWALL
Tamar Lake (SS2911). Regional Wildfowl Refuge since 1951, 75 a., also gull-roost.

DEVON
Devon Trust for Nature Conservation has 14 reserves.
Woody Bay (SS6749). Nature Reserve, in effect, of National Trust and Exmoor Society, since 1966.
North Devon (N-E-SW SS5448 – 6244 – 2117). Area of Outstanding Natural Beauty confirmed 1960, 66 sq. mi.; marches with Cornish A.O.N.B. and Exmoor National Park.
Watersmeet (SS7448). National Trust.

Fine woodland (good birds) in East Lyn river gorge.

Ilfracombe Zoo Park (SS5246). Zoological gardens founded in 1949. About 160 species of animals. Admission fee.

Lundy (around SS1345). Many breeding sea-birds and rare migrants; one indigenous plant, the Lundy cabbage. Observatory since 1947 of Lundy Field Society, 1,100 a., National Trust Reserve. Fine sea-birds, key migration point, rare plants. Boats from Bideford and Ilfracombe.

Chapel Wood, Spreacombe (SS 4841). Nature Reserve, 13 a., of Royal Society for the Protection of Birds, and Devon Bird Watching and Preservation Society. By permit only.

Arlington Court, Barnstaple (SS 6140). Bird Reserve of National Trust, with heronry and duck refuge.

Braunton Burrows (SS4437 – 4631). National Nature Reserve since 1964, 560 a. with facilities for scientific research over further 932. Great sand dune system of deep botanical interest; danger from unexploded missiles.

Hartland Point to Speak Valley (SS2227 – 2223). Nature Reserve of Devon Trust for Nature Conservation, since 1966.

East Devon (N-E-S-W ST1800 – SY 3495 – 0379 – 0180). Area of Outstanding Natural Beauty confirmed 1963, 103 sq. mi. Marches with Dorset A.O.N.B.

Dartmoor National Park (N-E-S-W SX6195 – 8481 – 6556 – 4680). National Park confirmed 1951, 365 sq. mi. Magnificent moors and tors on granite upland, and very interesting botany. Full of prehistoric treasures.

Axmouth – Lyme Regis Undercliffs (SY2589 – 3391). National Nature Reserve since 1955, 793 a. Geology: the Dowlands Cliffs and Landslips; also interesting plant communities. By permit off footpaths.

Bicton Gardens, East Budleigh (SY 0786). A classic formal garden laid out in 1735 with later developments, including pinetum and waterfowl collection.

Bovey Valley Woodlands (SX7582 – 8078). National Nature Reserve since 1963, 179 a. Rudge, Woodash and Houndtor Woods, best Dartmoor native hardwoods. By permit off footpaths.

Exmouth (around SX9980). Exmouth Aquarium founded 1951 (about 70 species) and Exmouth Zoo founded 1957 (about 60 species); admission fees. Exe Estuary good bird-watching centre with wader passage and wintering wildfowl, including brent geese; a National Wildfowl Refuge of 1,022 a. since 1951.

Chudleigh (SX8678 – 8979). Geology: Dunscombe Farm quarry a famous locality for Upper Devonian goniatite-limestone; Chudleigh Cave, a classic fissure site, has yielded vast numbers of Pleistocene fossils.

Yarner Wood (SX7778). National Nature Reserve since 1952, 361 a. By permit only.

Wistman's Wood (SX6177). Forest Nature Reserve since 1961, 63 a. of Duchy of Cornwall and Nature Conservancy.

Black Tor Copse (SX5770). Forest Nature Reserve since 1961, 72 a. of Duchy of Cornwall and Nature Conservancy.

Dendles Wood (SX6161). National Nature Reserve since 1965, 73 a. By permit only.

Buckfastleigh (SX7466). Geology: caves, including famous Joint Mitnor, yielding important Pleistocene fossils, now in Society for the Promotion of Nature Reserves' 11 a. reserve; also Pengelly Caves (Higher Kiln Quarry), reserve of D.T.N.C.

Torquay (around SX9164). Aquarium: Aqualand, Beacon Quay, founded

1955; admission fee. Gardens: Torre Abbey (9063). Geology: Lummaton Quarry (9266) shows rich Devonian fossil fauna; Kent's Hole (9263) a classic Pleistocene-Stone Age bone site first excavated in 1824.
Dartington Hall (SX 7962). School estate managed so as to amount to a local nature reserve.
South Devon (N-E-S-W SX8260 – 9456 – 7734 – 4850). Area of Outstanding Natural Beauty confirmed 1960, 128 sq. mi. Nearly marches with Dartmoor National Park.
Paignton (around SX8860). Gardens: Oldway; Italian and grotto. Aquarium; Paignton Seashore Aquarium, South Quay, founded 1954; admission fee. Zoo: Paignton Zoological and Botanical Gardens, founded 1923; very fine, well-housed collection of about 570 species, good tropical animals; admission fee.
Plymouth (SX4654 – 5053). Aquarium: Marine Biological Association of the United Kingdom; founded 1888, famous research collection of about 90 species; small admission fee. At Oreston interesting Pleistocene bone cave.
Slapton (SX8244). Slapton Ley Field Centre, Field Studies Council; birds, insects, plants, ecological research. Associated Bird Observatory also at Slapton Bird Cabin, D.B.W.P.S.
Overbecks, Salcombe (SX7338). National Trust museum and gardens.

DORSET
Dorset Naturalists' Trust has 9 reserves.
Dorset. Area of Outstanding Natural Beauty confirmed 1959, 400 sq. mi. A thick strip of virtually the whole coast save Weymouth and Portland and the western interior south of a line from Yeominster to (ST8210) Shillingstone. Marches with E. Devon A.O.N.B.
Minterne, Cerne Abbas (ST6604).

N.C.B.

Classic rhododendron collection, with over a thousand species and hybrids.
Morden Bog (SY9091). National Nature Reserve since 1956, now 367 a. Bird Sanctuary. By permit only.
Arne (SY9586 – 9889). National Nature Reserve in Big Wood since 1954, 9 a.; and Nature Reserve of Royal Society for the Protection of Birds, 680 a. Mainly for birds, a classic Dartford warbler place. By permit only.
Brownsea Island (SZ0288). Nature Reserve of National Trust and D.N.T. Mainly for birds, heronry. Poole Harbour is a great wader and wildfowl refuge.
Hartland Moor (SY9485). National Nature Reserve since 1954, now 637 a. Permit needed, and danger from unexploded bombs.
Studland Heath (SZ0184). National Nature Reserve since 1962, 429 a. Interesting heathland ecology and rare birds and reptiles. No permit needed. Unexploded missile danger.
Abbotsbury (SY5785–5784). Garden: fine collection of subtropical exotics. Swannery: part of second oldest nature reserve in the kingdom, flourishing in 1393 and sole breeding place of a great herd of mute swans in England. Access seasonal; admission fee.
Chesil Beach (SY5683 – 6675). Geology: an 18-mile unbroken pebble ridge about 170 yd. wide and to 35 ft. high, the finest coastal formation of its kind in Europe.
Furzebrook Research Station, Wareham (SY9383). Nature Conservancy. Lowland heath and physiographic research.
Radipole Lake (SY6779 – 6780). Nature Reserve of Weymouth Corporation since 1948. A Regional Wildfowl Refuge of 70 a.
Lulworth Cove (SY8279). Geology: classic example of the marine erosion of chalk. East of cove Fossil Forest;

Q

domed tufa masses with hollows once occupied by tree trunks.
Portland Bill (SY6868). Geology: Portland building stone quarries; 20 – 50 ft raised beach. Ornithology: Portland Bird Observatory and Field Centre, important link in our chain of migration-study stations.

DURHAM
Northumberland and Durham Naturalists' Trust has 4 reserves.
Marsden Rock (NZ4064). Fine stack with breeding sea-birds. Cave at Whitburn Lizards nearby (4163) disclosed evidence of Stone Age hunters who ate sea-birds.
Hawthorn Dene (NZ4345). Nature Reserve of N.D.N.T.
Castle Eden Denes (NZ4138 – 4540). Local Nature Reserve since 1954 of Durham County Council, other authorities and Nature Conservancy, 517 a. Only surviving good example of Co. Durham woodlands in gorges running to coast. Rare plants and insects and unique geology. By permit off footpaths.
Black Halls Rocks (NZ4738). Nature Reserve of N.D.N.T.
Dryerdale, Hamsterley (NZ0833). Fine private arboretum.
Teesmouth (NZ5328 – 5025). Bird Observatory. Nature Reserve planned embracing Seaton Common, North Gare Sands, part of Cowpen Marsh and Greatham Creek section of c 1500 a. Seal Sands.
Wynyard Forest (NZ4027 – 4115). State Forest of Forestry Commission with associated private woodland.
Raby Castle, Staindrop (NZ1221). Fine gardens with good trees, 10 a. Access seasonal; admission fee.

ESSEX
Essex Naturalists' Trust has 10 reserves.

Hales Wood (TL5740). National Nature Reserve since 1955, 20 a.; wardened by Saffron Walden Countryside Association; access by permit.
Tewes, Little Sampford (TL6433). Fine house and garden, waterfowl moat. Access seasonal; admission fee.
Mole Hall, Widdington (TL5431). Small but interesting zoo, opened 1965. Admission fee.
Stansted Wildlife Reserve (TL 5126). Almost a park zoo, 50 a. Nature Reserve in effect, plus fine exotic waterfowl. Access seasonal; admission fee.
Colchester (TL9925). Zoo here from 1965: admission fee.
Hamford Water Saltings (Horsey I. TM2324). Long proposed as Nature Reserve, though not yet so. Fine waterfowl at all seasons, including feral greylag flock.
Hatfield Forest (TL5319). Nature Reserve, in effect, of the National Trust. Fine old woodland with varied bird community.
Abberton Reservoir (TL9818). E. Anglia's largest lake. Great duck population and rare breeding waterbirds. Most active Duck Ringing Station in Britain.
Blackwater Marshes (Mersea I. TM 0415, The Ray TM0014, Salcott Channel TL9812). No part yet Nature Reserve or Refuge; should be. Fine area for winter wader and wildfowl watching.
Bradwell (TM0007). Bird Observatory manned in migration season at key watching point.
Epping Forest (TQ3895 – TL4400). Nature Reserve in effect, and long proposed as official one; owned by Corporation of City of London, and the nearest semi-natural forest (with nightingales and deer) to St. Paul's. High Beech Field Study Centre, sponsored by Walthamstow, in heart (4097).
Hainault Forest (TQ4894). Nature

Reserve, in effect, of Greater London Council.

South Essex Woodlands (TQ8392 – 7887). Nature Reserves of public-spirited local authorities at Bull Wood, Hockley (Rochford), Belfairs Great Wood, Hadleigh (Southend-on-Sea), and Shipwrights Wood and The Glen, Thundersley (Benfleet).

Hadleigh Marshes (TQ8185). Nature Reserve of Essex County and Benfleet Urban District Councils.

Gray's Chalk Quarry (TQ5979). Nature Reserve of E.N.T., since 1966.

Flatford Mill. Field Centre; *see* Suffolk.

Lea Valley, *see* Greater London.

GLOUCESTERSHIRE

Gloucestershire Trust for Nature Conservation has 24 reserves.

Cotswolds. Area of Outstanding Natural Beauty, *see* Worcestershire.

Hidcote Manor (SP1742). National Trust. Beautiful garden with fine tree collection. Access seasonal; admission fee.

Batsford Park (SP1833). Private arboretum of merit.

Bourton-on-the-Water Zoo (SP 1620). The Birdland Zoo Gardens, founded 1957, 2½ a. A bird zoo under tender management; many exotics at liberty. Penguins to humming birds. Admission fee.

Forest of Dean, *see* Wales, Monmouth.

Wildfowl Trust, Slimbridge (SO 7204 – 7207). Zoo; and a special one. Founded 1946, 35 a., the main wildfowl (flamingos, swans, geese, ducks) collection of the Trust, by far the most comprehensive (85 per cent of all living species) the world has known. More free-winged birds than not. Big Russian whitefront flock winters on the Dumbles. Duck decoy for ringing. Admission fee, and privileges for Trust members.

Westonbirt Arboretum (ST8489). A remarkable collection of exotic trees planted from 1829 and in their prime and beautifully disposed. Forestry Commission since 1956, 116 a. Free admission.

Clifton Zoo (ST5674). The Gardens of the Bristol, Clifton and West of England Zoological Society, 12 a., founded 1835. A gem of a zoo with beautiful gardens and well-managed collection of about 330 species; admission fee.

GREATER LONDON

On 1 April 1965 the new Greater London absorbed most of Middlesex and parts of Essex, Kent and Surrey. The rest of Middlesex passed to Hertfordshire and Surrey. As most naturalists, and some County Naturalists' Trusts, are likely to continue to observe the more ancient boundaries when logging their records, the old counties are mentioned.

Kent Naturalists' Trust has 2 reserves in this area.

Ruislip and Bourne Farm (TQ 0689 – 0889, *ex* Mdx.). Local Nature Reserve since 1959, 11 a. Under local authority and Nature Conservancy; Nature Reserve of l.a. (reservoir); and Nature Reserve of Hertfordshire and Middlesex Trust for Nature Conservation and l.a. (Bourne Farm) since 1966. Access to parts by permit.

London Zoo (TQ2883). The gardens of the Zoological Society of London in the Regent's Park, 36 a. The kingdom's oldest (opened 1828) and finest mainstream living animal collection. Over 1400 species, including inhabitants of magnificent aquarium. Admission fee.

Tower of London (TQ3380). Ravens represent the relics of the Royal Menagerie, the oldest surviving zoo in the world, founded in or before 1252.

Inner London Parks (Hyde Park

Corner TQ2879). Nature Reserves, in effect, and managed as such by Ministry of Works, with surprisingly varied wild bird fauna in Regent's, Green and Hyde Parks and Kensington Gardens. St James's Park (2979) has been Nature Reserve of a sort since 1536; present exotic royal waterfowl collection has continuous history since restoration of, and by, Charles II in 1660. Nearby, at 19 Belgrave Square, s.w.1, H.Q. of the Nature Conservancy.

Osterley Park (TQ1478, *ex* Mdx.). National Trust. Present waterfowl collection founded in late 18th C. Free admission to gardens.

Barn Elms Reservoir (TQ2277, *ex* Surrey). Wildfowl Refuge in effect; rare wintering duck and gull roost.

Battersea Park Children's Zoo (TQ 2877). Founded 1951, ⅓ a. About 80 species. Access seasonal; admission fee.

Greenwich Park (TQ3977). Nature Reserve in effect, under Ministry of Works.

Syon House, Brentford (TQ1776, *ex* Mdx.). Remarkable exotic plant collection. Access seasonal; admission fee.

Royal Botanic Gardens, Kew (TQ 1876, *ex* Surrey). The great national collection of living plants, 300 a., 25,000 species and varieties. Arboretum and magnificent tropical house and alpines. Founded 1759; had menagerie until present century; and still has exotic waterfowl. Nominal admission fee.

Richmond Park (TQ2073, *ex* Surrey). Nature Reserve, in effect, under Ministry of Works. Fine deer herds, heronry and rare wildfowl.

Crystal Palace Children's Zoo (TQ 3470, *ex* Kent). Founded 1953, ¾ a. About 80 species. Access seasonal; admission fee.

Hampton Court (TQ1568, *ex* Mdx.). One of world's greatest formal gardens, with amazing collection of exotics from 4151. Admission free.

The Wood, Surbiton (TQ1967, *ex* Surrey). Nature Reserve of Surbiton Corporation.

Chessington Zoo (TQ1762, *ex* Surrey). Founded 1931, 65 a. About 310 species, in fine flower garden. Admission fee.

Downe (TQ4361, *ex* Kent). Down House the home and workplace of Charles Darwin, held by the Royal College of Surgeons of England, not open Fridays; admission fee.

GREATER LONDON and ESSEX

Lea Valley Reservoirs (TQ3488 – 3797). Wildfowl Refuges, in effect, of Metropolitan Water Board. Access by permit. A large lower Lea Valley area may be made a Regional Park, if the thoughtful advice of the London Natural History Society is appreciated.

HAMPSHIRE (MAINLAND)

Hampshire and Isle of Wight Naturalists' Trust has 12 reserves.

East Hampshire (N-E-S-W SU7536–8029 – 7412 – 4826). Area of Outstanding Natural Beauty confirmed 1962, 151 sq. mi.

Waggoners' Wells and Ludshott Common (SU8534 – 8435). Nature Reserves, in effect, of National Trust; interesting heath and woodland, and hammer ponds.

Selborne Common and Hanger (SU 7333). Nature Reserve of National Trust, still in the inspiring natural state that fired Gilbert White to study and write of the animals and plants of the Hampshire scarplands.

Pigeon Copse, Liss (SU7728). Nature Reserve of R.S.P.B., 21 a.; access by permit.

Old Winchester Hill (SU6421). National Nature Reserve since 1954, 140 a., some danger from unexploded bombs.

Oxenbourne Down (SU7119). Nature Reserve of H.I.W.N.T., since 1966, 126 a.
New Forest (north to SU1717 – 2517). This vast relict of England's ancient wilderness (somewhat modified) is a paradise for every kind of naturalist, from mycologist to herpetologist, bryologist to lepidopterist. Within its 100 sq. mi. (and more) are Bramshaw Forest Nature Reserve, since 1959, 525 a. (2516), Mark Ash F.N.R., since 1959, 226 a. (2407), and Matley and Denny F.N.R., since 1959, 2,557 a. (3206 – 3906); also Long Aldermoor Nature Reserve of H.I.W.N.T., 6½ a., since 1966 (2809). Noble beech stands at Eyeworth (2215), Bushey Bratley (2208) and Mark Ash (2407), and yew in Sloden Inclosure (2013).
Catherington Down (SU6914). Nature Reserve of the Hampshire C.C. and H.I.W.N.T.
Farlington Marshes (SU 6804 – 6803). Nature Reserve of H.I.W.N.T., 300 a.; waders, and wildfowl in Langstone Harbour.
Exbury Gardens (SU4200). Fine arboretum and rhododendron-azalea collection, 250 a. Access seasonal, admission fee.
Stanpit Marsh (SZ1691). Local Nature Reserve since 1964, 145 a., of H.I.W.N.T., Christchurch B.C. and Nature Conservancy. Access restricted in bird breeding season.

HAMPSHIRE and SUSSEX
Chichester Harbour (N-E-S-W SU 7206 – 8502 – SZ7697 – SU7105). Area of Outstanding Natural Beauty confirmed 1964, 29 sq. mi.

ISLE OF WIGHT
Isle of Wight. Area of Outstanding Natural Beauty confirmed 1963, 73 sq. mi. Stretches to extremities of the is-

land, but not Parkhurst Forest or main towns.
Osborne (SZ5194). Nature Reserve, in effect, under Ministry of Works.
Town Copse, Newtown (SZ4290). Nature Reserve, in effect, of National Trust; estuarine woodland; good birds.
The Needles to Tennyson Down (SZ 2984 – 3385). Geology: magnificent example of marine erosion of chalk. T. Down is National Trust scenic cliffland.
Isle of Wight Zoo, Sandown (SZ 5984). Founded 1955. About 100 species; admission fee.
St. Catherine's Point (SZ4975). Bird Ringing Station manned at migration time.

HEREFORDSHIRE
Croft Castle (SO4465). National Trust. Arboretum with finest Spanish chestnut avenue in Britain. Access seasonal; admission fee.
Eastnor Castle (SO7336). Arboretum, with first Atlas cedars to be grown in England. Access seasonal; admission fee.

HERTFORDSHIRE
Hertfordshire and Middlesex Trust for Nature Conservation has 11 reserves.
Tring Reservoirs (SP9213 – 9012). National Nature Reserve and Regional Wildfowl Refuge since 1955, 49 a. Rare plants, relics of marsh flora; but mainly for breeding, passage and wintering waders and water birds; gull roost. By permit off footpaths.
Beech Grove, Tring (SP9211). The headquarters of the British Trust for Ornithology, to organize field research. Nearby, Tring Park, with branch of the Natural History Museum.
Hertford Heath (TL3511). Though not a nature reserve, is thought by H.M.T.N.C. to be 'the most important botanical site in the county'.

Rye Meads, Lea Valley (TL3810). Bird Ringing Station.

HUNTINGDONSHIRE and PETERBOROUGH

Peakirk Waterfowl Gardens and Borough Fen Decoy (TF1606, 2008). The satellite exotic wildfowl collection of the Wildfowl Trust, opened 1957; very comprehensive. Admission fee. The decoy is used for migration research; access by permit.

Barnack Hills and Holes (TF0704). Nature Reserve of the Northamptonshire Naturalists' Trust; a classic orchid sward on a worked-out limestone quarry.

Castor Hanglands (TF1201). National Nature Reserve since 1945, 221 a. A valuable relict of the old Midland limy-soil oak-ash woodland plant community, and grass heath, with very rare butterflies. Access to part by permit.

Holme Fen (TL2288). National Nature Reserve since 1952, 640 a. Relict of ancient flora and fauna in measurably shrunken peat fen, basis of important ecological study. By permit only.

Woodwalton Fen (TL2284). National Nature Reserve since 1954 of S.P.N.R. (since 1919) and Nature Conservancy, 514 a. Rich fen flora, with three extremely rare plants and one butterfly unique in England; and the subject of profound pollen-analysis research into its history since the last Ice Age. By permit only.

Monks Wood (TL1879 – 1980). National Nature Reserve since 1953, 387 a. Beautiful relict of old east English woodland with very fine insect fauna. By permit only. Nearby is the Nature Conservancy's Monks Wood Experimental Station.

Grafham Water (TL1568). Part is Nature Reserve of Bedfordshire and Huntingdonshire Naturalists' Trust and the Great Ouse Water Authority, since 1966.

KENT

Kent Naturalists' Trust has 23 reserves.

Northward Hill, High Halstow (TQ7876). National Nature Reserve since 1957 of Royal Society for the Protection of Birds; with Nature Conservancy, 131 a. By permit off footpaths. Neighbouring estuarine marsh and foreshore to north and west, may become a wildfowl refuge.

Swanscombe Skull Site (TQ6174). National Nature Reserve, 5 a., since 1954. Site of the oldest fossil known referable by palaeontologists to *Homo sapiens*, Swanscombe Man, probably between 250,000 and 300,000 years old, and other Pleistocene fossils. Inner enclosure by permit.

Blean Woods (TR1664 – 1864). National Nature Reserve since 1953, 165 a. By permit off footpaths.

Burham (TQ7162-7262). Nature Reserve of K.N.T. since 1966, over 300 a.

Stodmarsh (TR2261). National Nature Reserve since 1968; for rare plants and birds.

Sandwich Bay (TR3560). Nature Reserve of K.N.T., fine plants; and Bird Observatory at key migration point.

Ightham (TQ5956). The Fissure is a classic Late Pleistocene cave in which many fossils of birds and mammals have been discovered. Nearby the great (127 a.) hill fort of Oldbury Hill (5856), probably 3rd C. B.C.

Knole (TQ5354). Largest private house in England, dating from 1456; fine gardens: National Trust.

Zealds, Church St., Wye (TR0546). Nature Conservancy H.Q., S.E. Region of England.

Hothfield Common (TQ9745). Local Nature Reserve of K.N.T., West Ashford R.D.C. and Nature Conservancy since 1961, 143 a.

Wye and Crundale Downs (TR 0745). National Nature Reserve since 1961, 250 a. Classic chalk plant and insect locality. By permit in parts.

Bedgebury Forest (around TQ7233). Forest 2,375 a. National Pinetum, c. 64 a., in Bedgebury Park, of the Royal Botanical Gardens, Kew. Free admission.

Ham Street Woods (TR0033 – 0034). National Nature Reserve since 1952, 240 a. A woodland Nature Reserve of K.N.T. in same system. By permit off footpaths.

Benenden (TQ8033). The Collingwood Ingram Bird Sanctuary of K.N.T. since 1965, c. 30 a.

Dungeness (TR0916). Nature Reserve of R.S.P.B., 1,233 a. Shingle of deep interest to coastal physiographers. Rare breeding birds, including only common gull colony s. of Scottish Border country. By permit only. Bird Observatory also at this key migration point, logging average of 170 bird species a season.

LANCASHIRE

*In Lake District National Park (see Cumberland also).

*Blelham Bog (NY3700). National Nature Reserve since 1954, 5 a. National Trust and Nature Conservancy. Unusual plants and insects on *Sphagnum* bog developing from alder-willow carr.

*Hinning House Close (SD2399). The part of Hardknott National Forest Park in Lancashire.

*Esthwaite North Fen (SD3597). National Nature Reserve since 1955, 4 a. National Trust and Nature Conservancy. Woodland transition to *Sphagnum* bog; interesting hydrology and ecology.

Grizedale (SD3394). Nature Reserve of Forestry Commission, with deer, research nursery and museum.

*Ferry House, Windermere (SD 3995). Research Station of Freshwater Biological Association.

*Rusland Moss (SD3388). National Nature Reserve since 1958, 58 a. Woodland on best surviving 'moss' in region. Heronry in pines, and deer. By permit only off footpaths.

*Roudsea Wood (around SD3382). National Nature Reserve since 1955, 287 a. One of the most varied woodlands in the kingdom, with complex ecology and transitions of plant community from zone to zone. All three species of native deer. By permit off footpaths.

Merlewood Research Station (SD 4079). Nature Conservancy North Region of England H.Q., at Grange-over-Sands.

Leighton Moss (SD4875). Nature Reserve of the Royal Society for the Protection of Birds, 400 a. Reedbeds, waterfowl, duck refuge. By permit off footpaths.

Walney (SD1873 – 2361). Joint Nature Reserves of L.D.N.T. and Lancashire Naturalists' Trust; and Bird Observatory. Huge herring gull colony.

Wyre - Lune Sanctuary (SD4254 – 3448). National Wildfowl Refuge since 1963, 9,100 a., for geese on intertidal area.

Blackpool Aquarium and Zoo (SD 3036). Founded 1894, in the Tower. Aquarium specializes in British fishes and small tropicals; fine tanks: c. 360 species. Admission fee.

Southport Sanctuary (SD3118). National Wildfowl Refuge since 1956, 14,500 a., for both wild geese and ducks, which winter here in numbers.

Southport (SD3216 – 3718). Zoo in Princess Park, founded 1928, c. 80 species; admission fee: and good Botanic Garden.

Ainsdale Sand Dunes (SD2912). National Nature Reserve since 1965, 1,216 a., with plants and birds of ecological interest.

Holden Clough, Oldham (SD9401). Nature Reserve of Oldham Microscopical Society and Field Club.

Belle Vue Zoological Park (SJ8896). Manchester's Zoo, founded 1836, 35 a., *c.* 280 species, including good monkey collection and fine birds. Admission fee.

LANCASHIRE - YORKSHIRE
Forest of Bowland (N-E-S-W SD 5570 – 8541 – 6637 – 5049). Area of Outstanding Natural Beauty, confirmed 1964, 310 sq. mi. Marches with Yorkshire Dales National Park.

LEICESTERSHIRE
Leicestershire Trust for Nature Conservation has 12 reserves.

Stapleford Park (SK8117). Fine gardens with wildfowl. Access seasonal; admission fee.

Charnwood Forest (SK4615 – 5310). This noble area of woodland and moorland has a fine moor at Beacon Hill (5014) and two Nature Reserves of the Leicestershire C. C.; Bradgate Park and Swithland Wood (5310, 5312); woodland Ulverscroft, 80 a., since 1966 and moorland Charnwood Lodge (4615), Nature Reserves of L.T.N.C.

Twycross (SK3304). Zoo. Admission fee.

LEICESTERSHIRE - RUTLAND
Eye Brook Reservoir (SK8496 – 8594). A fine unofficial wildfowl refuge, with many rare ducks and waders on passage and in winter.

LINCOLNSHIRE
Lincolnshire Trust for Nature Conservation has over 20 reserves.

Cleethorpes (TA3008). Zoo opened 1965, with whale aquarium.

Stapleford Moor (SK8658). Nature Reserve of L.T.N.C. and Forestry Commission. By permit only.

Skegness – Gibraltar Point (TF 5661 – 5557). Local Nature Reserve and Regional Wildfowl Refuge, since 1952, of L.T.N.C., Lindsey County Council and Skegness Urban District Council, 1200 a. Bird Observatory at G.P., a key migration point. Public information centre by car park at G.P.

Spalding (TF2422). Bird Observatory.

NORFOLK
Norfolk Naturalists' Trust has 28 reserves.

North Norfolk Coast (from about Holme TF7044 to the Suffolk boundary at Caister TG 5310). This is perhaps the most interesting coast in Britain to the naturalist, with ts remarkable physiography and geology. 9,700 a. of marshes and sand dunes became Holkham NNR in 1967.

Scolt Head Island (around TF8046). National Nature Reserve and Regional Wildfowl Refuge since 1954, 1821 a. Norfolk Naturalists' Trust, National Trust and Nature Conservancy. Birds – breeding terns, key migration point, wintering brent geese; and very interesting shingle, dune formations and plant carpet. Access to ternery restricted May-July.

Blakeney Point (TF9845 – TG0445). Nature Reserve of National Trust and N.N.T. Terns and wintering brent geese. No permit, but access wardened in breeding season. Migration watch point.

Holme (TF7044). Nature Reserve since 1955. Most westerly station of the bearded tit; key migration point. Bird Observatory.

Wells Marshes (around TF9244). Not yet (1966) a reserve, but of National Nature Reserve quality.

Cley Marshes (TG0544). Nature Re-

serve of N.N.T. and National Trust, 435 a. Migration watch point. By permit off footpaths. Rare breeding birds and big migrant passage.
Weybourne (TG1143 and for miles along coast to e.). Geology. Cliff exposures of the greatest interest to students of the Pliocene and the Ice Ages of the Pleistocene; highly fossiliferous. Also the most southerly established colonies of fulmars in e. England.
Holkham Hall (TF8842). Large and fine formal garden, and exotic waterfowl. Access seasonal; admission fee.
Kelling Pines (TG0941). Zoo: Kelling Pheasantries and Tropical Aviary, opened 1964; admission fee.
Dersingham (TF6631). Duck Decoy; a Duck Ringing Station. Private; access by permit.
Blickling (TG1729 – 1728). National Trust. Hall and gardens; access seasonal, admission fee. Park and woods, Nature Reserve, in effect; free admission.
Norfolk Broads (N-E-S-W TG3429 – 5009 – TM4792 – TG2806 + 2818). Has been considered as a National Park, and should be a National Nature and Recreation Park. Of special biological interest are (among others) Calthorpe Broad (TG4025), Sutton Broad (TG3723), Burntfen Broad (TG 3318), Ranworth Marshes (TG3615 – 3715), Rockland Broad (TG3305) and Burgh St. Peter Fen (TM4792). The Broads constitute the greatest reservoir of wetland flora and fauna in the kingdom, with many relict rarities. Breydon Water (TG4706 – 5108), their outlet, may become a local Wildfowl Refuge.
Sandringham (TF6928). The Royal Estate. Fine woodland and lakes; good birds. To grounds (only) access seasonal; admission fee.
Hickling Broad (TG4122). National Nature Reserve and Regional Wild-

fowl Refuge since 1958, 1215 a. N.N.T. and Nature Conservancy. By permit ashore.
Horsey Mere (TG4522). Nature Reserve of National Trust. By permit off footpaths.
Winterton Dunes (TG4920). National Nature Reserve since 1956, 259 a. Plants and physiography. By permit off footpaths.
Norfolk Wildlife Park, Great Witchingham (TG1118). Zoo since 1962. The Ornamental Pheasant Trust's magnificent collection—the game birds' Slimbridge. Other exotic and fine native fauna. Admission fee.
Middleton Towers (TF6717). Fine moat and gardens; exotic birds. Access seasonal; admission fee.
Bure Marshes (TG3216 – 3515). National Nature Reserve and Regional Wildfowl Refuge since 1958, 1019 a. Decoy, Cockshoot and Ranworth Broads, N.N.T. and Nature Conservancy. By permit only.
Bishopgate, Norwich (TG2308). Nature Conservancy H.Q., East Anglia Region.
Talbot Manor (TF6806). Arboretum, and fine collection of other exotic plants. Private.
Weeting Heath (TL7888). National Nature Reserve since 1958, 338 a. N.N.T. and Nature Conservancy. By permit only.

NORFOLK – SUFFOLK
Breckland. About 240 sq. mi., of the western Norfolk-Suffolk border country, of peculiar dry heaths and forests with interesting fauna, flora, geology and archaeology, could be considered as yet another National Nature Park. Straddling the border, in its heart, is: **Thetford Chase** (N-E-S-W TF7800 – TL9883 – 7980 – 7392 with outlier at Mildenhall around TL7176 – 7474).

State Forest of Forestry Commission from 1922, 48,360 a.

NORTHAMPTONSHIRE

Northamptonshire Naturalists' Trust has 4 reserves.
Pitsford Reservoir (SP7771 – 7970). Wildfowl Refuge of N.N.T., north of the causeway.
Wellingborough Zoo (SP8967). Zoo since 1943. Animal collection in large town garden. Admission fee.
Buckingham Arm (SP7740 – 7536). Nature Reserve and Nature Trail of N.N.T. along this stretch of disused canal.

NORTHUMBERLAND

Northumberland and Durham Naturalists' Trust has 4 reserves.
Border Forests and Border National Forest Park, see Dumfries, Scotland.
Northumberland Coast (NU0150 – 2605). Area of Outstanding Natural Beauty confirmed 1958, 50 sq. mi., of coast from near Berwick to Amble, including Farne Islands and other nature reserve below.
Lindisfarne (NU0447 – 1435). National Nature Reserve since 1964, and National Wildfowl Refuge since 1966, 7378 a. Complex of estuarine sands and mudflats, and dunes of great botanical and physiographic interest. Migration watch point.
Farne Islands (N-E-S-W NU2539 – 2537 – 2135 – 2037). Nature Reserve of the National Trust and the Farne Islands Association, 80 a. The world's oldest sanctuary, first managed as such by St. Cuthbert in about 676. Great seabird populations (fine terns) and large grey seal colony. Access limited; by boat from Seahouses.
Northumberland National Park (N-E-S-W NT 8733 – NZ0699 + 0696 – NY6865 – 6368). National Park con-

firmed 1956, 398 sq. mi. Full of naturalists' and archaeologists' treasures; the north end of the Pennine Way, the Breamish and Coquet Valleys. The southern portion of this National Park includes the stretch of Hadrian's Wall from the Milecastle (no. 46) at NY 6666 to the Milecastle (no. 29) near Cilurnum at NY8871.
Chillingham Castle (NU0625). Private park with herd of ancient white park cattle since at least 1692, possibly 13th century.
Glanton (NU0714). Bird Research Station.
Lewisburn (NY6590). See Border Forests, under Dumfries.
Alnmouth (NU2410). Holiday Fellowship Centre; nature courses.
Coom Rigg Moss (NY6979). National Nature Reserve since 1960, 88 a. Forestry Commission and Nature Conservancy. In Northumberland National Park; Blanket bog at over 1,000 ft., with no history of human interference; a classic *Sphagnum* plant community. By permit only.
Dove Marine Laboratory, Cullercoats (NZ3671). Biological Research Station of King's College, Newcastle-upon-Tyne.

NOTTINGHAMSHIRE

Trent Valley (follow river SK5133 – 8174). From Stapleford to Dunham, a bird-watchers' paradise of water-meadows, marsh, pools and water-pits, including Nottingham Sewage Farm.
Welbeck Park (around SK5674). The Great Lake is a wildfowl refuge in effect, and the wilderness has a fine community of woodland birds.
Thoresby Hall and Lake (around SK6370). Wildfowl refuge in effect; and fine trees, some exotic. Access seasonal; admission fee.

Newstead Abbey (SK5453). Nottingham Corporation; gardens with many rare trees and shrubs.
Wollaton Hall and Park (around SK 5339). Nottingham Corporation; good bird-watchers' place, and Natural History Museum.
Attenborough Gravel Pits (SK 5324). Nature Reserve of Nottinghamshire Trust for Nature Conservation since 1966, 250 a.

OXFORDSHIRE
B.B.O.N.T., see Berkshire.
Cotswolds. Area of Outstanding Natural Beauty, see Worcestershire.
Chacombe Priory (SP4843). Fine gardens and collection of exotic ornamental birds. Access seasonal; admission fee.
Wychwood (SP3316). National Nature Reserve since 1955, 647 a. By permit only. One of the few remaining stands of ancient English forest, basically an oakwood but with many other species and a very rich flora and insect fauna.
Blenheim Palace (SP4416). Magnificent gardens and park, a nature reserve in effect. Access to palace seasonal; admission fee.
Oxford Botanic Gardens (SP5206). Earliest surviving botanic garden in the kingdom (1621), has a living plant collection worthy of the scholars of the great university in surroundings of beauty. Free admission.
Waterperry (SP6206). Forest Nature Reserve since 1954, 144 a. By permit only.
Aston Rowant etc. (SU7699 – 7497). National Nature Reserve since 1958, 166 a. (small part in Bucks.). Also Beacon Hill, Forest Nature Reserve since 1959, 13 a., and Chinnor Hill, Nature Reserve of B.B.O.N.T. since 1965, march with National Trust's

Aston Wood. Best example of Chiltern hillside woodland. By permit off footpaths.
Watlington Hill (SU7093). Farther down the same escarpment, this typical Chiltern downland summit is a nature reserve, in effect, of National Trust.

SHROPSHIRE
Ellesmere (around SJ4233). No reserve, but chain of meres of very great interest, formed among the moraines of the last Ice Age; some rare water plants, interesting wildfowl, and fine parks and plantations, including big Sequoias.
Preston Montford (SJ4314). Field Centre of the Field Studies Council.
Attingham Park, Shrewsbury (SJ 5409), National Trust; and H.Q. Midland Region of England, Nature Conservancy.
Shropshire Hills (NE-S-W SJ6309 – SO5772 + 2972 – 1683). Area of Outstanding Natural Beauty confirmed 1959, 300 sq. mi.
Pontesford and Earl's Hills (SJ4005–4104). Nature Reserve since 1965, 110 a., of Shropshire Conservation Trust.

SOMERSET
Leigh Woods and Nightingale Valley (ST5674). National Trust. Fine woodland with rare insects and plants, and overlooks geologists' panorama of Avon Gorge.
Clevedon (ST4172 – 4271). Clevedon Court and Gardens, National Trust; and Walton Cave (4172), whence interesting Pleistocene fossils.
Steep Holm (ST2260). Bird Observatory.
Chew Valley Lake (ST5760). A potential Regional Wildfowl Refuge. Ringing Station; access restricted.
Cheddar Gorge (ST4653 – 4654). Geology: a classic limestone gorge with

caves and small museum of fossils and antiquities. Cox's Stalactite Cave and Gough's Cave are famous.

Rode (ST8054). Zoo. Tropical Bird Gardens, founded 1963; admission fee; an excellent bird zoo with a well-housed, developing collection of exotic species.

Rodney Stoke (ST4849). National Nature Reserve since 1957, 86 a. Best surviving specimen of Mendip ash-wood. By permit off footpaths.

Wookey Hole (ST 5348). Geology: fine limestone cavern system with stalactites and stalagmites. Admission fee. A site of Old Stone Age hunters, which has yielded many bones. Ebbor Gorge nearby became National Nature Reserve, 1968; 101 a.

Bridgwater Bay (ST2246 - 2959). National Nature Reserve since 1954, and National Wildfowl Refuge since 1955, 6,076 a. Brean Down (ST2959) is National Trust property. Wildfowl and botany; Stert Island by permit.

Quantock Hills (N-E-S-W ST1444 - 2733 - 2129 - 0942). Area of Outstanding Natural Beauty confirmed 1957, 38 sq. mi.

Shapwick Heath (ST4240). National Nature Reserve since 1961, 546 a. Raised bog flora, rare plant species, many archaeological sites. By permit only.

Glastonbury (ST4940). Site of the best excavated and most important of the European lake villages, discovered in 1892, whence much evidence of England's fauna and flora 2000 years ago. Material in Tribunal museum (5039).

Sharpham Moor (ST4638). A small Nature Reserve of the Society for the Promotion of Nature Reserves.

Nettlecombe Court (ST0537). Field Centre of Field Studies Council, since 1967.

Seven Wells Bridge (ST1737). Quan-tock Forest Trail of Forestry Commission.

SOMERSET – DEVON

Exmoor National Park (N-E-S-W SS7551 - ST0934 - SS9325 - 5747). National Park confirmed 1954, 265 sq. mi. Moorland, wooded gorges and a lovely coast. Many naturalists' beauty spots within, e.g. National Trust's Bossington Hill (SS9148).

STAFFORDSHIRE

Peak District National Park, see Derbyshire.

Beeston Tor, Manifold Valley (SK 1054). Caves with fossil mammals, inhabited from Pleistocene to Dark Ages.

Coombes Valley, Leek (SK0052). Nature Reserve of the Royal Society for the Protection of Birds and the West Midlands Trust for Nature Conservation. 191 a. of mixed woodland. By permit only.

Hawksmoor Wood (SK0344). Nature Reserve of the National Trust.

Alton Towers (SK0743). Fine garden and trees; public recreation centre; admission fee.

Chartley Moss (SK0029). National Nature Reserve since 1963, 104 a. A *Sphagnum schwingmoor* or floating moss community 50 ft. deep formed about 10,000 years ago at the end of the last Ice Age. Scots pine and interesting botany. By permit only. Nearby Chartley Park once housed the famous Chartley herd of wild white cattle.

Blithfield (SK0524). New reservoir is a wildfowl stronghold.

Birch Wood (SK1124). An outlier of Cannock Chase State Forest.

Cannock Chase (N-E-SW SJ9822 - SK0610 - SJ9510). Area of Outstanding Natural Beauty confirmed 1958, 26 sq. mi., and chiefly composed of the Cannock Chase State Forest of the

Forestry Commission since 1920, 6,316 a.

Belvide Reservoir and Gailey Pool (SJ8610, 9310). Not official reserves, but fine refuges for very varied stock of winter wildfowl; also breeding Canada geese, inland cormorants, gull roost, heronry at Gailey.

STAFFORDSHIRE and WORCESTERSHIRE

Wren's Nest (SO9392 – 9391). National Nature Reserve since 1956, 74 a. A classic geological exposure. Upper Silurian Dudley limestone with a fossil fauna over 300 species strong in a most perfect state, about 330 million years old, and first studied in 1686. Research and collection by permit only.

SUFFOLK

Suffolk Naturalists' Trust has 4 reserves.

Thetford Heath (TL8579). National Nature Reserve since 1958, 243 a. N.N.T. and Nature Conservancy. By permit only.

Horn and Weather Heaths (TL 7877). Nature Reserve of the Royal Society for the Protection of Birds, 320 a. By permit only.

Cavenham Heath (TL7672). National Nature Reserve since 1952, 337 a. Permit required for Cavenham Poor's Heath and Tuddenham Heath.

Blythburgh – Walberswick (TM 4575 – 5074). Blyth Estuary a natural waterfowl and wader refuge. Walberswick has Ringing Station.

Westleton Heath (TM4569). National Nature Reserve since 1956, 117 a. By permit off footpaths.

Minsmere (around TM4667). Nature Reserve of R.S.P.B., 1,528 a. Generally held to be its finest. A Regional Wildfowl Refuge also. Britain's bearded tit headquarters; other very rare birds and fine plants. Permit required.

Mickfield Meadow (TM1362). Nature Reserve, 4½ a., of the Society for the Promotion of Nature Reserves. Permit required.

North Warren, Thorpeness (TM 4559). Nature Res rve of R.S.P.B., 196 a.

Orfordness – Havergate (TM4549, 4147). National Nature Reserve since 1954, and National Wildfowl Refuge, 514 a. Orfordness, 249 a., Nature Conservancy; access restricted. Havergate, 265 a., R.S.P.B., and N.C., headquarters of Britain's breeding avocets; other rare birds. By permit only.

Shingle Street (TM3642). Not a reserve but of special botanical and physiographical interest.

Flatford Mill (TM0733). Field Centre of the Field Studies Council, for nature teaching and research in the Constable country.

SURREY

Surrey Naturalists' Trust has 4 reserves.

West London Reservoirs (TQ0473, 0573, 0769, ex Mdx.). Wildfowl Refuges, in effect, of Metropolitan Water Board. Rare ducks regularly winter on King George VI, Staines and Queen Mary Reservoirs. Big gull roost. Access by permit; free causeway across Staines Reservoir.

Wisley (TQ0658). The Royal Horticultural Society's main, and magnificent, gardens, opened in 1904. Superb collection, including arboretum. Admission fee.

Juniper Hall and Box Hill (TQ1752, 1851). Juniper Hall a Field Centre of Field Studies Council. Box Hill a nature reserve, in effect, of National Trust; both perched on splendid wooded chalk escarpment of great ecological interest.

Surrey Hills (N-E-S-W TQ3358 – 4351 – SU9131 – 8241). Area of Outstanding Natural Beauty confirmed 1958, 160 sq. mi.

South-west Surrey (N-E-S-W SU 8848 – 9938 – 9034 – 8440). A classic area that should be scheduled as a Regional Nature Park, including the best remaining area of low-lying Surrey Heath, bogs and woodland. Treasures are found on The Hog's Back, and in the National Trust properties of Frensham Ponds and Commons (8643 – 8439), Witley Common (9341 – 9239), Hydon's Heath and Hydon's Ball (9740 – 9739), The Devil's Jumps (8639 – 8739), The Devil's Punchbowl, Gibbet Hill and Hindhead Common (8938 – 9034), Sandhills Common (9438), Whitmoor and Golden Valleys (8736 – 8735) and Nutcombe Valley (8835 – 8834).

Winkworth Arboretum (SU9941). A fine exotic tree collection with many rare novelties, 95 a., of National Trust. Free admission.

Grayswood Hill (SU9134). Private arboretum of very many species of flowering trees and shrubs. Access seasonal; admission fee.

Barfold Copse (SU9232). Nature Reserve, 13 a., of R.S.P.B.; access by permit.

SUSSEX

Sussex Naturalists' Trust has 16 reserves.

Sussex Downs (N-E-S-W SU8632 + 9432 – TV6098 – 5895 – SU7310). Area of Outstanding Natural Beauty confirmed 1966, 379 sq. mi. of the South Downs and Weald.

Marley and Black Down (N-W-E-S SU8832 – 9230 – 9228). A continuation of the Surrey Heath and Woodland complex embracing the National Trust properties of Shottermill Hammer Ponds; Marley Common, Wood and Heights; and Black Down Hill.

Borde Hill (TQ3226). Very fine private arboretum, rare shrub collection. Access seasonal; admission fee.

Leonardslee, Lower Beeding (TQ 2225). Magnificent private gardens with some exotic animals at large. Access seasonal; admission fee.

Pett Level (TQ9015). Should be a Nature Reserve. Fine coastal marsh, rare migrant and breeding birds.

Wood's Mill (TQ2113). Nature Reserve since 1966, 15 a., Nature Trail, H.Q. S.N.T. and site of Educational Museum.

Kingley Vale (SU8210). National Nature Reserve since 1952, 352 a. Magnificent stand of yews. No permit required, but danger of unexploded bombs.

Cissbury Ring (TQ1408). The largest prehistoric earthwork in England, 60 a., finished in 3rd C. B.C. In effect also fine downland nature reserve of National Trust.

Og's Wood, Polegate (TQ5805). Nature Reserve of Eastbourne College.

Brighton Aquarium (TQ3103). Founded 1872. Admission fee.

Lullington Heath (TQ5302). National Nature Reserve since 1956, 155 a. By permit off footpaths. Eastbourne College also has a reserve in neighbouring Cuckmere Valley.

The Mere, Hampden Park (TQ 6102). Nature Reserve of Eastbourne College.

Pagham Harbour (around SZ8796). Local Nature Reserve of West Sussex C.C., S.N.T. and Nature Conservancy since 1964; in effect a wildfowl and wader refuge.

Beachy Head (TV5995). Nature Reserve of downland and cliffs, of Eastbourne Corporation. Bird Observatory (lately at Selsey Bill) manned at migration time.

Selsey Bill (SZ8592). Migration watch point.

WARWICKSHIRE

West Midlands Trust for Nature Conservation has 3 reserves.
Edgbaston Park (SP0584). A fine, birdy, park and lake; and nearby the Birmingham Botanical, Horticultural and Zoological Gardens; admission fee.
Tile Hill Wood (SP2779). Nature Reserve of Coventry Corporation.
Charlecote Park (SP2656). National Trust. Deer park, and fine cedars and garden. Seasonal; admission fee.

WESTMORLAND

*In Lake District National Park (*see* Cumberland).
Moor House (around NY7729). National Nature Reserve since 1952, 10,000 a. Headquarters of national programme of ecological moor and peat research; embraces some head waters of Tees, and limestone escarpment of Pennines on west. By permit off footpaths. Within it, Moor House Field Station (7532) of the Nature Conservancy. See Teesdale.
*Whitbarrow Scar** (SD4389). Proposed Reserve by Lake District Naturalists' Trust; wild daffodil slopes.

WILTSHIRE

Wiltshire Trust for Nature Conservation has 3 reserves.
Cotswolds. Area of Outstanding Natural Beauty, *see* Worcestershire.
Fyfield Down (SU1470). National Nature Reserve since 1956, 612 a. Rich chalk downland with sarsen stones. By permit off footpaths.
Savernake Forest (around SU2266). A great old forest with rare insects and plants.
Blackmore Copse (ST9264). Nature Reserve of W.T.N.C.
Stourhead (ST7734). Gardens, National Trust: fine woodland.
White Sheet Hill (ST8034). Nature

Reserve of W.T.N.C. Iron Age hill fort.

WORCESTERSHIRE – HEREFORDSHIRE – GLOUCESTERSHIRE

Malvern Hills (N-E-S-W SO7355 – 8040 – 7633 – 7039). Area of Outstanding Natural Beauty confirmed 1959, 40 sq. mi.

WORCESTERSHIRE – OXFORDSHIRE – GLOUCESTERSHIRE – WILTSHIRE

Cotswolds. Area of Outstanding Natural Beauty confirmed 1966, 582 sq. mi.

WORCESTERSHIRE

West Midlands Trust for Nature Conservation has 2 reserves.
Dudley Zoo (SO9490). Zoo in grounds of ancient castle, 48 a., with clever architecture and conversion of moat to enclosures. Opened *c.* 1938. A comprehensive, well-tended and housed collection of *c.* 420 species, including fishes.
Clent Hills (SO9379). Potential Nature Reserve.
Bittell Reservoir (SP0175 – 0275). Potential Wildfowl Refuge.
Randan Wood (SO9172). Nature Reserve of W.M.T.N.C.
Spetchley Park (SO8953). Gardens with red and fallow deer, exotic waterfowl. Access seasonal; admission fee.

YORKSHIRE – CUMBERLAND – WESTMORLAND – DURHAM

Upper Teesdale (NY6933 – NZ0416). Rates National or Nature Park status; an Upper Teesdale Conservation area could march with the Yorkshire Dales National Park. Unique Ice Age plant community endangered by some water plans. Contains Moor House (Westmorland) National Nature Reserve and Upper Teesdale (Yorkshire) National Nature Reserve, below; magnificent moors and falls, some interesting ravine woodland; an archaeologist's and geologist's paradise. Ends at Barnard Castle, Durham, where interesting Bowes Museum; admission fee.

YORKSHIRE

Yorkshire Naturalists' Trust has 23 reserves.

Upper Teesdale (N.N.R.) (NY8429 – 8024). National Nature Reserve since 1963, 6,500 a., the third largest in England. Ancient rocks and complex geology support moorland with more rare plants than in any comparable area in the kingdom—species from north and south, some at edge of range, others in alpine meadows are woodland relicts. Research on water conservation. Yorkshire side of High Force fall (8828) in Reserve. By permit off footpaths.

North Yorkshire Forests (N-E-S-W NZ7618 – TA0378 – SE8770 + 4570 – 4598). State Forests of Hambleton (18,613 a.) and Allerston (36,717 a.); with associated private woodlands a complex of c. 70,000 a., much in North York Moors N.P. Outliers of Hambleton Forest at Kirk Leavington and East Rounton (NZ4210, 4202). Naturalists encouraged and advised by Forestry Commission.

North York Moors National Park (N-E-S-W NZ6315 – TA0294 – SE5376 – 4394). National Park, confirmed 1952, 553 sq. mi. From the glorious Cleveland Hills to Robin Hood's Bay, and Fylingdales Moor (common to the Parishes of Hawsker-cum-Stainsacre and Fylingdales, and the Early Warning System of the Atlantic West). Forest, moorland, dale and medieval architecture, from Rievaulx (5784) or wards and backwards.

Yorkshire Dales National Park (N-E-S-W NY9709 – NZ1500 + SE 1585 – SE0850 – SD6196). National Park, confirmed 1954, 680 sq. mi., third largest in the kingdom. A mosaic of limestone crags, gorges, sweeping moorland gouged by the Ice Age's ice, hidden woodlands, loved alike by hard-headed farmers, adventurous potholers, tender artists and dedicated naturalists. Places below marked * are within this paradise. The scenery is consistently moving.

Farndale (NZ6102 – SE7187). Local Nature Reserve of North Riding County Council and Nature Conservancy since 1955, 2,500 a. Along the R. Dove, probably the best wild daffodil slopes in England. Wardened in daffodil time.

Fen Bog (SE8598). Nature Reserve of Y.N.T.

Hayburn Wyke (TA0197). Nature Reserve of Y.N.T. since 1966, 34 a.

Silpho, Hackness and Snever Dale (SE9693, 9690, 8587). Nature Trails of F.C.

Kirkdale Cave (SE6785). Site of early (1821 on) excavation of Pleistocene fossil animals.

Hutton Buscel (SE9784). Field Centre of British Young Naturalists' Association.

Garbutt Wood (SE5083). Nature Reserve of Y.N.T. and F.C. on steep scarp of Hambleton Hills since 1966, 65 a.

Flamingo Park, Kirby Misperton (SE7779). Zoo founded 1961, 325 a., 170 species. Well-run park zoo in process of development.

*****Ling Gill** (SD7978). National Nature Reserve since 1958, 12 a. Steep eroded ravine at c. 1,000 ft., in limestone, with rich and rare flora under ash and birch.

*****Colt Park Wood** (SD7777). National Nature Reserve since 1962, 21 a. Ash-wood on long Ingleborough scar at 1,100 ft., one of the few remaining examples of such woods on high lime-stone pavement. By permit only.

Bempton Cliffs – Flamborough Head (TA1974) – 2570). Probable future Nature Reserve; great chalk cliffs (nearly 400 ft.) housing big sea-bird population, including only English breeding gannets, many kittiwakes and fulmars, big guillemot-razorbill colony. F.H. key bird migration point, manned as Observatory in season.

Forest of Bowland. Area of Out-standing Natural Beauty, *see* Lanca-shire.

Sewerby Hall (TA2069). Bridlington Corporation gardens (from 1714); hor-ticultural and botanical collection. Small admission fee.

*Wharfedale Bone Caves, Kilnsey (SD9568 – SE0061). Douky Bottom, Kilnsey Crag, Skythorns and Elbolton Caves, etc.; source of Pleistocene and Stone Age bones of men and other animals.

*Malham Tarn (SD8967). Field Centre of Field Studies Council, with gorgeous material at hand for natur-alist, palaeontologist, archaeologist, hydrologist.

*Ribblesdale Bone Caves, Settle (SD8365 – 8464). Victoria, Albert, Langcliffe Scar, Kelco and Attermire, etc. Classic digs of Stone Age fossils, including man and his culture.

Strensall Common (SE6561). Nature Reserve of Y.N.T. since 1965, *c.* 55 a.

Moorlands, Skelton (SE5858). Na-ture Reserve of Y.N.T., *c* 18 a. Admis-sion fee for non-members.

Knaresborough (SE3557). Bird Ring-ing Station.

Blubberhouses Moor (around SE 1354). Has been, and may still be, the greatest grouse moor in the king-dom.

Harlow Car Gardens (SE2754). Northern Horticultural Society, 40 a. of ornamental gardens and woodlands.

N.C.B.

The North's answer to Wisley. Admis-sion fee.

Hornsea Mere (TA1947). Probable future Nature Reserve; bird migration key watch point.

Kipling Cotes Chalk Pit (SE9143). Nature Reserve of Y.N.T. since 1966.

Rifle Butts Quarry (SE9042). Geo-logical Reserve of Y.N.T.

Fairburn Ings (SE4527 – 4726). Local Nature Reserve and Regional Wildfowl Refuge since 1957, 618 a., West Riding, County Council and Nature Conservancy. Large open water stretch due to mining subsidence; rich bird life especially migrant and winter-ing waterfowl. By permit only.

Spurn Point (TA4115 – 3910). Nature Reserve since 1959 of Y.N.T., *c.* 350 a. + 700 a. foreshore, and Bird Observa-tory at key migration point.

Brockadale (SE5017). Nature Re-serve of Y.N.T. and F.C. since 1966.

Sandall Beat (SE6103). Local Nature Reserve of Doncaster Corporation and Nature Conservancy since 1965.

Eccleshall Wood (SK3282). Bird Sanctuary of Sheffield Corporation.

YORKSHIRE – LINCOLNSHIRE

Humber Wildfowl Refuge (SE8623–9923). National Wildfowl Refuge since 1955, 3130 a., including Read's Island. Safeguards Humber pinkfoot flock. By permit only.

WALES
ANGLESEY

North Wales Naturalists' Trust has a reserve on this island.

Anglesey Coast. Area of Outstand-ing Natural Beauty confirmed 1966.

Cemlyn (SH3293). Hewitt Wild Bird Sanctuary.

South Stack, Holyhead (SH2082). Sea-bird stronghold.

R

Puffin Island (SH 6582). Potential Nature Reserve.

Newborough Warren – Ynys Llanddwyn (SH4165 – 3862). National Nature Reserve since 1955. 1,566 a. Botany and birds; tern colonies and heavy passage of migrant waders. By permit off footpaths.

BRECKNOCK

Brecknock County Naturalists' Trust has a reserve.

Nant Irfon (SN8355 – 8452). National Nature Reserve since 1962, 216 a. Upland sessile oakwood and moorland gorge. By permit only.

Craig Cerrig Gleisiad (SN9420 – 9621). National Nature Reserve since 1957, 698 a. Two great Old Red Sandstone crags with rare montane flora, several species here at s. end of world range. Permit needed.

Craig y Cilau (SO1915). National Nature Reserve since 1959, 157 a. Escarpment with rare trees, of which one (least white beam) is known only from this and a neighbouring crag. Vast cave system, Agen Allwedd, extending about 8 miles, is being scientifically and sportingly explored under permit.

Cwm Clydach (SO2012 – 2212). National Nature Reserve since 1962, 50 a. Hanger beechwoods of gorge are only self-regenerating mature stand of species in S. Wales.

Penmoelallt (SO0110). Forest Nature Reserve since 1961, 17a., remarkable for a few examples of the very rare Ley's white beam on a limestone escarpment. By permit off rides.

BRECKNOCK – CARMARTHEN – MONMOUTH

Brecon Beacons National Park (N-E-S-W SO 2242 – SO 3418– SN9705 – SN6321). Confirmed 1957, 520 sq. mi., the last of our chain of National Parks

in n gland and Wales. This beautiful mountain area deserves to be better known, and has several reserves within.

CAERNARVON

North Wales Naturalists' Trust has a reserve.

Penrhos Road, Bangor (SH5872). Nature Conservancy H.Q., Wales.

Penrhyn Castle (SH6071). National Trust. Fine forest of native and exotic trees in grounds. Access seasonal; admission fee.

Coed Gorswen (SH7571). National Nature Reserve since 1959, 33 a. Lowland oakwood on glacial drift, with interesting ground flora. By permit off footpaths.

Coed Dolgarrog (SH7667). National Nature Reserve since 1959, 170 a. The most impressive oakwood in North Wales. Varied geology has produced very interesting communities of lesser vegetation. By permit off footpaths.

Cwm Glas, Crafnant (SH7360). National Nature Reserve since 1960, 38 a. Rich flora with rare arctic-alpine species to over 1,250 ft. on Craig-Wen; and relict ashwood. Permit access only to experimental enclosure.

Cwm Idwal (SH6559). National Nature Reserve of National Trust and Nature Conservancy since 1954, 984 a. Amphitheatre (rock-climbers' paradise) to over 3,200 ft. with Ice Age floral relicts, some very rare.

Beddgelert Forest (N-E-S-W SH 5555 – 5848 – 5646 – 5451). The smaller of the two State Forests of the Snowdonia National Forest Park. Forestry Commission, c. 3,000 a.

Snowdon (NW-E-S SH6054 – 6452 – 6149). National Nature Reserve since 1964, 4,145 a. Y Wyddfa. The montane heartland of the National Park, from 176 ft to 3,560 ft. with foothill woodland and upland fauna and flora, complex geology. By permit where enclosed.

Coed Tremadoc (SH5841). National Nature Reserve since 1957, 49 a. Oak woodland on steep dolerite cliffs and scree with a complex undergrowth plant community. By permit only.
Lleyn. Area of Outstanding Natural Beauty confirmed 1957, 60 sq. mi. Practically the whole coast, and a large inland area of the promontory, on n. coast n. to SH4250 near Clynnog-Fawr, on s. coast e. to SH3432 near Llanbedrog. Includes Bardsey, below.
Bardsey (SH1222), 370 a. Bird and Field Observatory manned most effectively at this key migration point, and sea-bird station.

CAERNARVON - DENBIGH - MERIONETH
Snowdonia National Park (N-E-S-W SH7478 - SJ0130 - SH6495 + 6095 - 4748). National Park, 837 sq. mi., confirmed 1951, second largest in the kingdom. Most of the natural history treasures of the three counties lie within this glory of North Wales, haven of biologists, archaeologists, historians and climbers.

CAERNARVON - DENBIGH
Gwydr Forest (N-E-S-W SH7766 - 8257 - 7846 + 7546 - 7048 + 7056). The larger of the two State Forests comprising the Snowdonia National Forest Park—the Park within a Park. Forestry Commission, 19,473 a., and with few exceptions public access.

CARDIGAN
Cambrian Forests. Besides parts of Tarenig and Ystwyth State Forests, Cardigan has other vast tracts: Taliesin (6,700 a., e. of SN6589 Talybont), Rheidol (4,000 a., n. and e. of SN5881 Aberystwyth), Myherin (3,212 a. planted, e. of SN7376 Devil's Bridge) and Aeron. The State Forest of Aeron (new since 1954, c. 1,000 a.) is growing fast in the vale of the R. Aeron; mouth at SN4563 Aberayron.
Borth Bog (around SN6391). Nature Reserve of West Wales Naturalists' Trust, 95 a.
Coed Rheidol (SN7177). National Nature Reserve, the 'Devil's Bridge' gorge woodlands, since 1956, 107 a. Within Rheidol State Forest. Sessile oaks with rich and rare fern flora; Welsh poppy. By permit off footpaths. A Forest Nature Reserve since 1962 adds 8 a.
Pen-y-graig and Tyn-y-bwlch, Llanddeiniol. (SN5472 - 5573). Nature Reserve of W.W.N.T., 1966.
Cors Tregaron (around SN6863). National Nature Reserve and Regional Wildfowl Refuge, 'Tregaron Bog', since 1955, 1,898 a., one of finest raised bogs in Wales, with moss and carr vegetation. A wintering home of geese. By permit only.
Cardigan Island (SN1651). Nature Reserve of W.W.N.T., 40a.

CARMARTHEN
Allt Rhyd y Groes (SN7449 - 7747). National Nature Reserve since 1959, 153 a. Vigorous native sessile oak and rare mosses and flowers on w. side Afon Doethie. By permit off footpaths.
Carmarthen Bay (SN2407 - 4400). Interesting dune formations with special flora and fauna on Pendine, Laugharne, Tywyn and Pembrey Burrows, and the four estuaries, especially the Burry Estuary (border Glamorgan), are good places for waterfowl and waders.

DENBIGH
Welsh Mountain Zoo, Colwyn Bay (SH8579). Zoo, founded 1963, c. 100 species. Admission fee.
Bodnant, Tal-y-Cafn (SH8072). National Trust. Perhaps the finest garden in Wales, with a wonderful tree and shrub collection.

Rhyd-y-Creua (SH8057). Field Centre of Field Studies Council, since 1967. **Cilygroeslwyd Wood** (SJ1255). Nature Reserve of North Wales Naturalists' Trust, 10 a. **Perthichwareu, Llandegla** (SJ1853). Geology: cave of New Stone Age hunters, whence fossil mammals and birds excavated.

GLAMORGAN

Glamorgan Forests. State Forests (Forestry Commission), first planted in 1921, stretch to almost every corner of the county, belonging to one system. The classification of the last decade names Gower, Penllergaer, Coed Morgannwg, St. Gwynno, Llantrisant, Tair Onen and Coed Caerdydd. The great central forest of Coed Morgannwg, incorporating the older forest of Rheola and others, is the largest forest in Wales, with nearly 30,000 (eventually 40,000) a. under plantation.

Gower (w. of SS5295 – 6387). This remarkable peninsula was confirmed as an Area of Outstanding Natural Beauty in 1956, 73 sq. mi., w. of the line Llanmorlais – Mumbles Head, and could be made a special Nature Park on the strength of its abundant ecological, palaeontological and archaeological treasures. Within it are the three National Nature Reserves listed below. The Glamorgan County Naturalists' Trust have Nature Reserves at Llandmadoc Woods (4493), Broad Pool (5191), and on the south cliffs from Port Eynon (4684) to Overton (4584). The National Trust has three areas along the south coast. On or near this highly scenic coast at least eight caves and fissures have disclosed Stone Age cultures and associated mammal and bird bones, among them Paviland Cave (4385), first excavated in the early 1820s, which contained what is still the oldest cere-

monial human burial (Old Stone Age) known in the kingdom, Cat's Hole Cavern (5390), Mitchin Hole (5586), Bacon Hole (5686) with what is still the only known example of Old Stone Age cave painting in Britain, and Langland Bay (6287). Most of the woodland in Gower belongs to Gower Forest, part of the great State Forest system of the Glamorgan Forests under the Forestry Commission.

Whiteford (SS4496 – 4394). National Nature Reserve since 1964, 1,933 a., Nature Conservancy and G.C.N.T.; seawashed turf constituting the heart of the great Burry Estuary wildfowl wintering grounds, a National Wildfowl Refuge of 8,952 a. By permit only.

Gower Coast (SS3887 – 4087). National Nature Reserve since 1958, 116 a., with rare limestone plants and breeding sea-birds.

Oxwich (around SS5087). National Nature Reserve since 1963, 542 a., with interesting dune and fen flora, rare insects and a strong bird fauna. By permit off beach.

Parc Cefn On (ST1683). Pinetum and woodland dell with exotic shrubs, of Cardiff City.

Roath Park (around ST2077). Cardiff Botanical Gardens, with arboretum.

Pysgodlyn Mawr (ST0476). Nature Reserve of G.C.N.T., lake in woodland.

MERIONETH

Coed Cymerau (SH6842). National Nature Reserve since 1962, 65 a. High humidity sessile oakwood with dense moss carpet. By permit off footpaths. Part of the series of Merioneth woodlands of varying environment preserved for ecological comparison.

Coeddyd Maentwrog (SH6640). National Nature Reserve since 1966, 169 a. Natural oakwood.

Coed Camlyn (SH6539). National

Nature Reserve since 1959, 157a. Sessile oakwood with bilberry undergrowth. Permit required.

Portmeirion (SH5937). Exotic and subtropical flora—fine azaleas—surround this peninsula colony in a warm Welsh corner. Access seasonal; admission fee.

Coed y Rhygen (SH6836). National Nature Reserve since 1961, 68 a. Birch and stunted sessile oak woodland with luxuriant moss carpet. By permit only.

Morfa Harlech (SH5535 – 5633). National Nature Reserve since 1958, 1214 a. Active dune formation and plant colonization in course of study. By permit only.

Deudraeth and Coed y Brenin (N-E-S-W SH6631 – 8624 – 8218 + 7218 – 6529). State Forests of the Forestry Commission since 1922, part of the Cambrian Forests System, 16,841 a. Though rather less rugged than northern Snowdonia, scenically one of the most benign and beautiful areas of all Wales.

Rhinog (SH6530 – 6727; – 6724 with N.T. properties). National Nature Reserve since 1959, 991 a. Two National Trust properties adjoin. Rugged moor and mountain bog (1,000-2,632 ft.) of great botanical interest.

Morfa Dyffryn (SH5525 – 5623). National Nature Reserve since 1962, 500 a. Another dune sanctuary of interest to physiographers and botanists. By permit off foreshore and footpaths.

Coed Ganllwyd (SH7224). National Nature Reserve since 1962, 59 a., of National Trust and Nature Conservancy. Sessile oakwood; deep gorge of Rhaiadr Du (Black Falls) with deep mosses and ferns and rare flowering plants.

Cader Idris (around SH7113). National Nature Reserve since 1955, 969 a., with summit (2,927 ft.) and high lake; many species of arctic-alpine

plants. Permits needed for enclosed foothill woods.

Craig yr Aderyn (SH6406). Potential Nature Reserve; cormorant breeding station on 762 ft. inland crag.

Dovey Forest. Part of this State Forest (Forestry Commission) in the Cambrian Forests system lies in Merioneth; see under Montgomery.

MONMOUTH
Monmouthshire Naturalists' Trust has 9 reserves.

Tintern Forest (N-E-S-W SO5309 – ST5497 – 5296 + 4896 – 4797 + SO 4702). State Forest of the Forestry Commission, 4,902 a., since 1920; since 1938 part of Forest of Dean National Forest Park.

Blackcliff and Wyndcliff (ST5398, 5297). Forest Nature Reserve since 1959, 200 a., in Forest of Dean N.F.P. By permit off rides.

Whitewall-Magor (ST4384 – 4386). Nature Reserve of M.N.T. since 1966, 60 a., the largest remnant in county of extensive Severn Estuary fenland.

MONMOUTH – HEREFORDSHIRE – GLOUCESTERSHIRE
Forest of Dean (with other Wye Valley woodlands N-E-S-W SO6123 – 6916 – ST5291 – 4697). National Forest Park of the Forestry Commission, founded as such in 1938, c. 35,000 a. Magnificent Wye Valley woodlands, e.g. at Symond's Yat and Tidenham Chase; many palaeontological, archaeological and architectural remains. Very interesting flora with rare relict species. Vertebrate fauna rather interesting; insects good.

MONTGOMERY
Cambrian Forests. In this system of State Forests Montgomery has the Dovey Forest around Machynlleth

(19,000 a., part in Merioneth), the Hafren Forest (11,000 a.) up to SN 8289 the source of the Severn, and the Tarenig and Ystwyth Forests which it shares with Cardigan (c. 6,000 a.).

PEMBROKE
Pembrokeshire Coast National Park (from SN1549 in n. round most of coast to SN1807 in s.e., including islands). 144,000 a. Confirmed 1952, 225 sq. mi. of lovely sea-facing and sheltered coasts and inland hills of great ecological and archaeological interest.
Ramsey (SM7022 – 7025). Nature Reserve of Royal Society for the Protection of Birds, 688 a. Breeding bird list c. 50, over 30 regular, includes chough, guillemot, razorbill, four species of gulls, cormorant, shag, fulmar, peregrine. By permit only; admission fee.
Grassholm (SM5909). Nature Reserve of R.S.P.B., 22 a. Wardened by West Wales Naturalists' Trust. Seabird island; though has only about 10 breeding species, holds one of the four largest gannetries in the world, with over 15,000 occupied nests. By permit only.
Skomer (SM7209). National Nature Reserve from 1959, 759 a. Wardened by W.W.N.T. Landing fee. Over 30 bird species breed, including Manx shearwater (c. 35,000 pairs), cormorant, fulmar, other sea-birds, chough. Has own peculiar race of bank vole, breeding grey seals.
Skokholm (SM7305). Bird Observatory of the Field Studies Council, 272 a. Access restricted to members of W.W. N.T. 18-20 breeding bird species, including c. 20,000 pairs Manx shearwaters.
Dale Fort (SM8205). Field Centre of Field Studies Council, with big research and teaching programme. Warden arranges access to Skokholm and Grassholm.

Hoyle's Mouth, Tenby (SN1100). Interesting cave in Carboniferous limestone, inhabited by hunters from Old Stone to early Iron Ages.
Orielton (SR9599). Field Centre of F.S.C.: important task—duck ringing in own decoy.
St. Margaret's Island and Caldey (SS1297, 1496). Former is Nature Reserve of W.W.N.T. Latter has caves with prehistoric remains. Combined breeding bird list c. 50, c. 40 regular, including chough.

ISLE OF MAN
The Ayres (NX3902 – 4604). Pasture and dune area of interest to distributional botanists and entomologists.
The Curraghs (SC3695). Wildlife Park opened 1965.
Maughold Head (SC4991). Manx National Trust. Fine views, sea-bird colonies, prehistoric remains.
Manx Museum, Douglas (SC3776). Manx National Trust H.Q.; also good natural history collection.
Port Erin (SC1968). Marine Biological Station with Aquarium of the University of Liverpool. About 50 living species of sea animals on public exhibition.
Calf of Man (around SC1565). Nature Reserve of the Manx Museum and Manx National Trust, 616 a.; also Bird Observatory. Breeding bird list over 30, including fine sea-birds and choughs. Key migration point. Access restricted. Manx N.T. properties on mainland cliffs opposite are also interesting.

SCOTLAND
Scottish Wildlife Trust has 15 reserves.

ABERDEEN
Loch of Strathbeg (NK0559 – 0858). No reserve, but wildfowl harbourage and interesting plant community on extensive dune system.

Hatton Castle, Turiff (NJ7546). Site of what is, or has been, the largest rookery in Britain, perhaps in the world, c. 5,000 nests in some years.
Sands of Forvie (NK0229 – 0024). National Nature Reserve and National Wildfowl Refuge since 1959, 1,774 a. Classic series of dune plant communities with rich flora and interesting physiography. Prehistoric sites also. Wildfowl also on Cotehill Loch and at mouth R. Ythan, where large eider colony. Terneries. By permit from breeding season to autumn.
Balmoral Castle (NO2595). The Royal Residence has seasonal access; admission fee. Policies around embrace ancient Caledonian woodland.

ABERDEEN – PERTH – ANGUS
Caenlochan (N-E-S-W NO2079 – 2875 – 2673 – 1375). National Nature Reserve since 1961, 8,991 a. An arctic-alpine plant sanctuary rivalled only by Ben Lawers with very rare plants growing in lime-rich rock escarpments and a dry climate, up to 3,504 ft.

ANGUS
Montrose Basin (NO6859 – 7056). Potential Nature Reserve or Wildfowl Refuge for passage and wintering birds.

ARGYLL
Arriundle Oakwood (NM8464). Forest Nature Reserve since 1961, 288 a., of Department of Agriculture for Scotland and Nature Conservancy. High-level semi-natural oakwood rich in mosses and liverworts, where regeneration is studied under rotational fencing.
Ardgour (around NM9963). Deer forest with interesting stand of relict Caledonian pine.
Glencoe (N-E-S-W NN1358 – 2454 – 1851 – 1156). A recreation park of the National Trust for Scotland, 12,000 a.,

embracing the climbers' and botanists' mountains of Bidean nam Bian and Buachaille Etive Mor; access free.
Treshnish Isles (NM3044 – 2337). Private Nature Reserve, of ornithological, botanical and geological interest, centred on fine basalt islands of Lunga and Dutchman's Cap. Sea-birds, including Manx shearwaters; a wintering place for barnacle geese. By permit only.
Black Mount (NN2842). Deer forest, c. 80,000 a., with more stands of relict Caledonian pine.
Staffa (NM3235). In effect a geological monument, with famous Fingal's Cave, showing finest Tertiary columnar basalt outside Giant's Causeway in Antrim.
Iona (landing NM2823). Nature Reserve in effect, with interesting birds and good *machair* flora on Columba's isle.
Doire Donn (NN0469). Nature Reserve of Scottish Wildlife Trust since 1966, 70 a., oak woodland.
An Cala, Easdale (NM7417). Fine garden. Admission fee; seasonal.
Argyll National Forest Park (N-E-S-W NN2309 – 3007 – NS1880 – 0796). National Forest Park since 1936, of the Forestry Commission since 1922, 57,813 a., embracing the State Forests of Ardgartan, Ardgoil, Glenbranter, Loch Eck, Glenfinart and Benmore. Within this fine modern woodland, the Younger Botanic and Eckford Gardens, below.
Crarae Forest Garden, Minard (NR 9897). Arboretum, national property since 1955, 33 a., with fine conifers. Admission fee.
Kiloran, Colonsay (NR3996). Magnificent island garden and exotic plantations. Admission fee; seasonal.
Eilean nan Rón, Oronsay (NR3386). Classic breeding ground of Atlantic grey seal; in effect a sanctuary.
Younger Botanic Gardens, Ben-

more (NS1385). Arboretum in Glen Massan. Satellite of the Royal Botanic Garden in Edinburgh; a fine plant collection. Admission fee; seasonal.

Eckford (NS1484). Fine wild garden. Admission fee; seasonal.

Loch Gruinart, Islay (NR3073 – 2867). Wildfowl and wader ground (barnacle geese winter) and migration point.

Dunlossit, Port Askaig, Islay (NR 4369). Fine garden. Admission fee; seasonal.

Achamore, Gigha (NR6447). Very fine island garden with subtropical exotics. Admission fee. Ferry from Tayinloan (6946).

The Oa, Islay (around NR2641). Interesting peninsula, with lochs and bird cliffs; choughs.

Carradale House (NR8037). Fine garden. Admission fee; seasonal.

ARGYLL – PERTH

Ben Lui (NN2627 – 2725). National Nature Reserve since 1961, 925 a. One of a chain of N.N.R.'s, guarding high arctic-alpine vegetation of rare and interesting species, here luxuriant on escarpments near 3,708 ft. summit.

AYR

Horse Island (NS2142). Nature Reserve of Royal Society for the Protection of Birds, 5 a. By permit only. Boatman at Stevenston.

Lady Isle (NS2729). Nature Reserve of the Scottish Society for the Protection of Wild Birds.

Enterkine Wood (NS4223). Nature Reserve of Scottish Wildlife Trust since 1966, 12 a. beechwood.

Skeldon House, Dalrymple (NS 3713). Fine garden in woodland bend of R. Don. Access seasonal; admission fee.

Culzean Castle (NS2310). National Trust for Scotland. House and garden

park with fine native and exotic plants; access seasonal; admission fee.

Ailsa Craig (NS0200). Private Nature Reserve; a bold granite island of great geological interest, with big sea-bird community, including one of the largest gannetries in the world. Access from Girvan; by permit only.

Glenapp Castle, Ballantrae (NX 0980). Arboretum and fine gardens. Access seasonal; admission fee.

AYR – KIRKCUDBRIGHT

Glen Trool (N-E-S-W NS4202 – NX 6671 – 4563 – 2894). National Forest Park of the Forestry Commission, over 116,000 a., the State Forests of Carrick and Changue in Ayr; and Glen Trool and Kirroughtree in the Stewartry of Kirkcudbright. Contains Merrick (2,764 ft.), the highest peak in southern Scotland.

BERWICKSHIRE

St. Abb's Head (NT9169). Good sea-bird cliffs; accessible fulmar colony.

Duns Castle (NT7754). Nature Reserve of Scottish Wildlife Trust since 1966, 190 a. woodland, loch and marsh.

Gordon Moss (NT6644). Nature Reserve of S.W.T. since 1966, 102 a. peat bog.

BUTE

Millport, Isle of Cumbrae (NS 1754). Marine Station of the Scottish Marine Biological Association.

Glen Diomhan, Arran (NR9346). National Nature Reserve since 1956, 24 a. Steep-sided gorge with two species of white beam peculiar to the island of Arran.

Goat Fell and Brodick Castle, Arran (NR9941 – NS0037). National Trust for Scotland. Goat Fell is in the heart of one of Britain's greatest and most complex geological paradises. At

Brodick Castle a fine garden with semi-tropical exotics. Access seasonal; admission fee.
Lamlash, Arran (NS0231). Holiday Fellowship Centre; nature courses.

CAITHNESS
Duncansby Head (ND4073). Fine stretch of eroded Old Red Sandstone not far from John o' Groats; many noble detached stacks and a full sea-bird community. Other good cliffs on Caithness' northern headlands.
Berriedale (ND1122). From here some miles inland up valleys of Berriedale and Langwell Waters, an interesting deciduous woodland plant community; also many prehistoric cairns, mounds, brochs and hut circles.

CLACKMANNAN
Dollar Glen (NS9699). Nature Reserve, in effect, of the National Trust for Scotland, 60 a., leading to medieval Castle Campbell.

DUMFRIES
Forest of Ae (N-E-S-W NY0198 – 0390 – NX9989 – 9490). State Forest of the Forestry Commission since 1919, 10,683 a.
Tynron Juniper Wood (NX8293). National Nature Reserve since 1958, 12 a. A stand of juniper (fenced) unmatched in south Scotland.
Castle and High-tae Lochs (NY 0881, 0880). Local Nature Reserve and Regional Wildfowl Refuge of Dumfries County Council and Nature Conservancy since 1962, 339 a.
Caerlaverock (NY0066 – 0866). National Nature Reserve and National Wildfowl Refuge since 1957, 13,514 a. About 1,500 a. of Lowland saltmarsh, or 'merse', harbour great winter flocks of Iceland pinkfeet, Spitsbergen barnacles, greylags and other wildfowl and water birds. Access limited.

DUMFRIES – ROXBURGH – CUMBERLAND – NORTHUMBERLAND
Border Forests and Border National Forest Park (N-E-S-W NU 0626 – 0808 – NY6369 – 4281). The largest planted forest system in the kingdom, of 186,932 a., or nearly 300 sq. mi. Forestry Commission since 1920. Embraces the State Forests of Kielder, Wark, Redesdale, Kidland, Harwood, Chillingham and Rothbury in Northumberland; Kershope, Spadeadam and Longtown in Cumberland; Newcastleton in Roxburgh and Dumfries; and Wauchope in Roxburgh. In 1955 the Border National Forest Park was declared embracing most of the westerly forests. This marches on the east with the Northumberland National Park which embraces most of the easterly ones. National Forest Park Museum at Lewisburn, Northumberland, NY6590, access seasonal.

DUNBARTON
Ardmore (NS3178). Nature Reserve of Scottish Wildlife Trust since 1966, 480 a. of promontory and foreshore.

EAST LOTHIAN
Bass Rock (NT6087), 7 a. Classic gannetry, the oldest known; in the records since c. 705. Fine colonies of other sea-birds; also very interesting botany. Private Nature Reserve. Boats from North Berwick.
Eyebroughty, Fidra and the Lamb Island (NT4986 – 5386). Nature Reserve of R.S.P.B. Breeding sea-birds; by permit only.
Aberlady Bay (NT4582 – 4580). Local Nature Reserve and National Wildfowl Refuge since 1952, 1,439 a., of the East Lothian County Council and the Nature Conservancy; a migration point.

FIFE
Tentsmuir Point (NO4928 – 5326). National Nature Reserve since 1954, and National Wildfowl Refuge since 1962, 1,249 a. At the Point rapid coastal accretion of great botanical and physiographical interest. Abertay Sands are an important refuge for wildfowl, including geese. No vehicles.
Morton Lochs (NO 4626). National Nature Reserve and Regional Wildfowl Refuge since 1952, 59 a. Shallow artificial lochs on dry ground, of interest to botanists and invertebrate students; and a wildfowl migration refuge. By permit off roads.
Isle of May (NT6599). National Nature Reserve since 1956, 140 a. Sea-bird and migration station; also interesting botany. Bird Observatory of the Midlothian Ornithological Club.

INVERNESS (INNER ISLES)
Cuillin Hills, Skye (around NG4523). The only mountain range in Britain not fully explored until the present century, culminating in hidden peak of Sgurr Alasdair, 3,309 ft. Incredible 18-mile ridge system of continuous rock-climbing, mainly on gabbro. Paradise for the fit geologist and physiographer.
Canna and Sanday (around NG 2505). Benign, but presently depopulated islands with interesting communities of birds (good sea-birds) and plants.
Rhum (around NM3698). National Nature Reserve since 1957, 26,400 a., for both nature conservation and research on grazing ecology and deer management. Mountains of great interest to climbers and geologists; interesting relict woodland; sea-birds, with largest Manx shearwater colony in Britain on high escarpments. By permit away from Loch Scresort.

INVERNESS (OUTER ISLES)
Gasker (NA8711). Isolated skerry has large grey seal colony, second only to that on North Rona (Ross).
St. Kilda (NE-S-W NA1506 – NF1396 – NA0501). National Nature Reserve since 1957, 2,107 a. National Trust for Scotland and Nature Conservancy. The most westerly archipelago of Scotland. Highest sheer cliffs in Britain (several over ¼ mile high) on main islands of Hirta (old village), Soay and Boreray. Uninhabited since 1930, save by armed services and succession of busy researchers. Scenically and biologically the most exciting nature reserve in the North Atlantic, with indigenous races of wren and field mouse; indigenous breed of sheep, the Soay sheep, unchanged a thousand years; by far the largest gannetry in the world (30-40,000 nests) on Boreray and the prodigious rocks Stac Lee and Stac an Armin; the largest and most ancient fulmary in Britain (c. 40,000 nests); and the largest British puffinry and Leach's storm petrel colony. Interesting geology and archaeology. Access controlled, but N.T.S. arranges cruises and voluntary research and working parties.
Traighs Seilebost and Luskentyre, Harris (around NG0798). Estuary harbourage for wildfowl, wader and other migrant and wintering birds.
Haskeir (NF6182 – 5980). Dense sea-bird colonies on isolated, little-studied archipelago of islet and serried stacks.
Balranald Marshes, North Uist (NF 7170). Nature Reserve of Royal Society for the Protection of Birds, 1,500 a., since 1966, sheltering rare breeding marshland birds.
Lochmaddy (NF9168). The best centre for exploring North Uist's maze of sea and freshwater lochs, *machair* and hills.
Monach Islands or **Heisker** (around NF6321). National Nature Reserve since 1966, 1,425 a.

Wiay, Benbecula (around NF8746). Proposed island Nature Reserve, mainly as bird sanctuary. By permit only.
Loch Bee, South Uist (around NF 7743). Wildfowl and wader haven (big herd of mute swans), and interesting botany on *machair* sward.
Loch Druidibeg, South Uist (NF 7540 – 8037). National Nature Reserve and National Wildfowl Refuge since 1958, 4,145 a. The most important breeding ground in the kingdom of the greylag goose; and one of the finest examples of dunes and *machair* croft land. By permit in breeding season.
Lochboisdale, South Uist (NF7919). The best centre for exploring this great island, with its five breeding birds of prey and fascinating plant communities.
Berneray and Mingulay (around NL 5582). Islands with formidable Atlantic-facing cliffs, now uninhabited save for lighthouse on Barra Head. Vast seabird community, including big fulmar colony and perhaps the biggest kittiwakery in the kingdom.

INVERNESS (MAINLAND)
Loch Garten (NH9718 – 9717). Nature Reserve of Royal Society for the Protection of Birds, 677 a., dedicated to the protection of one of the breeding sites of the recently returned ospreys. Access encouraged but controlled by warden team through season.
Glen More (N-E-S-W NH9613 – NJ 0109 – NO0198 – NH9312). National Forest Park since 1948, managed by the Forestry Commission since 1923, 12,500 a. In the heart of the Cairngorms; almost marches with the Cairngorms National Nature Reserve, below.
Craigellachie (around NH8812). National Nature Reserve since 1960, 642 a. Stand of pure birchwoods, and moorland to 1,600 ft., with interesting herbs,

ferns and mosses and very rare moths. Achantoul, the Speyside research station of the Nature Conservancy, is hard by.
Pitmain Beag, Kingussie (NH7400). Field Centre of Highland and Overseas Field Holidays.

INVERNESS – ABERDEEN
Cairngorms (N-E-S-W NH9208 – NO0495 – NN9187 – 8492). National Nature Reserve since 1954, 64,118 a., the largest in the kingdom and one of the largest in Europe. Guards the most important relict fauna and flora of inland Scotland, ranging to 4,300 ft. Ben Macdhui, second highest mountain in Britain. Flora from Caledonian pine to rare arctic-alpines. Birds from native crossbills and crested tits to golden eagle, ptarmigan, dotterel, greenshank and snow bunting. Red deer, roe and wild cat. Access to parts of the ancient Forest of Mar restricted in autumn.

KINCARDINE
Crathes Castle (NO7396). Nature Reserve of National Trust for Scotland with stands of Caledonian pine. Fine formal garden and exotic shrubs. Access seasonal; admission fee.
Blackhall, Banchory (NO6795). Nature Conservancy's Mountain and Moorland Ecology Station.
Drumtochty (NO7086 – 6676). State Forest of the Forestry Commission since 1926, 9,998 a.

KINCARDINE – ANGUS
St. Cyrus (NO7564 – 7362). National Nature Reserve since 1962, 227 a. A botanist's paradise long surveyed ecologically by Aberdeen University students; foreshore, rocks, dune pastures and cliffs to 200 ft. Very rich flora with some species at northern limit; and rare insects.

KINROSS

Loch Leven (around NO1401). National Nature Reserve since 1964, 3,946 a. The most important freshwater area in the kingdom for migratory and breeding wildfowl; four species of wintering geese. Also famous trout. Limited access; but three public shoreline points.

KIRKCUDBRIGHT

Silver Flowe (NX4684 – 4781). National Nature Reserve since 1956, 472 a., of Glen Trool Forest. Seven upland bogs under e. side of Merrick, very inaccessible and quite undisturbed, showing all gradations from blanket to raised bog, most valuable for research.
Loch Ken (NX6375 – 6771). Unofficial wildfowl refuge; good place to see whooper swans or Greenland whitefronts in winter.
Kirkconnell Flow (NX9769). National Nature Reserve since 1959, 383 a. Estuarine peat moss including raised bog, with Scots pine and birch scrub. Interesting invertebrates. By permit only.

LANARK

Possil Marsh (NS5771 – 5869). Nature Reserve of Scottish Society for the Protection of Wild Birds.
Glasgow Zoo (NS6862). Calderpark Gardens of the Zoological Society of Glasgow and West of Scotland since 1947, 106 a. Balanced educational collection. Admission fee.
Hamilton Low Parks Sanctuary (NS7355). Regional Wildfowl Refuge, 336 a., of Hamilton Burgh.

MIDLOTHIAN

Inchmickery (NT2080). Nature Reserve of Royal Society for the Protection of Birds. Breeding sea-birds; by permit only.
Royal Botanic Garden, Edinburgh

(NT2475). World-famous exotic collection, with alpines and rhododendrons a speciality. Free admission.
Edinburgh (around NT2674). Scottish Centre for Ornithology and Bird Protection at 21 Regent Terrace, Edinburgh 7; is H.Q. of Scottish Ornithologists' Club and Scottish H.Q. of R.S.P.B. At 12 Hope Terrace, Edinburgh 9, Scottish H.Q. of Nature Conservancy. At 8 Duke Street, Edinburgh 1, H.Q. of Scottish Wildlife Trust.
Edinburgh Zoo (NT2073). Zoological Park and Carnegie Aquarium of the Royal Zoological Society of Scotland since 1913, 75 a. Fine collection of over 530 species. Probably the finest breeding group of penguins in any zoo. Admission fee.
Duddingston Loch (NT2872). Nature Reserve of 40 a. since 1923, a Royal Park Sanctuary and Regional Wildfowl Refuge.

MORAY – NAIRN

Culbin Forest (N-E-S-W NJ 0164 – 0463 – NH 9656 – 9257). State Forest of the Forestry Commission since 1921, 7,546 a. Increasing conquest of sand by 'dune fixing' techniques. Neighbouring sands and Findhorn Bay a wildfowl and wader harbourage.

ORKNEY

North Ronaldsay (HY 7856 – 7651). Fine bird island and migration watch point.
Papa Westray (HY5055 – 4849). Most northern isles of Orkney have good sea-bird cliff colonies; Papa Westray great and arctic skuas on interior moorland.
Eday and the Calf of Eday (HY 5640 – 5528). Fine sea-bird islands (fulmars, cormorants) patrolled by Royal Society for the Protection of Birds.
Eynhallow (HY3629). Private Nature

Reserve on this (now) uninhabited island, used for fulmar and other research by Aberdeen University.
Gairsay and its Holms (HY4322 – 4520). Fine sea-bird islands patrolled by R.S.P.B.
Sule Stack (HX5617). Bare rock-stack with crowded gannetry, 4 miles from Sule Skerry (where lighthouse), about 30 from anywhere else.
West cliffs of Hoy (HY1904 – 1700). A stupendous rock curtain of Old Red Sandstone, rising to *c.* 1,100 ft., at St John's Head: Old Man of Hoy is 450 ft., detached slender tower. Cliffs are crowded with vast fulmar colony and many other sea-birds; skuas breed on moorland behind.

PEEBLES
Glentress (N-E-SW NT2844 – 2940 – 2337). State Forest of the Forestry Commission since 1920, 2,349 a.

PERTH
Kindrogan, Strathardle (NO0563). Field Centre of Scottish Field Studies Association.
Rannoch Moor (NN4056 – 4252). National Nature Reserve since 1958, 3704 a. The largest area of blanket bog south of the Great Glen, at *c.* 1,000 ft. Important in the study of bog flora and the formation of peat. Rare plants and insects.
Garth, Glen Lyon (NN7547). Field Centre of S.F.S.A.
Ben Lawers (N-E-S-W NN6544 – 6942 – 6137 – 5941). Nature Reserve of the National Trust for Scotland, with co-operation from the Nature Conservancy, 8,000 a. On highest mountain in county, 3,984 ft., the finest arctic-alpine flora in the kingdom, including several species unique to our islands.
Meall nan Tarmachan (NN5839 – 5637). National Nature Reserve since 1964, 1,142 a. Rich arctic-alpine flora

on 3,421 ft. mountain with lime-bearing rock. Complementary to above. By permit in late summer and autumn.
Strathyre (NN5224 – 5816 + 5809 – 5708 – 5023). State Forest of the Forestry Commission since 1930, 10,461 a., at a gateway to the Highlands.
Kinnoul Hill (NO1322). Deer Park of Perth Burgh Council and British Deer Society since 1966, 30 a. Viewpoint at 729 ft.

PERTH – STIRLING
Queen Elizabeth Forest Park (N-E-S-W NN4008 – 5706 – NS4092 – NN 3304). National Forest Park since 1953, based on State Forests of Loch Ard and Rowardennan, Forestry Commission since 1921, 41,454 a. Contains some of the finest Loch Lomond and Trossachs scenery, and many ecological treasures.

RENFREW
Castle Semple Loch, Lochwinnoch (NS3960 – 3558). Nature Reserve, *c.* 207 a., of Renfrew County Council; a wildfowl refuge in effect.

ROSS and CROMARTY (OUTER ISLES)
North Rona and Sula Sgeir (HW 8132, 6130). National Nature Reserve since 1956, 320 a. combined. North Rona (47 mi.n.w. of Cape Wrath), uninhabited for close on a century, has the largest colony of breeding grey seals in the world (*c.* 3,000); and a big sea-bird community including a (now) large, early fulmary and Leach's storm petrel colony. Eleven mi. w., and even more inaccessible, Sula Sgeir has an ancient gannetry (5-6,000 nests) and an equally flourishing fulmary and Leach's storm petrel colony. These are the two most inaccessible islands in Britain regularly visited by scientific naturalists, weather permitting.
Butt of Lewis (NB5166). Bird migration watch point.

Flannan Isles (NA7246). Lighthouse-keepers are now most isolated citizens of the kingdom. A natural nature reserve of six sharp steep islets with many smaller stacks; big sea-bird colonies, and interesting vegetation, only recently ecologically surveyed owing to great difficulty of landing.

Melbost Sands, Stornoway, Lewis (NB4534). Good wildfowl and wader harbourage and migration watch point.

Lewis Castle, Stornoway, Lewis (NB4133). Parkland around contains only substantial woodland in Outer Hebrides: as plantation has developed most interesting floral and faunal (specially bird) changes and colonizations have taken place.

Shiant Islands (around NG4197). Private Nature Reserve with big fulmary and puffinry, other sea-birds; and 500 ft. columnar basalt cliff. Uninhabited.

ROSS AND CROMARTY (MAINLAND)

Inverpolly (NW-E-S NC0519 – 2111 – 1605). National Nature Reserve since 1961, 26,827 a. The heart of one of the two 200 sq. mi. areas of Britain (the other is in n.w. Sutherland) in which no man normally sleeps. Lewisian gneiss glaciated plateau with steep 'butte' type Torridonian sandstone mountains, e.g. Stac Polly. Relict woodland and montane plant carpets of great interest, with limestone oasis of Knockan at east corner. Important area for future land-use study. Loch Sionascaig, with wooded islets, in heart of this huge reserve. By permit in Drumrunie area late summer and autumn.

Ristol and the Summer Isles (N-E-SW NB9712 – NC0006 – NB9101). Private Nature Reserves (nearly whole archipelago) supporting a native population of greylag geese and other fine

birds; a barnacle goose harbourage in winter. By permit only.

Inverewe, Poolewe (NG8581). National Trust for Scotland since 1952; centenarian Highland garden, a rare and tender oasis of exotics including a record magnolia. Admission fee.

Corrieshalloch Gorge, Braemore (NH 2077). National Nature Reserve of 13 a. since 1967. Interesting plants, birds, insects in wooded gorge, and 150 ft. sheer Falls of Measach.

Beinn Eighe (N-E-S-W NG9767 – NH0262 – NG9656 – 9562). National Nature Reserve since 1951, 10,507 a., the first in the kingdom. Lowland to alpine (3,000 ft.) plant communities in this deer forest, and relict Caledonian pine woods. Rare animals, including pine marten. Interesting geology. The Nature Conservancy's Anancaun Field Station (NH0263) lies hard by.

Strathpeffer (NH4858). Holiday Fellowship Centre; nature courses.

Rassal Ashwood (NG8443). National Nature Reserve since 1956, 209 a. The most northerly ashwood in the kingdom, and one of the few natural ashwoods in Scotland. Complex plant community on smallish limestone outcrop.

Balmacara (N-E-S-W NG8034 – 8431 – 8126 – 7529). National Trust for Scotland's recreation park, 8,000 a., for highly scenic Highlands dedicated to the satisfaction of tourists and naturalists.

Kintail (N-E-S-W NH0126 – 0416 – NG9913 – 9319). A sister recreation park of N.T.S., along the road to the isles, 15,000 a. Embracing the highly scenic Five Sisters of Kintail and with free access for all.

ROXBURGH

Border Forests and Border National Forest Park, *see* Dumfries.

SELKIRK
Hare and Dunbog Mosses (NT 4625). Nature Reserve of Scottish Wildlife Trust since 1966, 10 a. of interesting bogs.

SHETLAND
Hermaness, Unst (HP6120 – 5912). National Nature Reserve since 1955, 2,383 a. Includes Out Stack, northernmost point, and Muckle Flugga, northernmost inhabited point (lighthouse) of Britain. Blanket moorland supporting skuas and other rare birds, and cliff-range with big sea-bird colonies, including increasing gannetry and fulmary. Wardened by Royal Society for the Protection of Birds.
Haaf Gruney (HU 6398). National Nature Reserve since 1959, 44 a. Rich plant community and sea-birds; uninhabited.
Fetlar (landings HU5792, 6290). Good bird island with breeding rarities, including whimbrel, snowy owl; birds also good on neighbouring, uninhabited Hascosay.
Richmond Cottage, Mid Yell (HU 5790). 'The John and Mary Birdwatchers' Hostel' of R.S.P.B.
Noss (landing HU5340). National Nature Reserve since 1955, 774 a. On east side 592 ft. Old Red Sandstone cliff (Noup) houses increasing gannetry and fulmary, and detached Holm has biggest colony of great blackbacks in the kingdom. Both native species of skuas breed on moor. Wardened by R.S.P.B., now uninhabited.
Foula (landing HT9738). This isolated inhabited isle has a quarter-mile sheer cliff (the Kame) emulating St. Kilda's (Inverness), with Britain's oldest and largest fulmary outside St. Kilda (8,000 nests or more) and a big skua colony, Manx shearwaters and other breeding sea-birds in great number.

Mousa (broch at HU4624). A gentle isle with the finest Iron Age broch still standing, an accessible sample of Shetland's fine sea-birds and waders, and an interesting plant community. Uninhabited.
Scousburgh (NU3717). Best centre to enjoy the rare breeding marsh birds and many of the rare plants of Shetland: close to good bird cliffs (e.g. Fitful Head 3413), the great Bronze Age to Norse Age ruins of Jarlshof (3909) whence excavated evidence of Shetland's prehistoric fauna, Shetland airport (3910), and Grutness (4010), departure point of Fair Isle's *Good Shepherd*.
Fair Isle (landing HZ2272), *c.* 5,000 a. National Trust for Scotland since 1954, with a small but progressing human community, among which are several generations of naturalists. Known to be perhaps the most important and interesting migration point in Britain for more than half a century, and has more 'first records' of new British birds than any other place in the kingdom. Bird Observatory and Ringing Station manned from early spring to late autumn, and in effect a Nature Reserve. Fine breeding sea-birds, including big fulmary and skuas; and a special race of wren.

STIRLING
Flanders Moss (NS5496 – 5795). Potential Wildfowl Refuge: goose grounds.

STIRLING – DUNBARTON
Loch Lomond (NS4190 – 3988 and 4487). National Nature Reserve since 1958, and Regional Wildfowl Refuge since 1962, now 624 a. Five islands in loch and a stretch of shore near mouth of Endrick River. Among best ungrazed semi-natural Scottish woodlands on larger islands (oak dominant,

rich herb flora) and near shore an important wildfowl refuge and migration watching point. By permit on mainland.

SUTHERLAND

Cló Mór (NC2973 – 3272). The highest mainland cliff in Britain, at least 800 ft. nearly sheer. Fine sea-bird colonies on the face and stacks.

Faraid Head to Smoo (NC3971 – 4167). Fine coast with sea-bird headland, interesting dune system, rare and beautiful limestone plants, and Smoo Cave, accessible and exciting.

Eilean Bulgach (Am Balg) (NC1866). Sea-bird islet very seldom visited, with crowded colonies and a rank and interesting growth of guano-fed plants.

Invernaver (NC6762 – 7059). National Nature Reserve since 1960, 1,363 a. The finest galaxy of boreal plant communities in northern Scotland on shell sand beach and limy hills. Rare plants and breeding birds.

Strathy Bog (NC7953). National Nature Reserve since 1960, 120 a. The least disturbed of a vast area of blanket bog in a very natural state. Rich plant community where effect of 'peat-slides' can be studied.

Handa (land at NC1447). Nature Reserve of the Royal Society for the Protection of Birds, 766 a. Fine sea-bird colonies on Torridonian sandstone cliffs. Bothy-observatory for students and wardens.

Inchnadamph (N-E-S-W NC2521 – 2920 – 2617 – 2419). National Nature Reserve since 1956, over 3,200 a. A limestone oasis with complex geology, rare flowers and willows, and cave Allt nan Uamh whence bones of late Pleistocene animals of different periods and traces of early man.

Dunrobin (NC8500). Fulmars breed on the (inhabited) castle roof. Surrounding plantations have interesting flowers and support several birds at northern end of range.

WIGTOWN

Mochrum and Castle Lochs (around NX2953). Unofficial wildfowl refuges; M. Loch has feral greylags and Scotland's largest (and only inland) cormorant colony.

Great Scaur (**Big Scar**) (NX2533). Small but increasing gannetry; other breeding sea-birds on this isolated stack.

Mull of Galloway (NX1530). Sea-bird colonies on cliffs near lighthouse.

NATIONAL WILDFOWL REFUGES
England

	Acres	
Humber Wildfowl Refuge, Yorks.	3,130	Sanctuary Order 1955
Southport Sanctuary, Lancs. ..	14,300	Sanctuary Order 1956
Bridgwater Bay, Somerset ..	6,076	NNR 1955
Orfordness-Havergate, Suffolk ..	514	NNR 1954
Exe Estuary, Devon	1,022	Sanctuary Order 1934-51
Rostherne Mere, Cheshire ..	327	NNR 1961
Wyre-Lune Sanctuary, Lancs. ..	9,100	Sanctuary Order 1963
Lindisfarne, Northumberland ..	7,210	NNR 1966

Wales

Burry Estuary, Glamorgan ..	8,952	Sanctuary Order 1948

Scotland

Caerlaverock, Dumfriesshire ..	13,514	NNR 1957
Loch Druidibeg, S. Uist ..	4,145	NNR 1958
Sands of Forvie, Aberdeen ..	1,774	NNR 1959
Aberlady Bay, East Lothian ..	1,439	LNR 1952
Tentsmuir Point, Fife	1,249	NNR 1962

REGIONAL WILDFOWL REFUGES
England

Scolt Head, Norfolk	1,821	NNR 1954
Bure Marshes, Norfolk	1,919	NNR 1958
Hickling Broad, Norfolk ..	1,204	NNR 1958
Tring Reservoirs, Herts.	49	NNR 1955
Gibraltar Point, Lincs.	500	LNR 1952
Fairburn Ings, Yorks.	618	LNR 1957
Walmsley Sanctuary, Cornwall	42	Sanctuary Order 1948
Tamar Lake, Devon	75	Sanctuary Order 1951
Radipole Lake, Dorset	c. 70	Sanctuary Order 1948
Wicken Sedge Fen, Cambs. ..	320	Sanctuary Order 1957
Minsmere, Suffolk	1,528	Reserve of Royal Soc. Prot. of Birds

Wales

Cors Tregaron, Cards.	1,842	NNR 1955

Scotland

Hamilton Low Parks, Lanarkshire	336	Sanctuary Order 1958
Duddingston Loch, Midlothian..	40	Sanctuary, Ministry of Works, 1923
Morton Lochs, Fife	59	NNR 1952
Loch Lomond, Dumbartonshire	624	NNR 1962
Castle and High-tae Lochs, Dumfriesshire	339	LNR 1962

INDEX

Main references in Appendix IV are included in the index. Abbreviations are as follows:

AONB	Area of Outstanding Natural Beauty	NNR	National Nature Reserve
BO	Bird Observatory	NT	National Trust
BS	Bird Sanctuary	NTS	National Trust for Scotland
FC	Forestry Commission	NWR	National Wildfowl Refuge
FNR	Forest Nature Reserve	Pr. NR	Private Nature Reserve
LNR	Local Nature Reserve	RWR	Regional Wildfowl Reserve
NC	Nature Conservancy	SF	State Forest
NR	Nature Reserve	SWT	Scottish Wildlife Trust
NFP	National Forest Park		

Abberton Reservoir, Essex 119 143 228

Abbotsbury Swannery 8 137 227

Aberdeen, University of 170 189

Aberdeenshire 171 176 248 249 253

Aberlady Bay, LNR, NWR 19 177 251 259

Aberystwyth 72 163 164 165

Achamore, Gigha 250

Acts of Parliament
Agriculture Act 1947 16
Agricultural Holdings Act 86
Countryside Acts 89
Destructive Imported Animals Act 1932 195
Electricity Act 1957 87
Game Act 1831 85 86
Game Licences Act 1860 86
Grey Seals Protection Act 1914 80
Grey Seals Protection Act 1932 80
National Parks and Access to the Countryside Act 1949 18 27 29 48
North Wales Hydro-

Electricity Acts 1952 and 1955 87
Opencast Coal Act 1958 87
Pipelines Act 1962 87
Protection of Birds Act 1954 86 87 119
Repeal Act of 1846 94
Tees Valley and Cleveland Water Act 1967 160
Tithe Redemption Act 1836 94
Town and Country Planning Act 1947 16 22 23 50
Water Resources Act 1963 87

Advisory Committee on Planning 1941 15

Agricultural Land Service 15

Agricultural Research Council 47

agricultural revolution 6 99-103

agricultural statistics 3 94-6

Ailsa Craig, Pr NR 178 250

Ainsdale Dunes, NNR 158 233

Alnmouth 236

Alston 159

Alton Towers 238

Ambleside 157

An Cala, Easdale 249

Anancaun Field Station 59

Anglesey 165 243

Anglesey Coast, AONB 243

Angus 249 253

animal introductions 193-7

Annet, Scilly, BS 130 224

Appleby Castle Estates 159

arable acreage 94-6

Ardgour (deer forest) 249

Ardmore, NR 251

Areas of Outstanding Natural Beauty (AONB) 27 29 (for individual Areas, see separate entries)

Argyll 176 178 249 250

Argyll National Forest Park 112 249

Arlington Court, Barnstable, NT 226

Arne, NNR 137 227

Arne Peninsula 137

Arran 175 177

Arriundle Oakwood, FNR 249

Ascott, Wing, NT 222

Ashford 141 142

Askham Bog 65

Aston Rowant, NNR 144 237

Aston Rowant Beechwood, NT 58 237

Atkinson-Willes, G. L. 119

Atomic Energy Authority 60
Attenborough Gravel Pits, NR 237
Attingham Park, Shrewsbury, NT 151 203 237
autecology 69 70
Aviemore 170 172
Avon Gorge 43
Axmouth-Lyme Regis Undercliffs, NNR 43 58 226
Ayr 177 250
Ayres, The 168 248
Ayrshire 177

Balmacara, NTS 177 256
Balmoral Castle 249
Balranald Marshes, North Uist, NR 252
Banchory 170
Bangor 163 164
Bardsey, BO 245
Barfold Copse, NR 240
Barlow Commission 12 13 169
Barlow, Sir Montague 12
Barlow Report 12
Barn Elms Reservoir 230
Barnack Hills and Holes, NR 232
Bass Rock, Pr. NR 178 251
Batsford Park 155 229
Battersea Park 126
Children's Zoo 230
Beachy Head, NR 140 240
Beacon Hill 144
Beddgelert Forest, FC 244
Bedfordshire 143 145 221
Bedgebury Forest 233
Beech Grove, Tring 231
Beeston Tor, Manifold Valley 238
Beinn Eighe, NNR 19 50 54 173 256
Belle Vue Zoological Park 234
Belvide Reservoir and Gailey Pool 239
Bempton Cliffs, Flamborough Head 243
Ben Lawers, NR 177 255
Ben Lui, NNR 176 250
Benenden, BS 233
Benfleet 143
Bere, Rennie 116

Berkeley estate 120
Berkeley New Decoy, Slimbridge 119
Berkshire 144 221
Berneray and Mingulay 253
Berriedale 251
Berry, Dr. John 49 54 170
Berwickshire 250
Bicton Gardens, East Budleigh 226
Bilston Burn 43
Biological Committee of the Royal Society 19
Biological Records Centre 150
Birch Wood 238
bird observatories 137 141 153 160 167 175
Birmingham University 153 196
Bishopgate, Norwich 235
Bittell Reservoir 241
Black, Prof. J. N. 62 192
Black Country 152 155
Black Halls Rocks, NR 228
Black Mount 178 249
Black Tor Copse, FNR 132 226
Blackcliff and Wyndcliff, FNR 247
Blackhall, Banchory, Fld. St. of NC 189 253
Blackmore Copse, NR 136 241
Blackpool Aquarium and Zoo 233
Blackwater Marshes 228
Blakeney Point, NR 34 146 234
Blean Woods, NNR 51 142 232
Blelham Bog, NNR 157 233
Blenheim Palace 237
Blickling, NT 235
Blithfield 238
Blubberhouses Moor 243
Blythburgh – Walberswick 239
Board of Agriculture 11 93-5
Boarstall 222
Bodnant, Tal-y-Cafn, NT 245
Boote, R. E. 53
Borde Hill 240
Border Forests and Border National Forest Park, FC 112 251
Borough Fen Decoy 120
Borth Bog, NR 66 166 245

Botanical Gardens 123-8
Cambridge University 148 222
Oxford University 154 237
Botanical Society of the British Isles 64
Botanical survey of Scotland 10
Bourton-on-the-Water Zoo 229
Bovey Valley Woodlands, NNR 132 226
Box Hill, NT 65 142 239
Boyd, A. W. 153 222
Bracondale 55
Bradwell, BO 228
Bramshaw, FNR 114 138 231
Brancaster Staithes 146
Brassington-Bradbourne Caves 225
Braunton Burrows, NNR 58 133 226
Breckland 145 148 149 235
Brecknock 244
Brecon Beacons, NP 27 165 244
Brecon County Council 165
Bridgwater Bay, NNR, NWR 58 238 259
Brighton 140
Brighton Aquarium 240
Brimpton 55
British Ecological Society 10 19 64
British Museum (Natural History) 127
Broads, The 145 147-8
Brockadale, NR 243
Brodick Castle, NTS 177
'brown land' 24
Brownsea Island, Poole Harbour, NR 34 196 227
Buckfastleigh 226
Buckingham Arm, NR 236
Buckinghamshire 144 222
Bude-Stratton Urban District Council 131-2
Budworth Mere 223
Bure Marshes, NNR, RWR 58 147 235 259
Bureau of Animal Population 154
Burham, NR 232

Burnham Beeches 222
Burrator Reservoir 132
Burrington Combe 133
Burry Estuary, NWR 167 259
Burton Wood, NR 223
Burwell Fen, NR 34
Bute 250
Butterburn Flow, Gilsland, FC 224
Butterfly Valley, Cornwall 76
Butt of Lewis 255
Buxton, Aubrey 64

Cader Idris, NNR 165 247
Caenlochan, NNR 176 249
Caerlaverock, NNR, NWR 55 62 120-1 176 251 259
Caernarvon 165 245
Cairngorms, NNR 54 55 170-2 173 178 183 253
Caithness 251
Calderwood, W. L. 80
Caledonian Forest 108
Calf of Man, NR 34 167 248
Calthorpe Broad 51
Cambrian Forests 245 247
Cambridge 145 148 150
Cambridge University Botanic Gardens 148 222
Cambridgeshire 145 222
Cambridgeshire and Isle of Ely County Council, Survey Report 59
Campbell, Dr. Bruce 67-8
Canna and Sanday 252
Cannock Chase, AONB 238
Canterbury 141 142
Cape Wrath 174
Capel Curig 164
Cardiff 163 164
Cardigan 165 245
Cardigan Island, NR 167 245
Carmarthen 244
Carmarthen Bay 245
Carradale House 250
Carrigill 159
Carson, Rachel 63 104 187
Castle and High-tae Lochs, LNR, RWR 251 259
Castle Eden Denes, LNR 161 228
Castle Island 176

Castle Loch 177
Castle Semple Loch, Lochwinnoch, NR 255
Castleton Caves 225
Castor Hanglands, NNR 149 232
Catherington Down, NR 138 231
Cavenham Heath, NNR 51 149 239
Cemlyn 243
Central Electricity Generating Board 140 141 152 203
Chacombe Priory 237
Champion, Sir Harry G. 154
Chapel Wood, Spreacombe, NR 226
Charlecote Park, NT 241
Charlton Sand Pit 44
Charnwood Forest 153 234
Chartley Moss, NNR 58 152 153 238
Chatsworth 225
Chaucer 8
Cheddar Gorge 133 237
Cheesewring, The 223
chemicalization 6 63 101-5
Cheshire 151 152 153 222 225
Chesil Beach 137 189 227
Chessington Zoo 230
Chester Zoo 223
Chew Valley Lake 237
Chichester Harbour, AONB 139 140 231
Chillingham Castle 236
Chilterns, AONB 143 221
Chinnor Hill 154
Chipp, T. F. 11
Chippenham Fen, NNR 59 148 222
Chislehurst common 126
Chudleigh 226
Church Wood, Hedgerley, NR 222
Cilygroeslwyd Wood, NR 246
Cissbury Ring, NR 240
City of London Corporation 127 143
Clackmannan 177 251
Clapham, Prof. A. R. 53
classification of land, 12 13 185
Clee Hills 154

Cleethorpes 234
Clements, F. E. 74
Clent Hills 241
Clevedon, NT 237
Cley Marshes, NR 146 234
Clicker Tor Quarry, Menheniot 223
Clifton Zoo 229
Cligga Head and St. Agnes 223
climax vegetation 71-2
Cliveden, NT 222
Cló Mór 258
Clyde 178
Coalbrookdale 152
Coastguards' Path, Cornwall 131
Cobbett, William 9 94
Cockshoot Broad 147
Coed Camlyn, NNR 165 246
Coed Cymerau, NNR 165 246
Coed Dolgarrog, NNR 164 244
Coed Ganllwyd, NNR 165 247
Coed Gorswen, NR 164 244
Coed Rheidol, NNR 165 245
Coed Tremadoc, NNR 164 245
Coed y Rhygen, NNR 165 247
Coeddyd Maentwrog, NNR 246
Colchester 228
Coleman, Miss Alice 185-6
Colt Park Wood, NNR 242
Committee for the Promotion of Field Studies 20
Committee for the Study of British Vegetation 10
Committee of the British Association for the Advancement of Science 18
Committee on Land Utilization in Rural Areas, see Scott Committee
common land 3 9 14 25-7 92-3 126 132 142 143
agricultural land 27
arable land 92 93
definition of 26
forest and woodland 27
grazing 92 93
grazing land 27
recreational land 26
rough grazing 27 95 96 185 186
use of 26

Commons, Open Spaces and
Footpaths Preservation
Society 9
Commons Registration Bill 27
Condry, William 36
Connell, Sir Charles 52
conservation:
as a career 62 190-2
history of 7-21
international aspects of 1-4
20-1
of arctic-alpine flora 42 160
164 171 172
of wildfowl, Chapter 11
of wildlife 84-9
of sites of geological im-
portance 42-6
opposition to, Chapter 23
research, Chapter 21
Conservation Corps 19-20 65
Conservation Report 44
Conway Valley 164
Coom Rigg Moss, NNR 236
Coombe Hill, NT 222
Coombes Valley, Leek, NR
238
Corn Laws 94
Cornwall 66 129 130 131 223
225
Corrieshalloch Gorge, Braemore, NTS 256
Cors Tregaron, NNR, RWR 165
245 259
Cothill, NNR 221
Cotswolds, AONB 241
Cotterill Clough, NR 222
Council for Nature 19 64-6
128 Appendix I
Council for the Preservation
of Rural England (CPRE) 31
64 110 112
Country Parks 89
Countryside Commission 29
89
Countryside in 1970 Con-
ferences:
1963, 60 65
1965, 29 60 65 202 203
County Naturalists' Trusts 6 7
11 12 19 42 64-6 139 151
182 189 199
(Trusts' Secretaries are
given in Appendix I)

Bedfordshire and Hunting-
donshire 65 221
Berkshire, Buckinghamshire
and Oxfordshire 144 154
221
Cambridge and Isle of Ely
222
Cheshire Conservation Trust
222
Cornwall 66 76 131 198 223
Devon Trust for Nature
Conservation 76 225
Dorset 137 196 227
Essex 142 228
Gloucestershire Trust for
Nature Conservation 229
Hampshire and Isle of
Wight 138 230
Hertfordshire and Middle-
sex Trust for Nature Con-
servation 155 231
Kent Naturalists' Trust 141
229 232
Lake District 157 224
Leicestershire Trust for
Nature Conservation 234
Lincolnshire Trust for
Nature Conservation 65 234
Monmouthshire 247
Norfolk 11 58 145 147 149
234
Northamptonshire 236
Northumberland and
Durham 162 228 236
North Wales 165 243 244
Shropshire Conservation
Trust 154
Suffolk 239
Surrey 239
Sussex 240
West Midlands Trust for
Nature Conservation 241
West Wales 66 163
Wiltshire Trust for Nature
Conservation 241
Yorkshire 65 160 242
Scottish Wildlife Trust 66
248
County War Agricultural
Executive Committees
(CWAEC) 24 25 186
Court of Verderers 138
Cow Green reservoir 71 74

Cragg, J. B. 54
Craig Cerrig Gleisiad, NNR
165 244
Craig y Cilau, NNR 165 244
Craig yr Aderyn 247
Craigellachie, NNR 172 253
Crarae Forest Garden,
Minard 249
Crathes Castle, NR 253
Crewe 152
Criffell 121
Croft Castle, NT 231
Cross Fell 159
Crown Estate Commission 121
Crystal Palace Children's Zoo
230
Cuckmere Valley 140
Cuillin Hills, Skye 252
Culbin Forest, FC 254
Culzean Castle, NTS 177 250
Cumberland 157 224 241 251
County Council 158
Curraghs, The 168 248
Cwm Clydach, NNR 165 244
Cwm Glas, Crafnant, NNR 164
244
Cwm Idwal, NNR 164 183 244

Daily Mail, the 198
Dale Fort Field Centre 20
167 248
Dancer's End, NR 222
Darling, F. F. 36
Dartington Hall 227
Dartmoor, NP 27 132 183
226
Dartmoor Preservation Associ-
ation 132
Davies, Dr. William 72 186
Dawley 152
Daysh, Prof. G. H. J. 161
Dee estuary 163
deer:
red 55 82-3 87 170 171 173
176 181
roe 82 171 173
Denbigh 245
Dendles Wood, NNR 226
Department of Agriculture
for Scotland 3 195
Derbyshire 151 225
Dersingham 235

Deudraeth and Coed y Brenin, FC 247
Devil's Punch Bowl 142
Devon 20 129 133 225 238
Dial House 146
Diver, Captain Cyril 19 49
Dodman Point 224
Doire Donn, NR 249
Dolgellau 165
Dollar Glen, NTS 177 251
Domesday Book 154
Dorrien-Smith, Cmdr. 130
Dorset, AONB 137 138 227
Douglas 168
Dove, River 160
Dove Marine Laboratory, Cullercoats 236
Dover 141
Dovey Forest, FC 247
Dower, John 16 17
Dower Report 16 17
Dowlands Cliffs and Landslips 133
Downe 230
Drigg Dunes, LNR 158 225
Dropmore House 222
Drumtochty, FC 253
Dryerdale, Hamsterley 228
duck-ringing 119 120 143 146 158 167
Duddingston Loch, NR, RWR 254 259
Dudley 152
Dudley Zoo 241
Duke of Bedford 124
Duke of Edinburgh 60 64
Duke of Norfolk 120
Dumfriesshire 177 251
Dunbarton 251 257
Duncan, A. B. 52
Duncansby Head 251
Dungeness, NR 139 140 233
Dunham, K. C. 158
Dunlossit, Islay 250
Dunrobin 258
Duns Castle, NR 250
Dunwich 146
Durham 161 228 241

eagle, golden 171 173 176 188
Earl's Hills 154

Easington Rural District Council 161
East Devon, AONB 226
East Hampshire AONB 230
East Lothian 177 251
East Riding 160
East Suffolk 146 181
East Wood, Stalybridge, NR 222
Eastbourne 140
Corporation 140
College 140
Eastnor Castle 231
Ebbor Gorge 133
Eccleshall Wood, BS 243
Eckford 250
Ecology (Journal) 11
ecology 9-11 36 52 62 63 69 70 71 161 166 173 181 187 191
animal- 10 70
applied- 70 191
heathland- 181
meaning of 9-11 69
plant- 71
study of 9 10
ecosystem 5 11 36 62 69 124 127 139 188 193
Eday and the Calf of Eday 254
Edgbaston Park 241
Edinburgh 169 170 174 176 254
University 172 191-2
Zoo 254
Edlin, H. L. 25 114 115
Edward VII 83
Edwards, Prof. K. C. 36 151
Egerton Estate 153
Eggeling, Dr. W. J. 54
Eilean Bulgach 258
Eilean nan Rón, Oronsay 249
Ellesmere 237
Elliot, Dr. R. J. 164
Ellis, E. A. 36
Elton, C. S. 154
Ely 145
Engholm, Basil 15
Enterkine Wood, NR 250
Enterprise Neptune 30 34 141
Epping Forest 127 143 228
Essex 142 145 228 230
Esthwaite North Fen, NNR 233

Evelyn, John 108
Exbury Gardens 231
Exe Estuary Wildfowl Refuge 133 226 259
Exmoor, NP 27 83 133 238
Exmouth 226
Eye Brook Reservoir 234
Eyebroughty, Fidra and the Lamb Island, NR 251
Eynhallow, Pr. NR 254

Fairburn Ings, LNR, RWR 160 243 259
Fair Isle, NTS 179 257
falconry 85
Faraid Head 258
Farlington Marshes, NR 231
farming, Chapter 9:
agricultural neglect 98 99
and conservation 200-1
applied genetics 105
chemicalization 100-3 105
farming development in Scotland 96
hedgerows 100
herbicides 105
'high farming', 94
history 90-100
hydroponics 103
mechanization 99 100
pesticides 103-105
Farndale 160
Farne Islands, NR 34 81 82 161 236
Fen Bog, NR 242
Fenham Flats 121
Fens, The 148
Ferry House, Windermere 158 233
Fetlar 257
Field Studies Council 20 167
Appendix III
Centres 20 146 152
stations 20 133 142 156 · 7
Fife 176 252
Firth of Forth 175 176 178
Firth of Tay 176
Fisher, James 36 119 120 126 148 153 166 221
Fitter, R. S. R. 125 136
Flamingo Park, Kirby Misperton 242

Flanders Moss 257
Flannan Isles 256
Flashes, Northwich 153
Flatford Mill Field Centre 20
  146 239
Folkestone 34 141
Footpaths and Access Sub-
  committee 18
Forest Nature Reserve (FNR),
  definition of, 59
Forest of Ae, FC 251
Forest of Bowland, AONB 234
Forest of Dean, NFP 32 72 112
  116 155 247
forestry, Chapter 10:
  depletion 107 108
  reforestation 108
  and wild life 114 115
Forestry Commission (FC) 14
  30 31 32 40 51 59 83 109-
  117 132 138 144 149 155
  157 158 161 177 188 199
  history of, 30-1
  policy towards wildlife 116-
  17
Forth Road Bridge 176
Foula 257
fox-hunting 71 199
Frampton estate 120
Freshwater Biological
  Station 158
Frohawk, F. W. 76
Furzebrook Research Station,
  Wareham, NC 54 135 136
  188 227
Fyfield Down, NNR 58 136 241
Fylingdales Early Warning
  Station 161

Gairsay and its Holms 255
gamekeepers 77-9 85
Garbutt Wood, NR 242
Garth, Glen Lyon 255
Gasker 252
Geddes, Dr. Arthur 172
geological history of Britain
  4-5
geological 'monuments' 43-4
George, Dr. Martin 182
George VI 18
Gibraltar Point, LNR, RWR 19
  65 150 234 259

Gilmour, John 18 148
Glamorgan 246
Glamorgan Forests, FC 246
Glamorgan Trust 166
Glanton 236
Glasgow 171 175 178 254
  Zoo 254
Glastonbury 238
Glen Affric 169
Glen Diomhan, Arran, NNR
  175 250
Glen More, NFP 112 253
Glen Trool, NFP 112 250
Glenapp Castle, Ballantrae
  250
Glencoe, NTS 169 177 249
Glentress, FC 255
Gloucestershire 154 155 229
  241 247
Goat Fell, NTS 177
  and Brodick Castle, Arran
  250
Goldring, F. 36 136
Gordon, Prof. W. J. 43
Gordon Moss, NR 250
Gower, AONB 164 166 246
Gower Coast, NNR 246
Grafham Water 232
Grafnant 164
Grampians 171
Grand Junction Canal 143
Grassholm, NR 167 248
grasslands 41
Gray's Chalk Quarry, NR 229
Grayswood Hill 142 240
Great Gable, NT 158
Great Glen 171
Great Scaur (Big Scar) 258
Greater London 229 230
Green Belts 27-30
Green, F. H. W. 54
Green Park, London 126
Greenwich Park 126 230
grey seals 79-82, 161 162 167
  170 174
Grizedale, NR 233
Grune Point, Skinburness 224
Gwydr Forest, FC 245

Haaf Gruney, NNR 175 257
habitats, classification of 37-42
Hadleigh Marshes, NR 143 229

Hainault Forest 228
Hales Wood, NNR 142 228
Ham Street Woods, NNR 51
  142 233
Hamford Water Saltings 228
Hamilton Low Parks Sanc-
  tuary, RWR 254 259
Hampshire 138 230 231
Hampstead Heath 126
Hampton Court 230
Handa, NR 258
Hardknott, FC 112 158 225
Hardy, Sir Alister 35
Hardy, Marcel 10 172
Hare and Dunbog Mosses, NR
  257
Harlech 165 166
Harlow Car Gardens 243
Harrock Wood, Irby, NR 222
Hartland Moor, NNR 137 227
Hartland Point, NR 226
Harvey, L. A. 36 133
Haskeir 252
Haslemere Educational
  Museum 127 142
Hatchmere 153
Hatfield Forest, NT 143 228
Hatton Castle, Turiff 249
Havergate Island 146 182
Hawke's Wood, Wadebridge,
  NR 131 223
Hawksmoor Wood, NR 238
Hawthorn Dene, NR 162 228
Hayburn Wyke, NR 242
Hayle Estuary 224
Heck, H. J. W. 131
Helford River and Glendur-
  gan 224
Henry VII 85
Henry VIII 85 122
Hepburn, Ian 36
herbicides 105 188
Herefordshire 151 154 231
  241 247
Hermaness, Unst, NNR 175
  257
Hertford Heath 231
Hertfordshire 143 221 231
Hickling Broad, NNR, RWR 58
  147 235 259
Hidcote Manor, NT 155 229
High Standing Hill 144
Highland Society 108

Highlands, 169 171 172 173
188
High-tae Loch 177 251
Hilbre Islands, NR 222
Hill, Miss Octavia 32
Hindhead 9 142
Hinning House Close 233
Hobhouse, Sir Arthur 17 18
Holden Clough, Oldham 234
Holkham Hall 235
Holme, NR 234
Holme Fen, NNR 51 149 150
232
Holy Island 161
Sands 121
Horn and Weather Heaths, NR
239
Hornsea Mere 243
Horse Island, NR 177 250
Horsey Mere, NR 34 147 235
Hosking, Eric 53
Hoskins, Prof. W. G. 25 59
93
Hothfield Common, LNR
232
House of Commons 47 52 93
160
Hoyle's Mouth, Tenby 248
Hudson, Lord 13
Hughes, Dr. R. Elfyn 54 164
Humber Wildfowl Refuge,
NWR 118 160 243 259
Hunter, Sir Robert 32
Huntingdon 145 149
Huntingdon-Peterborough 149
Huntingdonshire 145 232
Hurcomb, Lord 53 64
Hutton Buscel 242
Huxley, Sir Julian 17 18 64
Hyde Park 126
hydroponics 103

Ightham 232
Ilfracombe Zoo Park 226
Inchmikery, NR 254
Inchnadamph, NNR 173 258
Inner London Parks 126 229
insecticides 188
International Botanical Congress 60
International Congress of
Zoology 60

International Congress of
Bird Preservation 119
International Geographical
Congress 60
International Union for Conservation of Nature and
Natural Resources (IUCN)
20 59
Inverewe, NTS 256
Invernaver, NNR 173 258
Inverness 173
Inverness-shire 171 252 253
Inverpolly, NNR 58 173 256
Iona 249

Johnson, G. A. L. 158
Johnson, Samuel 9
Journal of Animal Ecology 10
Journal of Ecology 10
Juniper Hall Field Centre 20
142 239

Keele, University of 202
Kelling Pines 235
Kensington Park 112
Kent 138 139 140 142 232
Kent's Hole, Torquay 43
Kenwood 126
Keswick 156
Kiloran, Colonsay 249
Kincardine 253
Kindrogan, Strathardle 255
Kingley Vale, NNR 139 183
240
Kinlochleven 170
Kinnoul Hill 255
Kinross 176 254
Kintail 177 256
Kipling Cotes Chalk Pit, NR
243
Kirk and Wasdale Fells, NT
225
Kirkconnell Flow, NNR 177
254
Kirkcudbright 177 252 254
Kirkdale Cave 242
Knaresborough 243
Knockan cliff 173
Knocking Hoe, NNR 144 221
Knole, NT 232
Knutsford 152

Lady Isle 177 250
Lake District, NP 83 156 157
158 224
Lakes Urban District Council
157
Lamlash, Arran 251
Lanark 177 254
Lancashire 157 158 224 233
234
Lancaster, University of 62
Land Utilisation Survey of
Britain 12 98 185 186
Lanhydrock House, NT 223
large blue butterfly 42 75-7
Launchy Gill 158 224
Lea Valley 126 143 199 230
League against Cruel Sports
199
Leeds 160
Leicestershire 151 153 234
Leigh Woods and Nightingale
Valley, NT 237
Leighton Moss, NR 233
Leith Hill 142
Leonardslee, Lower Beeding
240
Lerwick 174
Lewis Castle, Stornoway 256
Lewisburn 236
Lincolnshire 145 150 234 243
Lindisfarne, NNR, NWR 58 121
161 236 259
Lindsey County Council 150
Ling Gill, NNR 158 242
litter 88
Lizard, NT 224
Llanwrtyd Wells 165
Lleyn, AONB 245
Local Nature Reserves (LNR)
19 27
(for individual Reserves, see
respective entries)
Loch an Eilean 183
Loch Bee, South Uist 253
Loch Druidibeg, South Uist,
NNR, NWR 175 253 259
Loch Garten, NR 171 253
Loch Gigha 25
Loch Gruinart, Islay 250
Loch Ken 254
Loch Kishorn 173
Loch Leven, NNR 58 176
254

Loch Lomond, NNR, RWR 169
175 257
Loch of Strathbeg 248
Loch Scresort 174
Loch Sionascaig 173 256
Lochar Water 121
Lochboisdale, South Uist 253
Lochmaddy 252
Lockley, R. M. 36
Loe, The 224
London 126-7 135
London University 62 191 192
London Zoo 127 229
Longmynd 154
Lord of the Manor 25
Lousley, J. E. 36 64 136
Lowland Point 224
Luckett, Stoke Climsland, NR
131 223
Luckett woods 198
Lullington Heath, NNR 139 240
Lulworth Cove 138 227
Lundy 133 226
Lyme Park 222
Lymm Dam 153

Macan, T. T. 35
Magdalen Meadow 154
Malham Tarn Field Centre
20 161 243
Malltreath Pool 166
Malvern Hills, AONB 154 241
Man, Isle of 167 168 248
Management Plan (NNR)
179-83 186
Manchester 157
Corporation 158
Manley, Gordon 35
Manx Museum, Douglas 167
168 248
Manx National Trust 167 168
Maps Research Office 15
Marbury 153 223
Mark Ash, FNR 114 138
Marley and Black Down 240
Marsden Rock 228
Matley-Denny, FNR 114 138
Matthews, Prof. J. R. 52
Maughold Head 168 248
May, Isle of, NNR 175 252
McCowan, Dan 20
McVean, D. N. 170

Meall nan Tarmachan, NNR
176 255
Meathorp Moss 65
mechanization 6 99-100
Medway 141
Melbost Sands, Stornoway 256
Melbourne Hill 225
Meldon Quarry 132
Mellanby, Dr. Kenneth 54
104 150 187
Mendip, NNR 133 134
Meopham, Kent 96
Mere, The 140 240
Merioneth 165 166 245 246
Merlewood, Grange-over-
Sands 53-4 156 157 233
Mickfield Meadow 239
Mickle Fell 159
Middleton Towers 235
Midlothian 254
Milford Haven 164
Millook Haven 223
Millport, Isle of Cumbrae 250
Ministry of Agriculture 3 14
15 16
Ministry of Agriculture and
Fisheries (MAF) 23 24 25
182 195
Ministry of Agriculture,
Fisheries and Food (MAFF)
23 27
Ministry of Housing and
Local Government
(MHLG) 23 27 30
Ministry of Land and
Natural Resources (MLNR)
3 27 29 185 186
Ministry of Town and
Country Planning (MTCP)
22 23 24
Ministry of Works and Plan-
ning 22
Minsmere, NR, RWR 148 239
259
Minterne, Cerne Abbas 227
Mochrum and Castle Lochs
258
Mole Hall, Widdington 228
Monach Islands, NNR 252
Monks Wood, NNR 150 187
232
Experimental Station 54 145
149 187

Monmouth 244 247
Montgomery 247
Montrose Basin 176 249
Moor House, NNR 156 158 159
241
Field Station 159
Moore, Dr. N. W. 188
Moorlands, Skelton, NR 243
Moray 254
Morden Bog, NNR 137 227
Morecambe Bay 156 158
Morfa Dyffryn, NNR 166 247
Morfa Harlech, NNR 58 166
247
Morton Boyd, J. 36
Morton Lochs, NNR, RWR 50
176 252 259
Moss, C. E. 10
Mousa, 257
Mulchrone, Vincent 198
Mull of Galloway 258
Murchison Falls 125
Museum of Geology 127

Nairn 254
Nant Irfon, NNR 165 244
National Atlas 18-19
National Forest Parks 14 31
112 161 177
National Museum of Wales
128 163
National Nature Reserves
(NNR) 19 23 43 44 49 50 51
55 58 179 181-3
National Nature Reserves of
Nature Conservancy 120 139
National Nature Week 65 67
183 198 202
National Parks 15 16 17 27-9
31 132 133 139 146 147 157
161 164 165 166 169 170
183
Brecon Beacons 27 165 244
Dartmoor 27 132 183 226
Exmoor 27 83 133 238
Lake District 27 83 158 224
North York Moors 27 161
242
Northumberland 27 236
Peak District 27 151 222 225
Pembrokeshire Coast 27 164
248

National Parks (cont.)
Snowdonia 27 36 112 163 164 183 245
Yorkshire Dales 27 161 242
National Parks Commission 16 17 18 27 29 89 199
National Planning Series 187
National Trust for Places of Historic Interest or Natural Beauty (NT) 9 14 30 32-4 65 131 140 142 146 148 153 155 158 161 167 168 170 196 199
status and functions 32-4
National Trust for Scotland (NTS) 34 170 175 177
Natural Environment Research Council (NERC) 60 89 183
Nature Conservancy 18 19 36 37 41-6 Chapter 5 64-6 71 75 79-81 87 112 114 119 121 122 132 134 137-9 141 144-7 149 151-3 156-9 164 166 167 169 170 172 179 185 187-9 190 191 196 199 202; Appendix II
acquisitions 50 51 55 58
administration 54-5
Advisory Committee on Photography 53
Committee for England and Wales 53
Conservation Committee 149
Finance Committee 53
First Report 47
Land Agent 179
National Collection of Nature Photographs 53
Physiographic Unit 188
Regional Divisions 54-5
Royal Charter 18 47-9 60
Scientific Policy Committee 51 52 53
Scottish Committee 49 52 53 169
Staff Selection Committee 53
Study Group on Education and Field Biology 36
Welsh Committee 164
Wildfowl Conservation Committee 119

nature conservation, see conservation
Nature Reserve Agreement 146 170 179 182
Nature Reserves 23 34 42 44 47 52 61 66
Nature Trails 158 161 183
Naver 174
Needles 138 231
Ness 174 223
Nettlecombe Court Field Centre 238
Neven-Spence, Sir Basil 52
Newcastle-upon-Tyne, University of 161
New Forest 32 72 83 114 136 138 231
New Galloway 177
Newmarket 148
New Naturalist Series x-xiv 35-6 61 132 136 147 151
New Scientist, The 75
New Statistical Account of Scotland 94
Newborough Warren – Ynys Llanddwyn, NNR 58 165 183 244
Newbould, Dr. P. J. 191
Newlands Corner 142
Newstead Abbey 237
Nicholson, Dr. E. M. 19 49 60 61 63 66
Nith, River 121 177
Norfolk 145-8 188 195 235
Norfolk Broads 145 147-8
Norfolk Wildlife Park, Great Witchingham 235
North Downs 144
North, Dr. F. J. 164
North Fen 157
North Riding 160
North Rona 82 174 and Sula Sgeir, NNR 255
North Ronaldsay 254
North Sea 147
North Warren, Thorpeness, NR 239
North York Moors, NP 27 161 242
North Yorkshire Forests, SF 242
Northamptonshire 151 161 236

Northumberland 224 236 251
Northumberland Coast, AONB 236
Northward Hill, High Halstow, NNR 142 232
Norwich 145 147
Noss, NNR 174 257
Nottinghamshire 151 236
Nottinghamshire Border Caves 225

Oa, The 250
Og's Wood, Polegate 140
Old Winchester Hill, NNR 138 230
Ordnance Survey 32 94 184 186
Orford Beach 182
Orfordness-Havergate, NNR, NWR 146 182 239 259
Orielton Field Centre, Pembrokeshire 119 167 248
Orkney 254
Ornamental Pheasant Trust, The 196
Osborne 231
Osterley Park, NT 126 230
Overbecks, Salcombe, NT 227
Oxenbourne Down, NR 231
Oxford 154 194
Botanic Garden 154 237
School of Forestry 154
Oxfordshire 154 221 237 241
Oxwich, NNR 166 246

Pagham Harbour, LNR 140 240
Paignton 227
Pan's Garden, Ashover 225
Papa Westray 254
Parc Cefn On 246
Parkhurst Forest 138
Peacehaven 140
Peak District, NP 27 151 222 225
Peakirk Waterfowl Gardens and Borough Fen Decoy 232
Pearsall, Prof. W. H. 35 53 64
Peebles 255
Pembroke 167 248

Penjerrick 224
Penmoelallt, FNR 244
Pennines 151 156 158 159 160
Penrhos Road, Bangor, NC 244
Penrhyn Castle, NT 244
Pentire Point 43 223
Pen-y-graig and Tyn-y-bwlch, Llanddeiniol, NR 245
Pepler, G. L. 22
Perth 176 177 249 250 255
Perthichwareu, Llandegla 246
pesticides, 79-80 103-5 188
Peterborough 145 149 232
Peterlee Development Corporation 161
Peter's Wood, Boscastle, NR 131 223
Pett Level 240
Pick Mere 153
Pigeon Copse, Liss, NR 230
Piltdown Skull site 43
Pitmain Beag, Kingussie 253
Pitsford Reservoir 236
plant introductions 193-7
Plymouth 227
pollution 88-9
Pontesford and Earl's Hills, NR 154 237
Poole Harbour 137 196 227
Poore, Prof. Duncan 170
population density in Britain 2-4
Port Erin 248
Portland Bill, BO 137 228
Port Meadow 154
Portmadoc 164
Portmeirion 247
Possil Marsh, NR 177 254
Preston Montford Field Centre 20 152 237
Pritchard, Dr. Tom 153
Proposed National Nature Reserves (PNNR) 59
Puffin Island 244
Purbeck 138 189
Psygodlyn Mawr, NR 246

Quantock Hills, AONB 83 133 134 238
Queen Elizabeth Forest Park, NFP 112 169 255

Raby Castle, Staindrop 228
Radipole Lake, NR, RWR 132 227 259
Ramsbottom, J. 115
Ramsey, NR 248
Randan Wood, NR 241
Rannoch Moor, NNR 176 255
Ranworth Broad 147
Rassal, NNR 173 256
Ratcliffe, D. A. 170
Raven, John 36
Ravenglass 158 225
Rawnsley, Canon 32
Redes Mere 153
Regent's Park 126
Reith, Lord 13 15
Renfrew 255
Rhinog, NNR 165 247
Rhum, Isle of, NNR 54 55 170 174 198 252
Rhyd-y-Creua Field Centre 246
Rhynie Chert 44
Ribble, River 158
Ribblesdale Bone Caves, Settle 243
Richards, Prof. P. W. 53
Richmond Cottage, Mid Yell 257
Richmond Park 126 230
Rifle Butts Quarry 243
Ristol and the Summer Isles, Pr. NR 256
Ritchie, Prof. James 80 177
River Boards 122
River Fal and Trelissick 224
Roath Park 246
Roberts, Prof. R. Alun 53
Robinson, Lord 109
Roche Rock 223
Rochford 143
Rockcliffe Marsh 158
Rode 238
Rodney Stoke, NNR 133 238
Ross and Cromarty 173 177 255 256
Rostherne Mere, NNR, NWR 58 152 153 222 259
Rothschild, Hon. Charles 10
Roudsea Wood, NNR 157 233
Round Island 130
Roxburgh 251 256

Royal Botanic Garden, Edinburgh 254
Royal Botanic Gardens, Kew 126 142 230
Royal Commission on Common Land 25-7 60 93 169
Royal Commission on the Distribution of the Industrial Population 12
Royal Horticultural Society 142
Royal Society for the Prevention of Cruelty to Animals (RSPCA) 199
Royal Society for the Protection of Birds (RSPB) 64 104 137 141 142 146 148 149 167 177 182 199
Royal Society of Arts (1963) 60
Ruislip and Bourne Farm, LNR 229
Ruislip Reservoir 126
Rural Land Utilisation Officers (RLUO's) 15 24
Ruskin Reserve, Cothill 144
Rusland Moss, NNR 58 157 233
Rusland Valley 157
Russell, Sir John 35 63
Rutland 151 234
Rye Meads, Lea Valley 232
Ryle, G. B. 116

St. Abb's Head 250
St. Agnes, Scilly, BO 224
St. Andrews, 176
St. Bee's Head 158 225
St. Catherine's Point 231
St. Cyrus, NNR 176 253
St. Erth 224
St. James's Park 122 123 126
St. John's Lake, Torpoint 223
St. Kilda, NNR 55 174 252
St. Leger Gordon, D. 36 133
St. Margaret's Bay 141
St. Margaret's Island and Caldey 248
St. Paul's Cray Commons 126
Salisbury, Sir Edward 194
Salthouse Broad 34 146
Sandall Beat, LNR 243

Sandringham 235
Sands of Forvie, NNR, NWR 176 249 259
Sandwich Bay, NR 141 232
Sandy 221
Savernake Forest 136 241
Sayer, Lady Sylvia 132
Sca Fell, NT 158 225
Schimper, A. F. W. 10
Schlich, Sir William 109
Scilly, Isles of 129 224
Scolt Head Island, NNR, RWR 19 34 145 146 188 234 259
Scotland 169-78 248-58
Scott Committee 13 15-18 22 43 169
Scott Report 16 43
Scott, Lord Justice 13
Scott, Peter 64 119
Scottish Dept. of Agriculture (SDA) 24
Scottish Dept. of Health 23
Scottish Society for the Protection of Birds 177
Scottish Tourist Board 34
Scottish Wild Life Conservation Committee 50
Scottish Wildlife Trust 66
Scousburgh 259
seals, grey 79-82 161 162 167 170 174
Second World War, effects of 24-5 30 109-10
Secretary of State for Scotland 31 48 80
Selborne Common and Hanger, NR 230
Selkirk 257
Selsey Bill 240
Seven Sisters 140
Seven Wells Bridge 238
Severn estuary 155 163
Sewerby Hall 243
Shakespeare Cliff 141
Shap Fell 156
Shapwick Heath, NNR 58 134 238
Sharp, Dr. Thomas 15
Shgrpham Moor, NR 238
Sheppey, Isle of 141
Shetland, 174 175 257
Shiant Islands, Pr. NR 256
Shinale Street 146 239

Shrewsbury 151
Shropshire 20 151 154 237
Shropshire Hills, AONB 154 237
Silkin, Lord 18
Silpho, Hackness and Snever Dale 242
Silver Flowe, NNR 176 254
Sinclair, Sir John 93
Sites of Special Scientific Interest (SSSI) 23 27 50 58 59 141
Skegness-Gibraltar Point, LNR, RWR 234
Skeldon House, Dalrymple 250
Skinburness 158
Skokholm, BO 66 167 248
Skomer Island, NNR 58 65 66 167 248
Slapton Ley Field Centre 20 133 227
Slimbridge Wildfowl Trust 119 120 124 196 229
Smith, Guy-Harold 190
Smith, Robert 10
Smith, W. G. 10
Snowdon, NNR 163 164 244
Social Science Research Council 60
Society for the Promotion of Nature Reserves (SPNR) 10 12 61 150 214; Appendix I
Solway Coast, AONB 224
Solway Firth 158
Somerset 129 133 134 237 238
Somerset Levels 134
Somerset Rivers Board 134
South Downs, AONB 139
South Essex Woodlands, NR 229
South Stack, Holyhead 243
South Uist 175
Southampton 29
Southend-on-Sea 143
Southport 233
Southport Sanctuary, NWR 233 259
Spalding, BO 234
Spetchley Park 241
Speyside 54
Spurn Point 160 243
squirrel, grey 63 79 194

Stac Polly 173
Staffa 249
Stafford 152
Staffordshire 151 152 225 238 239
stag hunting 199
Stamp, Lord 67
Stamp, L. D. (publications) 35 59 91 93 94 98 136 172 173 193 194
Standing Committee on National Parks 31
Stanpit Marsh, LNR 231
Stansted Wildlife Reserve 143 228
Stapledon, Sir George 72 73 98 164 186
Stapleford Moor, NR 234
Stapleford Park 234
Statistical Account of Scotland 93
Steep Holm, BO 237
Steers, Prof. J. A. 35 145
Stirling 255 257
Stodmarsh, NNR 141 232
Stour, River 141 147
Stourhead, NT 241
Stratford-on-Avon Canal 153
Strathpeffer 256
Strathy Bog, NNR 174 258
Strathyre, FC 255
Strensall Common, NR 243
Studland Heath, NNR 58 137 227
Studland sand-dunes 183
Suffolk 20 145 146 148 235 239
Sula Sgeir, NNR 174 255
Sule Stack 255
Surrey 126 138 139 142 143 239
Surrey, South-west 240
Surrey Hills, AONB 142 239
Sussex 138 139 140 240
Sussex Downs, AONB 240
Sutherland 173 174 258
Swale 139
Swanscombe Skull 142 Site, NNR 232
Swansea 163 164
Swirls and Launchy Gill, Thirlmere 158 225
Syon House, Brentford 126 230

Talbot Manor 235
Tamar 131 132 198
Tamar Lake, RWR 132 225
259
Tansley, Prof. Sir Arthur G.
10 11 18 19 37 40 41 49 69
145 186
Tatton Mere 153 223
Taylor, E. W. 64
Tees 159
Teesdale 160 162
Teesmouth, BO 228
Tentsmuir Point, NNR, NWR
176 252 259
Tewes, Little Sampford 228
Thames 141 142
Thanet, Isle of 141
Thanet Sand 44
Thetford Chase, FC 149 235
Thetford Heath, NNR 239
Thirlmere 157 158
Thomson, Sir Landsborough
64
Thoresby Hall and Lake 236
Thornthwaite Forest, FC 158
224
Tile Hill Wood, NR 241
Tintern Forest, FC 247
Tithe Redemption Com-
mission 94 186
Torquay 226
Totternhoe Knolls, LNR 221
Tower of London 126 229
Town Copse, Newtown, NT
231
Traighs Seilebost and
Luskentyre, Harris 252
Trawsfynydd Lake 165
Trebetherick Point 223
Tree Preservation Orders 110
Tregargus Quarry, St.
Stephen 223
Trengwainton House, NT 224
Trent College, Long Eaton
225
Trent Valley 236
Tresco Abbey 130 224
Treshnish Isles, Pr. NR 249
Trethias Island, NR 223
Trevelyan, Sir Charles 16
Trewithen, Probus 223
Tring Reservoirs, NNR, RWR
126 143 183 231 259

Trueman, Dr. A. E. 43
Twycross 234
Tynron Juniper Wood, NNR
177 251

Ullswater 157
Unit of Grouse and Moor-
land Ecology 189
United Nations Educational
Scientific and Cultural
Organization (UNESCO) 193
Upper Teesdale, NNR 159 241
Usk valley 165
Uthwatt Committee 23

vegetation, classification of
37-42
Vegetation Map of Scotland
10 172-3
Vesey-Fitzgerald, Brian 78-9
84 86
Victoria Cave, Settle 43

Wadebridge 131
Waggoners' Wells and Lud-
shott Common, NT 230
Walberswick 146
Wales 163-8 243-48
Walmsley Sanctuary, Wade-
bridge, RWR 122 131 223 259
Walney Island, NR 157 233
Walters, Max 36
Wandlebury 222
Warren, The 43 141
Warwickshire 151 153 241
Waterperry, FNR 237
Watersmeet, NT 225
Watlington Hill 237
Wayre, Philip 196
Weald (Selborne) 138 139
Weeting Heath, NNR 149 235
Welbeck Park 236
Wellingborough Zoo 236
Wells Marshes 146 234
Welsh Mountain Zoo,
Colwyn Bay 245
Wenlock Edge 154
West cliffs of Hoy 255
West London Reservoirs 239
West Riding 160

West Wales Field Society 65
66 80 163
West Wales Trust 166
Wester Ross 169 173
Westleton Heath, NNR 146 181
239
Westmorland 156 157 159 241
Weston Marsh, Runcorn, NR
222
Westonbirt Arboretum, FC 159
229
wetlands 6 40 118-22 148
Weybourne 146 235
Wharfedale Bone Caves,
Kilnsey 243
Whipsnade Zoo 125 143 221
Whitbarrow Scar 241
Whitby 160
White, D. A. 181
White, Gilbert 67
White Sheet Hill, NR 136 241
Whiteford, NNR 166 246
Whitewall-Magor, NR 247
Whittlesey Mere 150
Wiay, Benbecula 253
Wicken Fen, NR, RWR 34 59
148 222 259
Wight, Isle of, AONB 138 231
Zoo, Sandown 231
Wigtown 258
wildfowl 118-22 134 166 167
176 195
Wildfowl Refuges 19 118 153
158 161
Wildfowl Trust 119 120
Slimbridge 124 229
Wildfowlers' Association of
Gt. Britain and Ireland 119
199
Wild Life Conservation
Committee 43 44 50
Wild Life Conservation
Special Committee 18
Wild Life Special Committees
47
Willatts, Dr. E. C. 15
Wiltshire 241
Wimbledon common 126
Windermere 158
Windsor Forest and Park 144
221
Winkworth Arboretum, NT
142 240

Winterton Dunes, NNR 146 235
Wisley 142 239
Wistman's Wood, FNR 132 226
Woburn Park 124 143 221
Wolfson Foundation 64
Wollaton Hall and Park 237
Wood, The (Surbiton), NR 230
Wood's Mill, NR 240
Woodwalton Fen, NNR 65 150 187 232
Woody Bay 225
Wookey Hole 133 238
Wooldridge, Prof. S. W. 20 36 136
Worcestershire 151 154 239 241
Worm's Head 166
Worthington, Dr. E. B. 35 53 60 81

Wray Castle, Windermere 158
Wrekin 154
Wren's Nest, Dudley, NNR 152 155 239
Wybunbury Moss, NNR 152 223
Wychwood, NNR 154 237
Wye and Crundale Downs, NNR 141 233
Wye Downs 58
Wye, Kent 135
Wye Valley Caves, Buxton 225
Wyre-Lune Sanctuary, NWR 233 259

Yapp, Brunsdon 196
Yarmouth 146
Yarner Wood, NNR 50 132 226

Ynys Llanddwyn 166
Yonge, Dr. C. M. 35
Yorkshire 20 159 160 161 225 234 241 242 243
Yorkshire Dales, NP 27 161 242
Young, Arthur 93
Younger Botanic Gardens, Benmore 249
Y Wyddfa (Snowdon) 164

Zealds, Church St., Wye, NC 232
Zennor and Zennor Quoit, NT 224
zoological gardens 123-8
Zoological Society of London 126